image comics presents

THE WALKING DEAD™

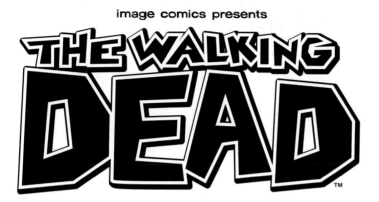

for image comics:

Erik Larsen
Publisher
Todd McFarlane
President
Marc Silvestri
CEO
Jim Valentino
Vice-President

Eric Stephenson
Executive Director
Missie Miranda
Controller
Brett Evans
Production Manager
B. Clay Moore
PR & Marketing
Coordinator
Allen Hui
Production Artist
Joe Keatinge
Traffic Manager
Mia MacHatton
Administrative
Assistant

THE WALKING DEAD,
VOL. 1: DAYS GONE BYE.
April 2005. Fourth Printing.
Published by Image Comics,
Inc. Office of Publication: 1942
University Ave., Suite 305,
Berkeley, CA 94704. Image
and its logos are ® and ©
2005, Image Comics, Inc. All
Rights Reserved. THE
WALKING DEAD is ™ and ©
2005, Robert Kirkman.
Originally published in single
magazine format as The
Walking Dead #1-6. The story
and characters presented in
this publication are fictional.
Any similarities to events or
persons living and/or dead are
purely coincidental. With the
exception of artwork used for
review purposes, none of the
contents herein may be
reproduced without the
expressed written permission
of the copyright holder.
PRINTED IN CANADA

ROBERT KIRKMAN
CREATOR, WRITER, LETTERER

TONY MOORE
PENCILER, INKER, GRAY TONES

CLIFF RATHBURN
ADDDITIONAL GRAY TONES

INTRODUCTION

I'm not trying to scare anybody. If that
somehow happens as a result of reading this
comic that's great, but really... that's not what
this book is about. What you now hold in your
hands is the most serious piece of work I've
done so far in my career. I'm the guy that
created Battle Pope; I hope you guys realize
what a stretch this is for me. It's really not
that hard to believe when you realize that I'm
delving into subject matter that is so utterly
serious and dramatic...

Zombies.

To me, the best zombie movies aren't the
splatter fests of gore and violence with goofy
characters and tongue in cheek antics. Good
zombie movies show us how messed up we
are, they make us question our station in
society... and our society's station in the
world. They show us gore and violence and
all that cool stuff too... but there's always
an undercurrent of social commentary
and thoughtfulness.

Give me "Dawn of the Dead" over "Return of
the Living Dead" any day. To me zombie

movies are thought provoking, dramatic fiction, on par with any Oscar worthy garbage that's rolled out year after year. Movies that make you question the fabric of our very society are what I like. And in GOOD zombie movies... you get that by the truckload.

With **THE WALKING DEAD** I want to explore how people deal with extreme situations and how these events CHANGE them. I'm in this for the long haul. You guys are going to get to see Rick change and mature to the point that when you look back on this book you won't even recognize him. I hope you guys are looking forward to a sprawling epic, because that's the idea with this one.

Everything in this book is an attempt at showing the natural progression of events that I think would occur in these situations. This is a very character driven endeavor. How these characters get there is much more important than them getting there. I hope to show you reflections of your friends, your neighbors, your families, and yourselves, and what their reactions are to the extreme situations on this book.

So, if anything scares you... great, but this is not a horror book. And by that I do not mean we think we're above that genre. Far from it, we're just setting out on a different path here. This book is more about watching Rick survive than it is about watching zombies pop around the corner and scare you. I hope that's what you guys are into.

All story commentary aside, at the very least, even if you hate the thing... you've got to admit... it at least looks good. I've been working with Tony Moore for as long as I can remember. I've SEEN Tony's work, I KNOW Tony's work, I know it better than anyone, and I've got to say... just in case you didn't notice... Tony really pulled out all the stops one this one. I can really tell that he shares my immense love for the subject matter. This book is really a thing of beauty. I couldn't be more pleased with how it turned out. I hope you all agree.

For me the worst part of every zombie movie is the end. I always want to know what happens next. Even when all the characters die at the end... I just want it to keep going.

More often than not zombie movies feel like a slice of a person's life shown until whoever is in charge of the movie gets bored. So we get to know the character, they have an adventure and then, BOOM, as soon as things start getting good... those pesky credits start rolling.

The idea behind The Walking Dead is to stay with the character, in this case, Rick Grimes for as long as is humanly possible. I want The Walking Dead to be a chronicle of years of Rick's life. We will NEVER wonder what happens to Rick next, we will see it. The Walking Dead will be the zombie movie that never ends.

Well... not for a good long time at least.

-Robert Kirkman

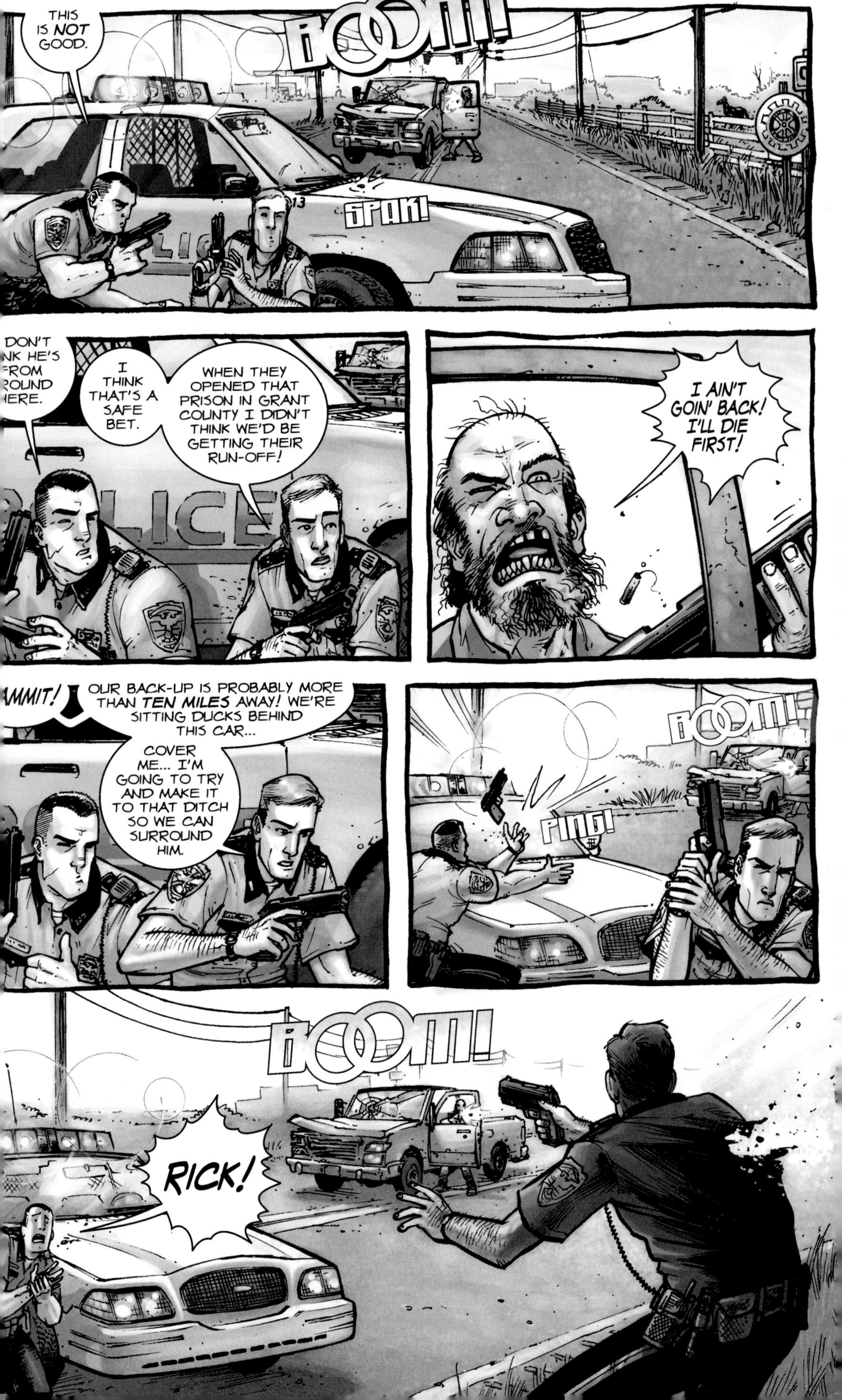
THIS IS NOT GOOD.
BOOM!
SPAK!
DON'T
NK HE'S
FROM
ROUND
HERE.
I THINK THAT'S A SAFE BET.
WHEN THEY OPENED THAT PRISON IN GRANT COUNTY I DIDN'T THINK WE'D BE GETTING THEIR RUN-OFF!
I AIN'T GOIN' BACK! I'LL DIE FIRST!
AMMIT!
OUR BACK-UP IS PROBABLY MORE THAN TEN MILES AWAY! WE'RE SITTING DUCKS BEHIND THIS CAR...
COVER ME... I'M GOING TO TRY AND MAKE IT TO THAT DITCH SO WE CAN SURROUND HIM.
BOOM!
PING!
BOOM!
RICK!

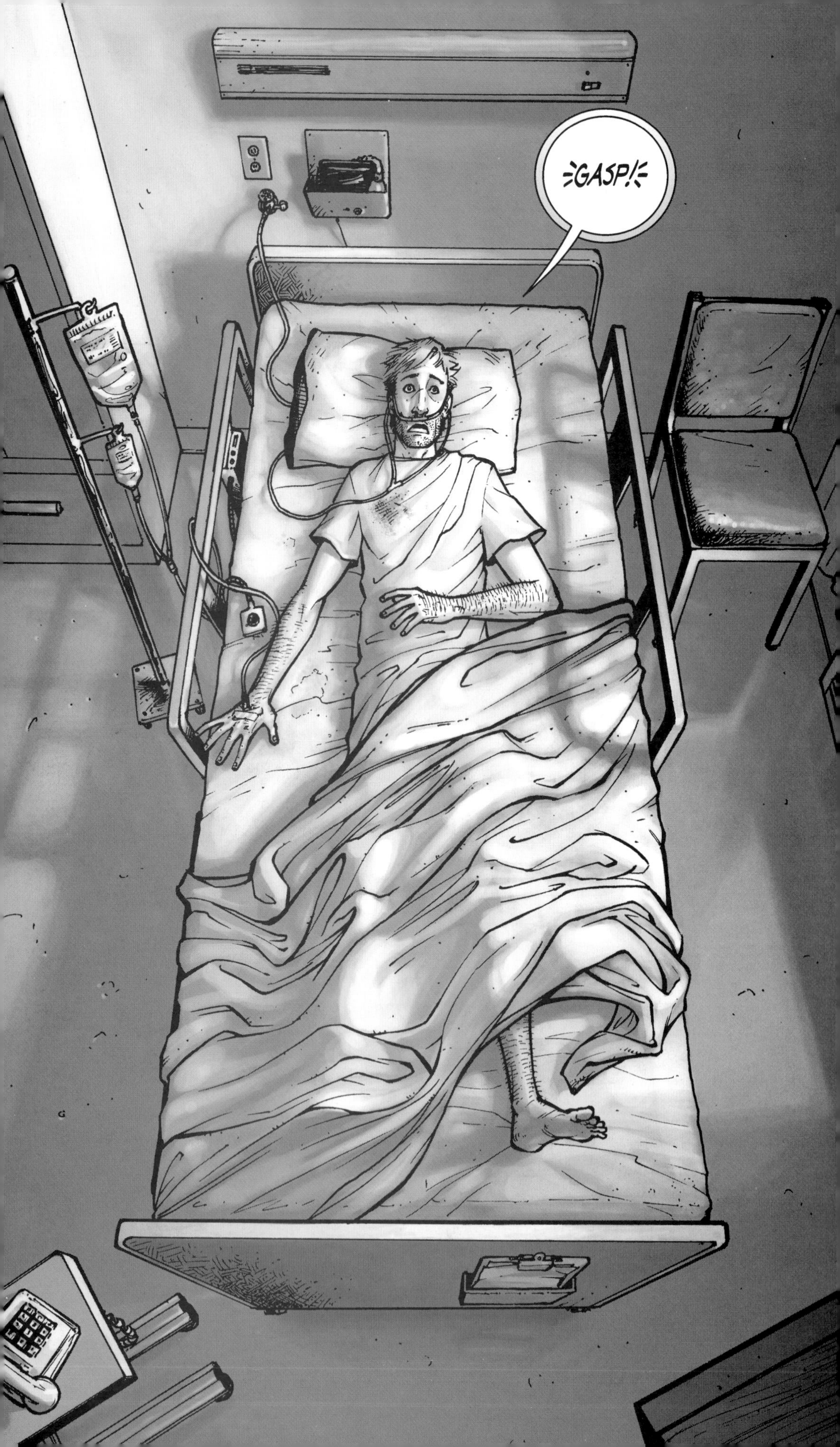
GASP!

NURSE!

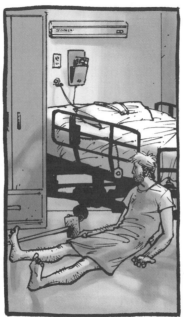

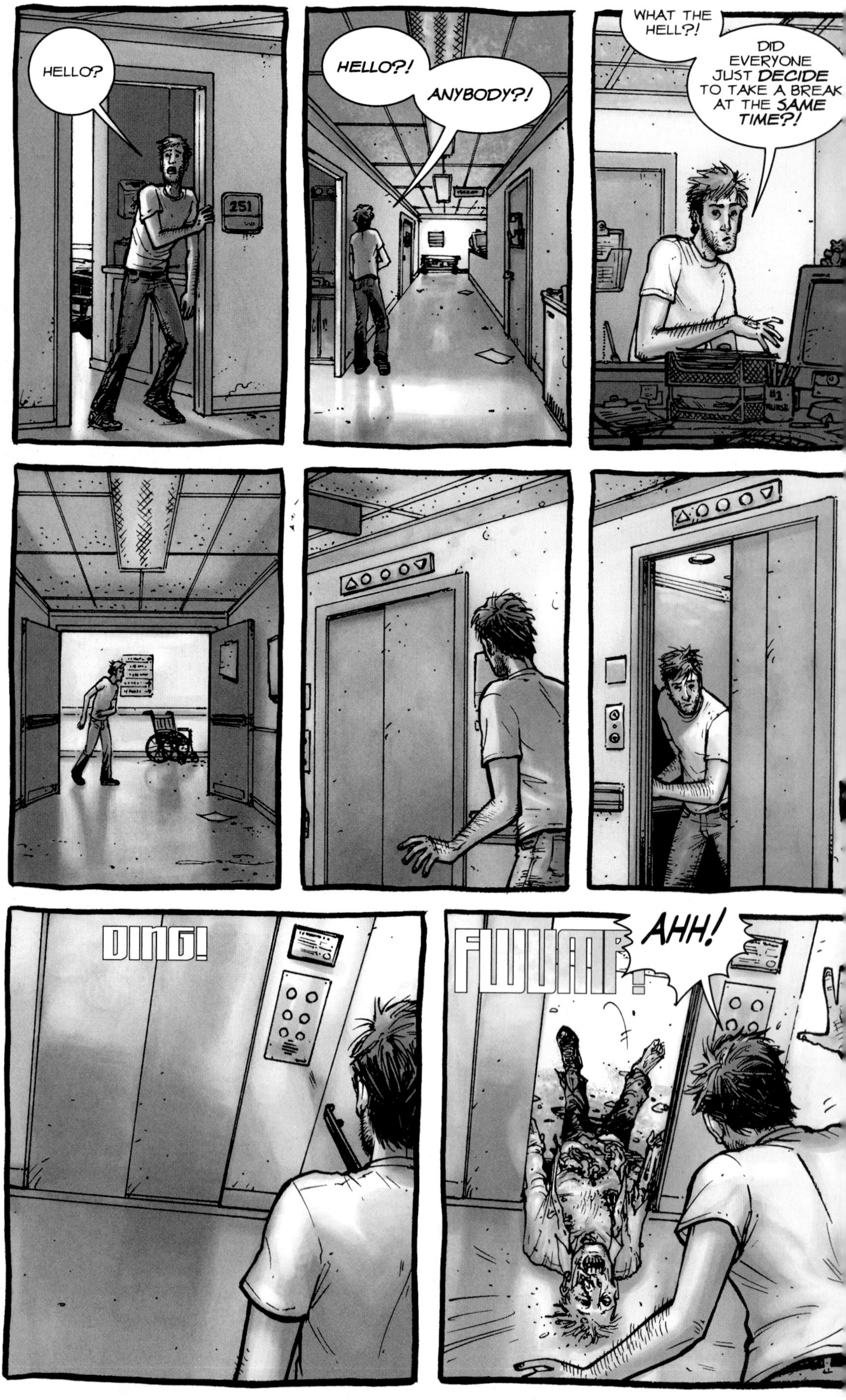
HELLO?
HELLO?!
ANYBODY?!
WHAT THE HELL?!
DID EVERYONE JUST DECIDE TO TAKE A BREAK AT THE SAME TIME?!
251
#1 NURSE
DING!
FWUMP!
AHH!

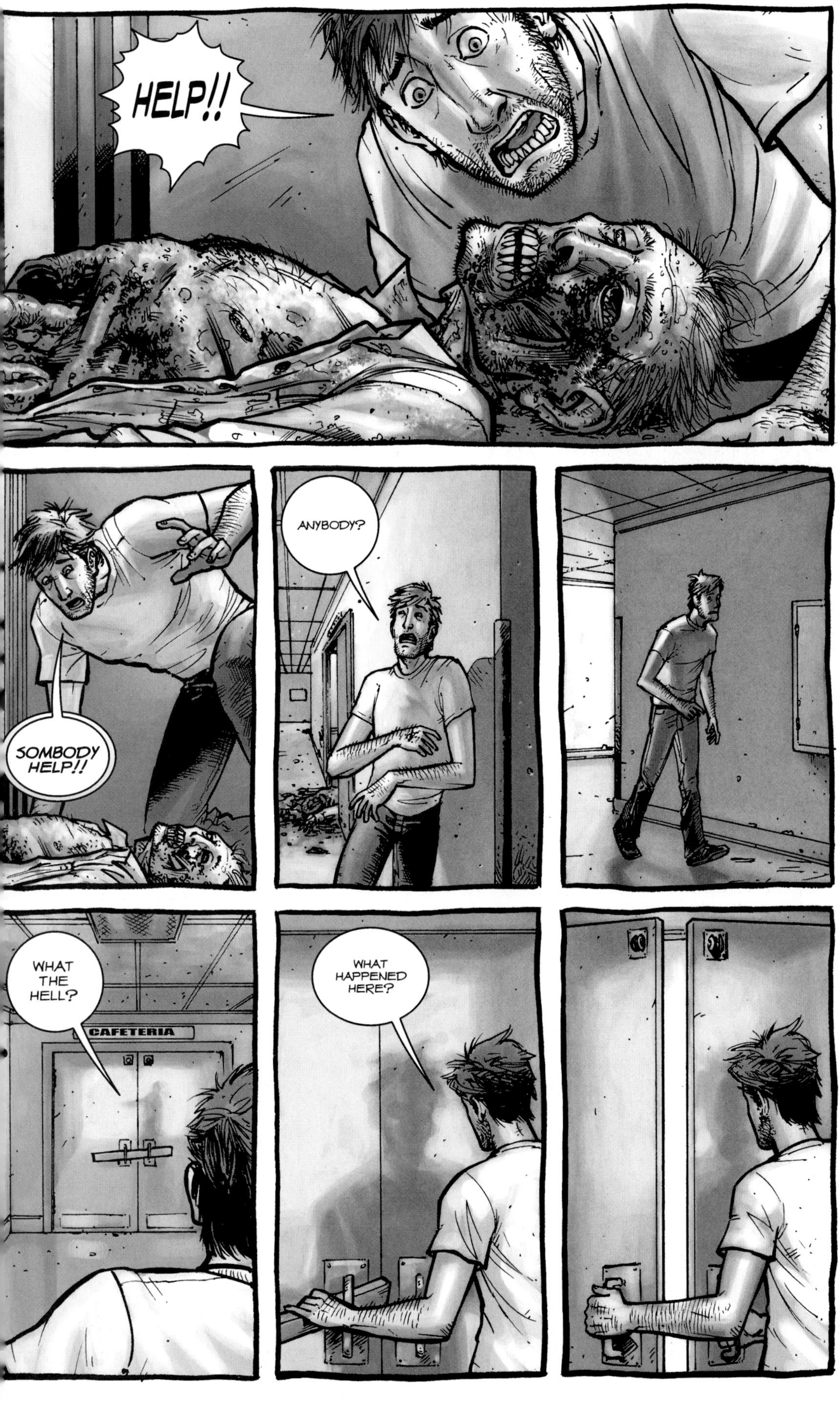
HELP!!
SOMBODY HELP!!
ANYBODY?
WHAT THE HELL?
CAFETERIA
WHAT HAPPENED HERE?

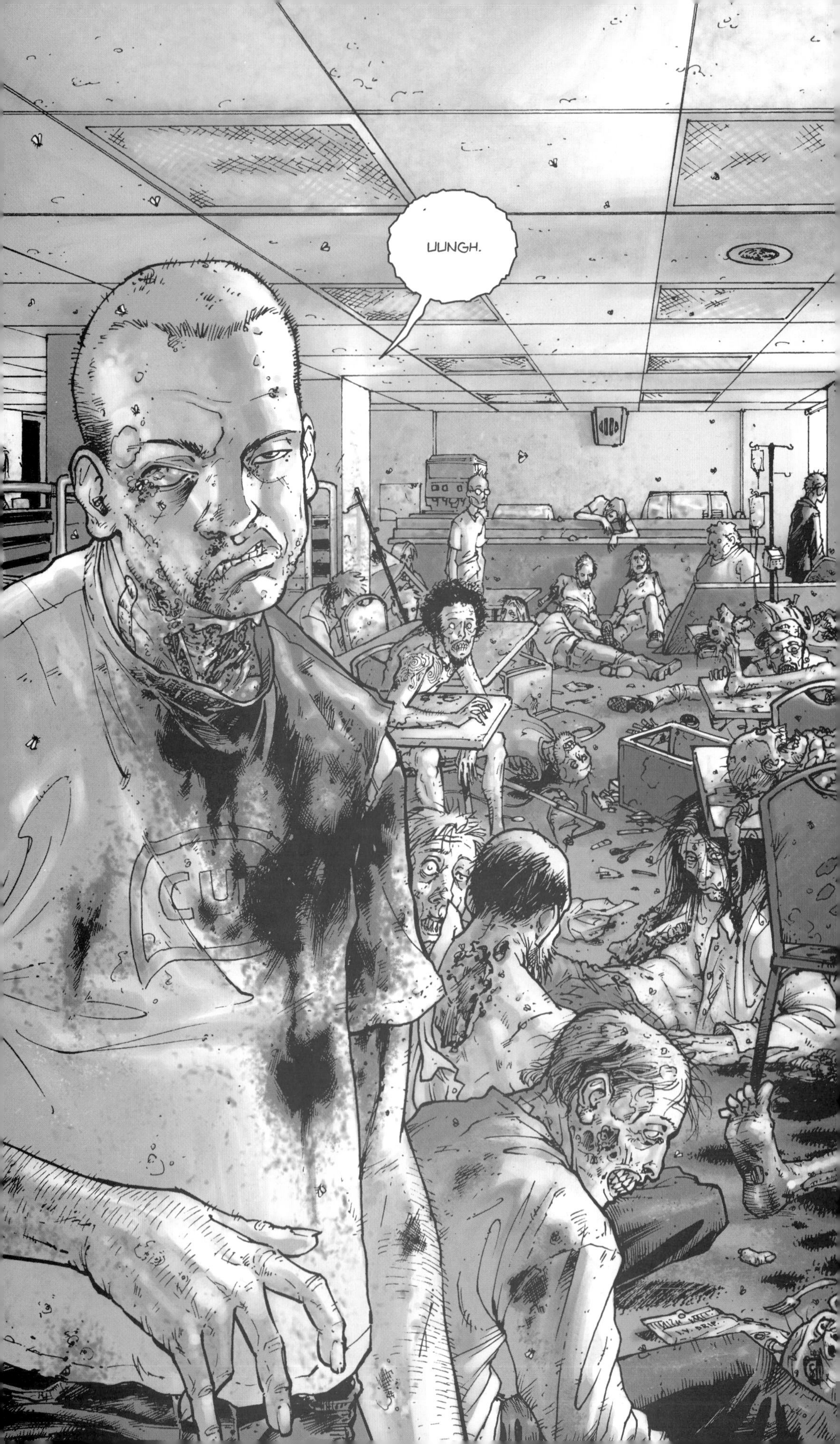
UUNGH.

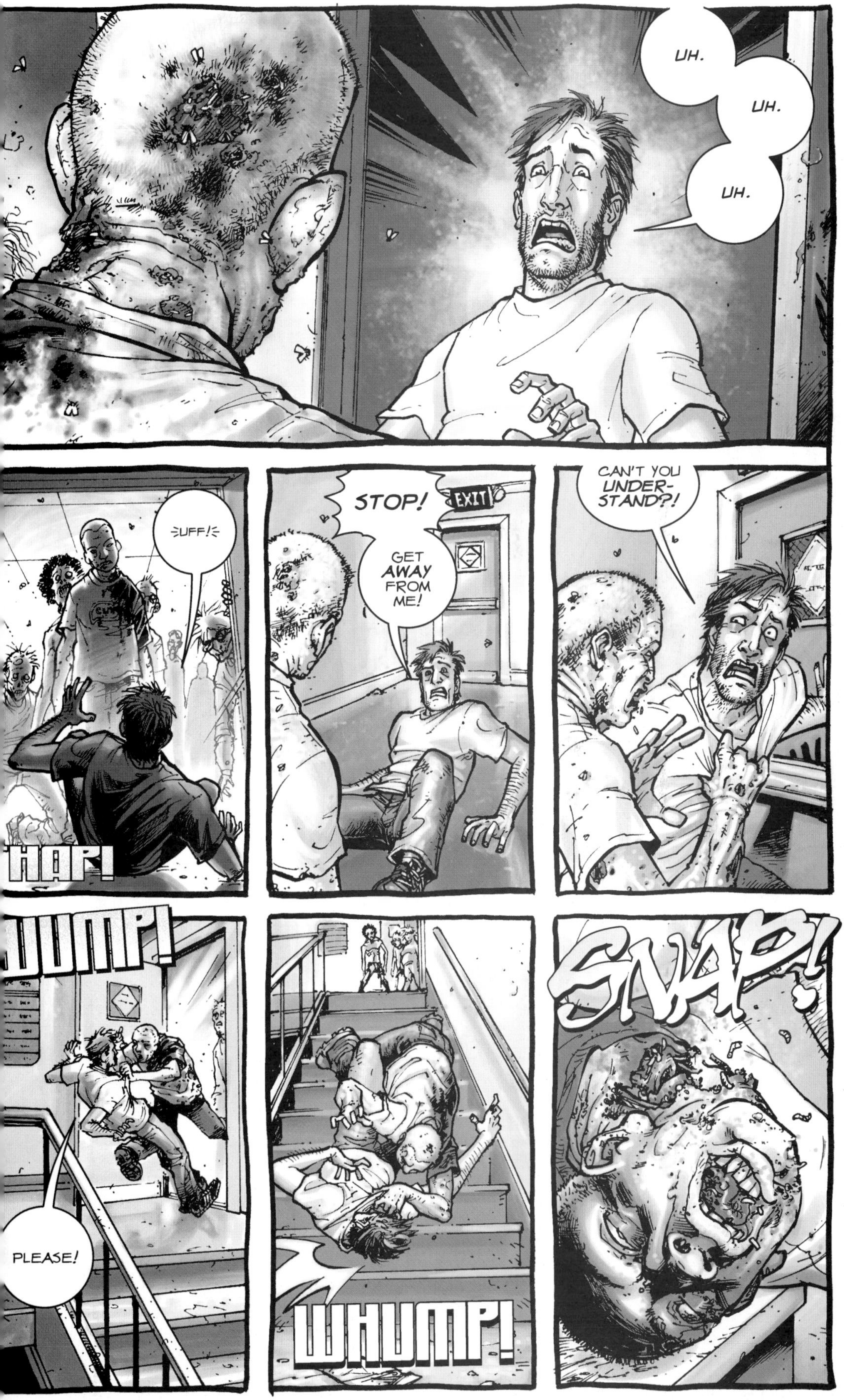
UH.
UH.
UH.
=UFF!=
HAP!
STOP!
EXIT
GET AWAY FROM ME!
CAN'T YOU UNDER-STAND?!
WUMP!
PLEASE!
WHUMP!
SNAP!

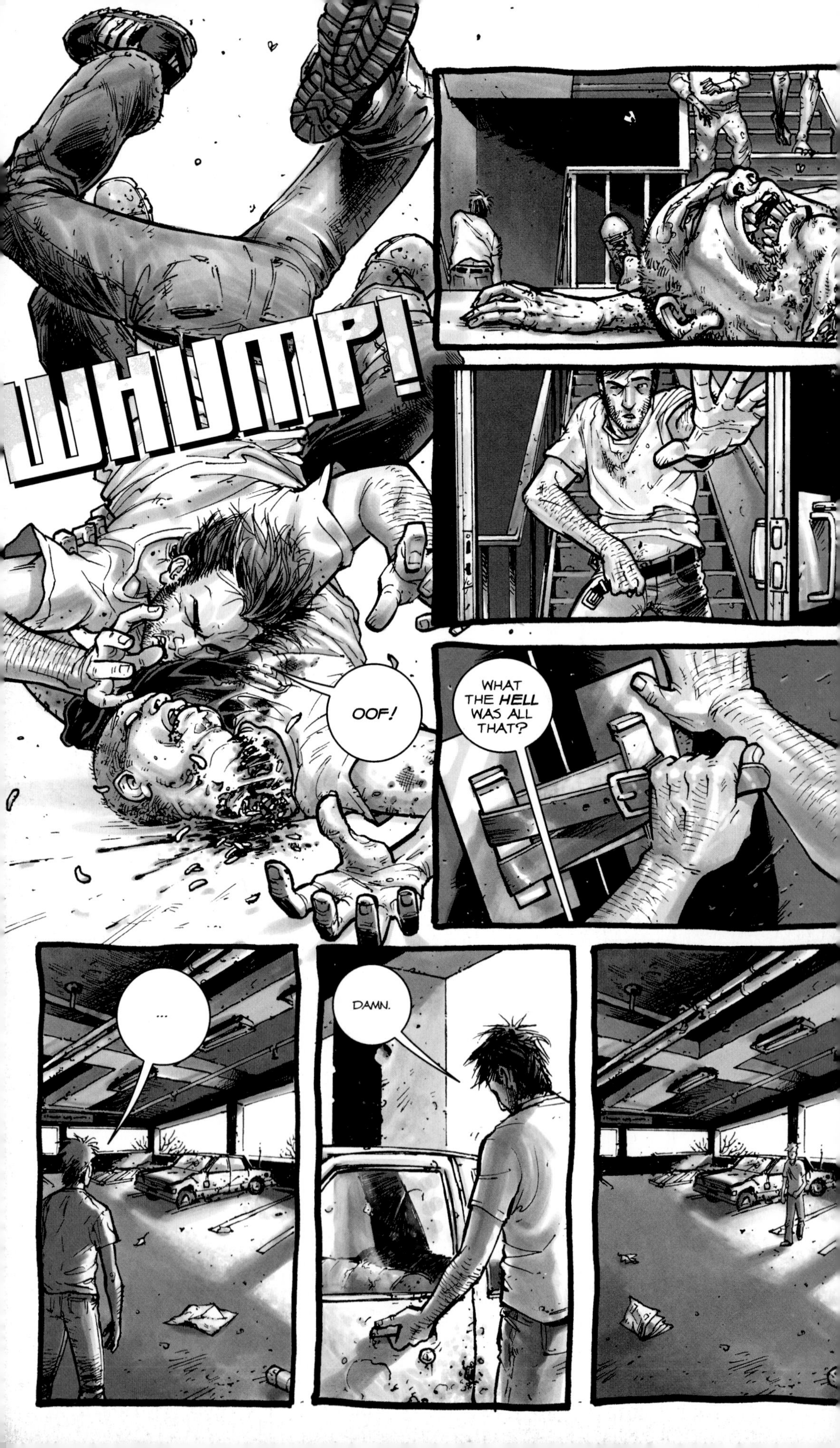
WHUMP!
OOF!
WHAT THE *HELL* WAS ALL THAT?
...
DAMN.

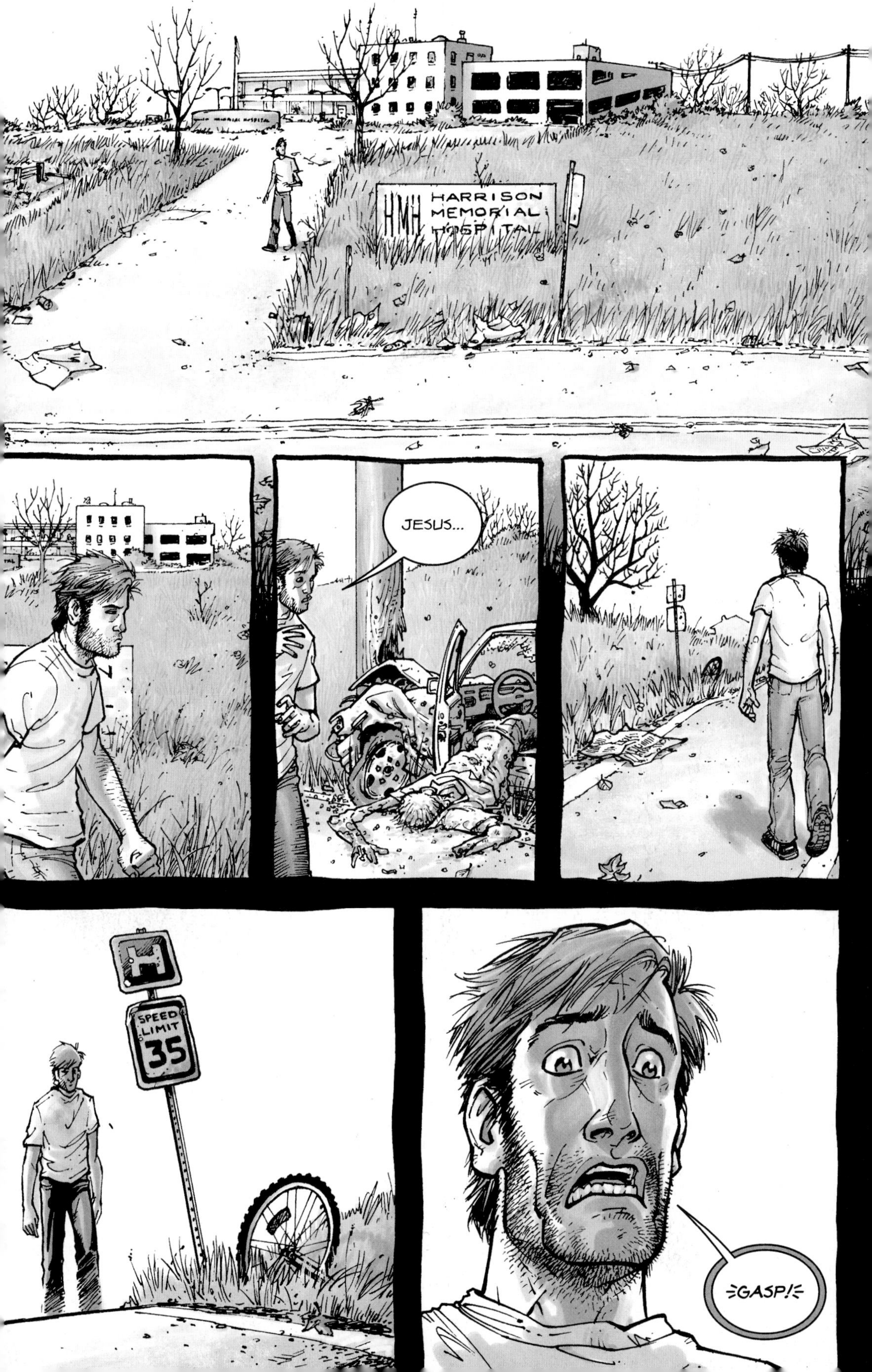
HMH HARRISON MEMORIAL HOSPITAL
JESUS...
SPEED LIMIT 35
GASP!

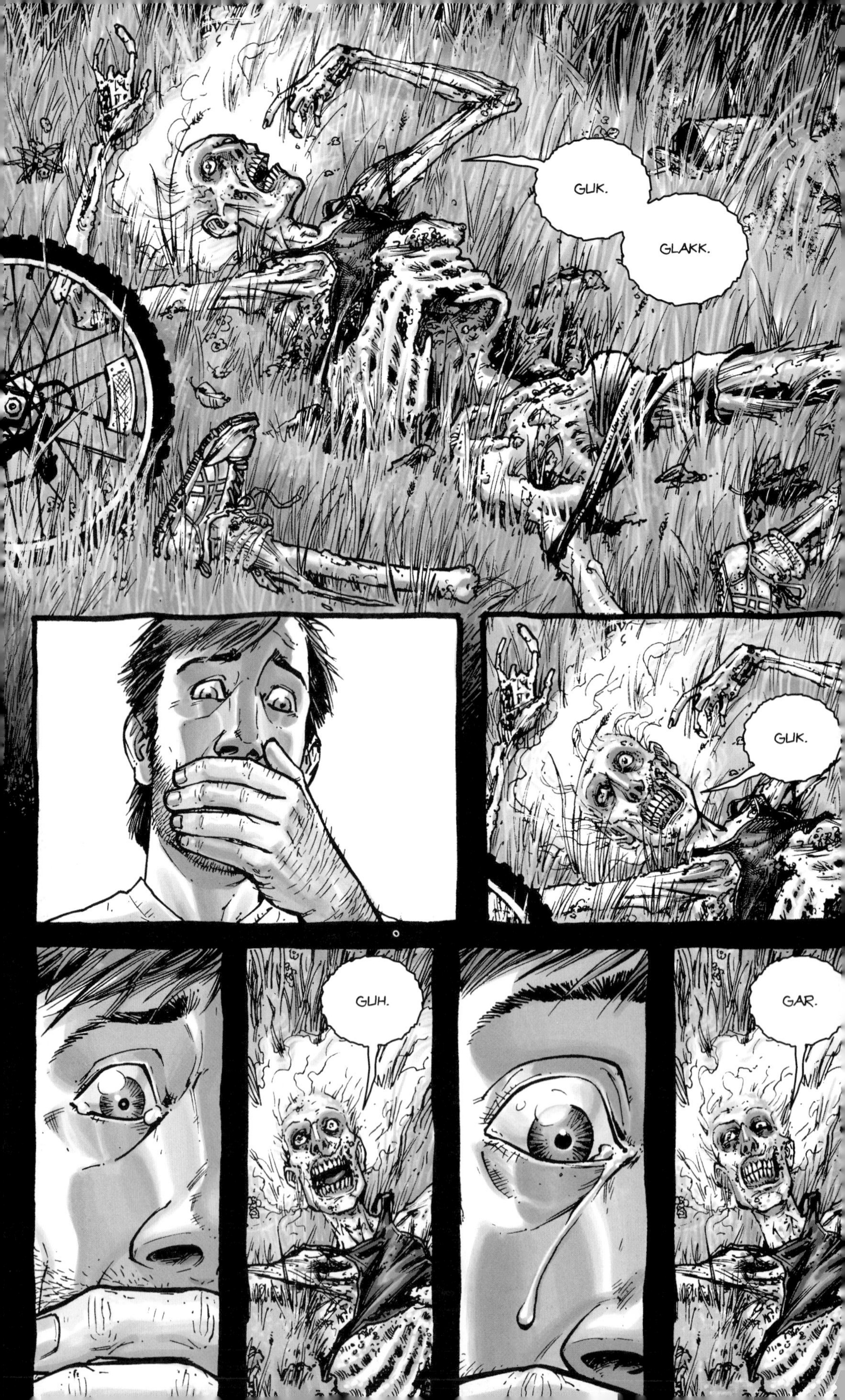
GUK.
GLAKK.
GUK.
GUH.
GAR.

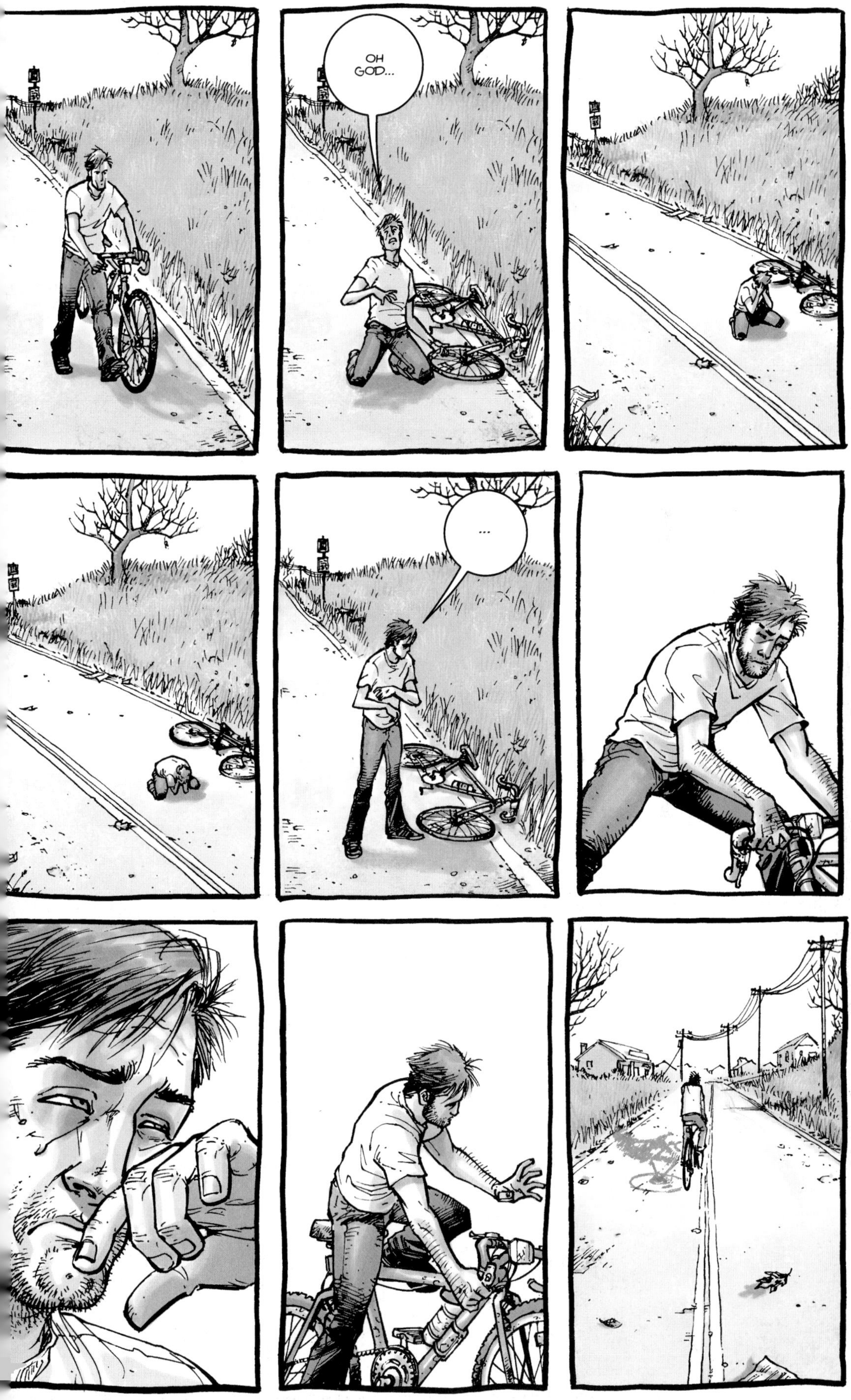
OH GOD...
...

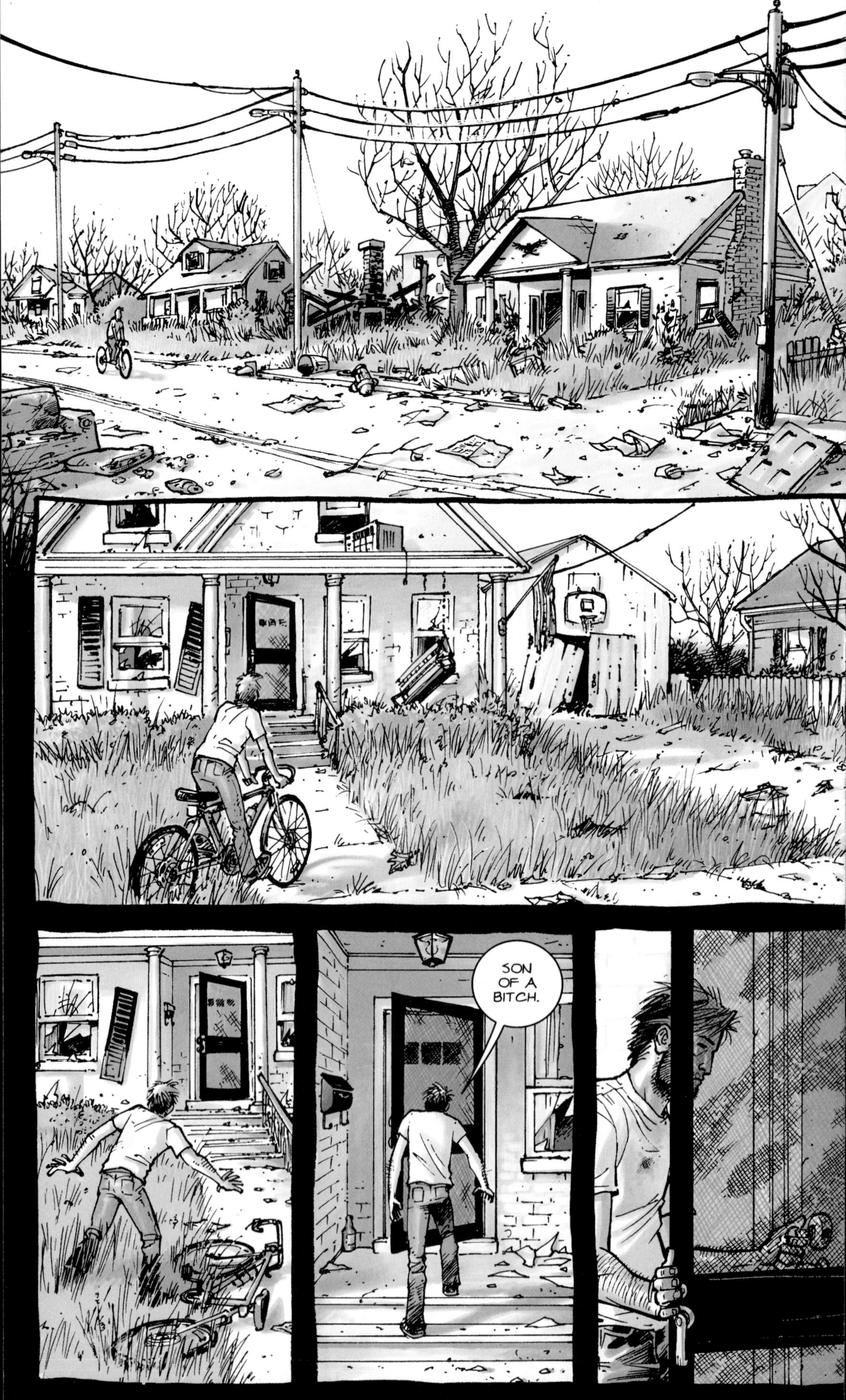
SON OF A BITCH.

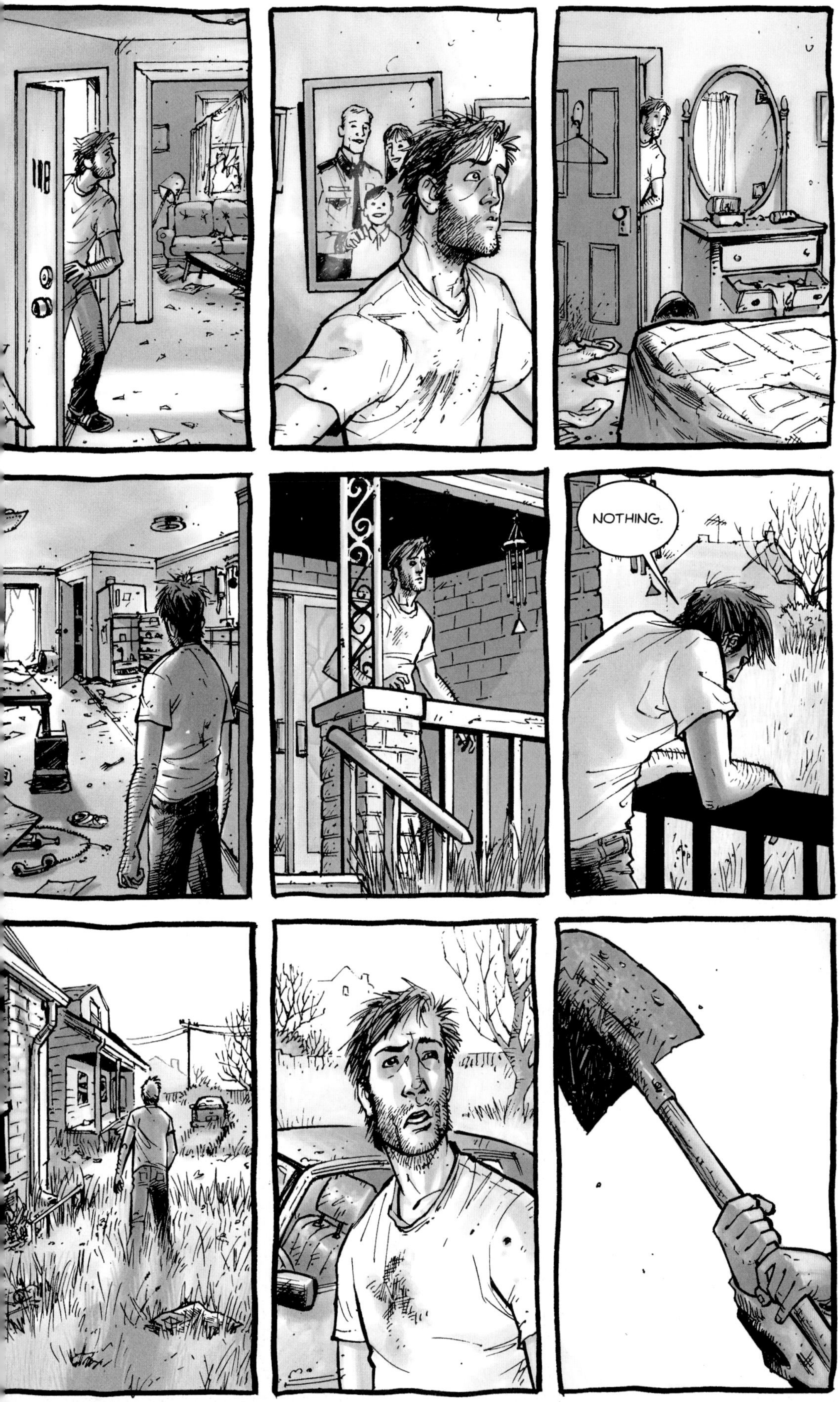
NOTHING.

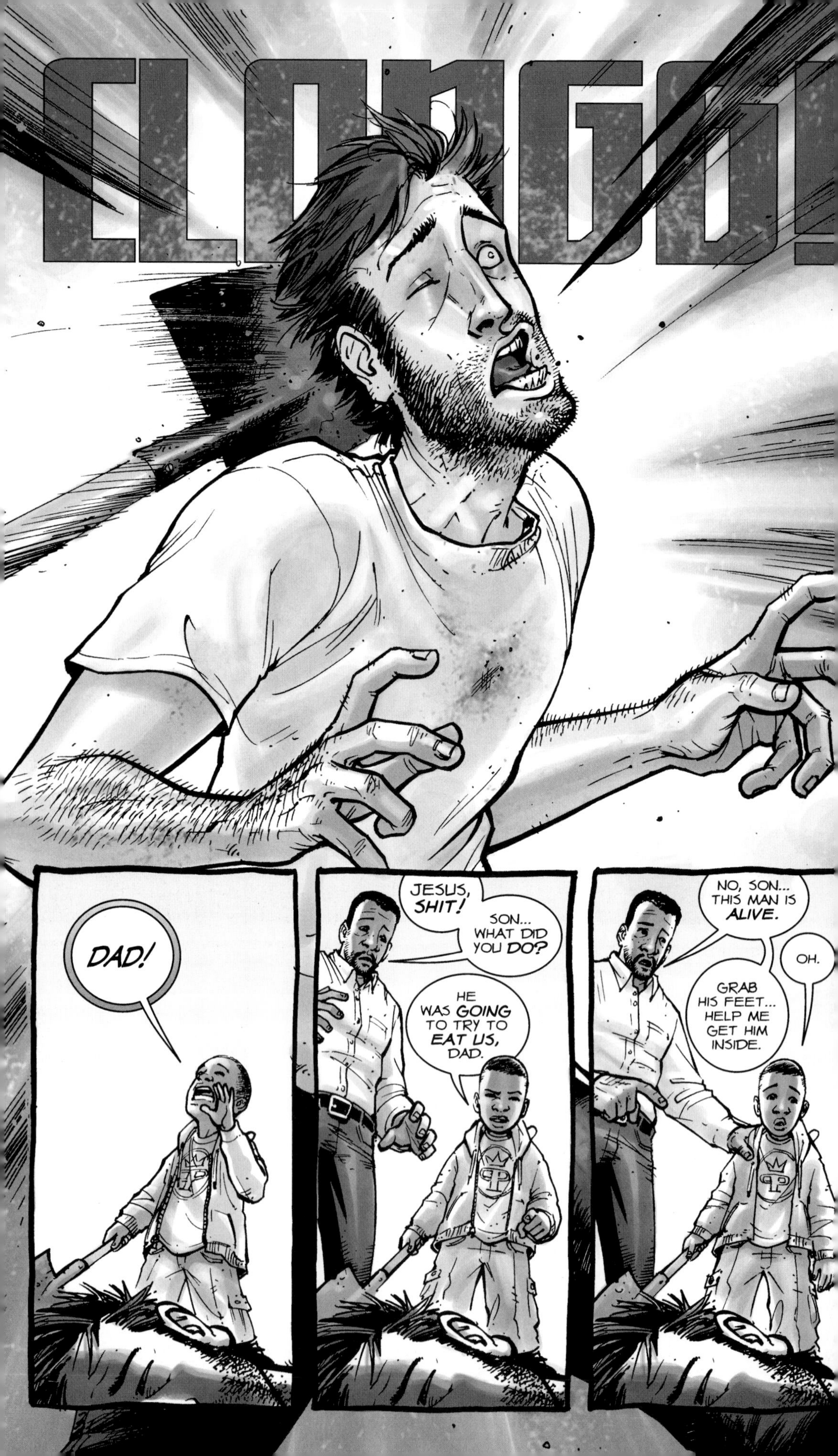
DAD!
JESUS, SHIT!
SON... WHAT DID YOU DO?
HE WAS GOING TO TRY TO EAT US, DAD.
NO, SON... THIS MAN IS ALIVE.
OH.
GRAB HIS FEET... HELP ME GET HIM INSIDE.

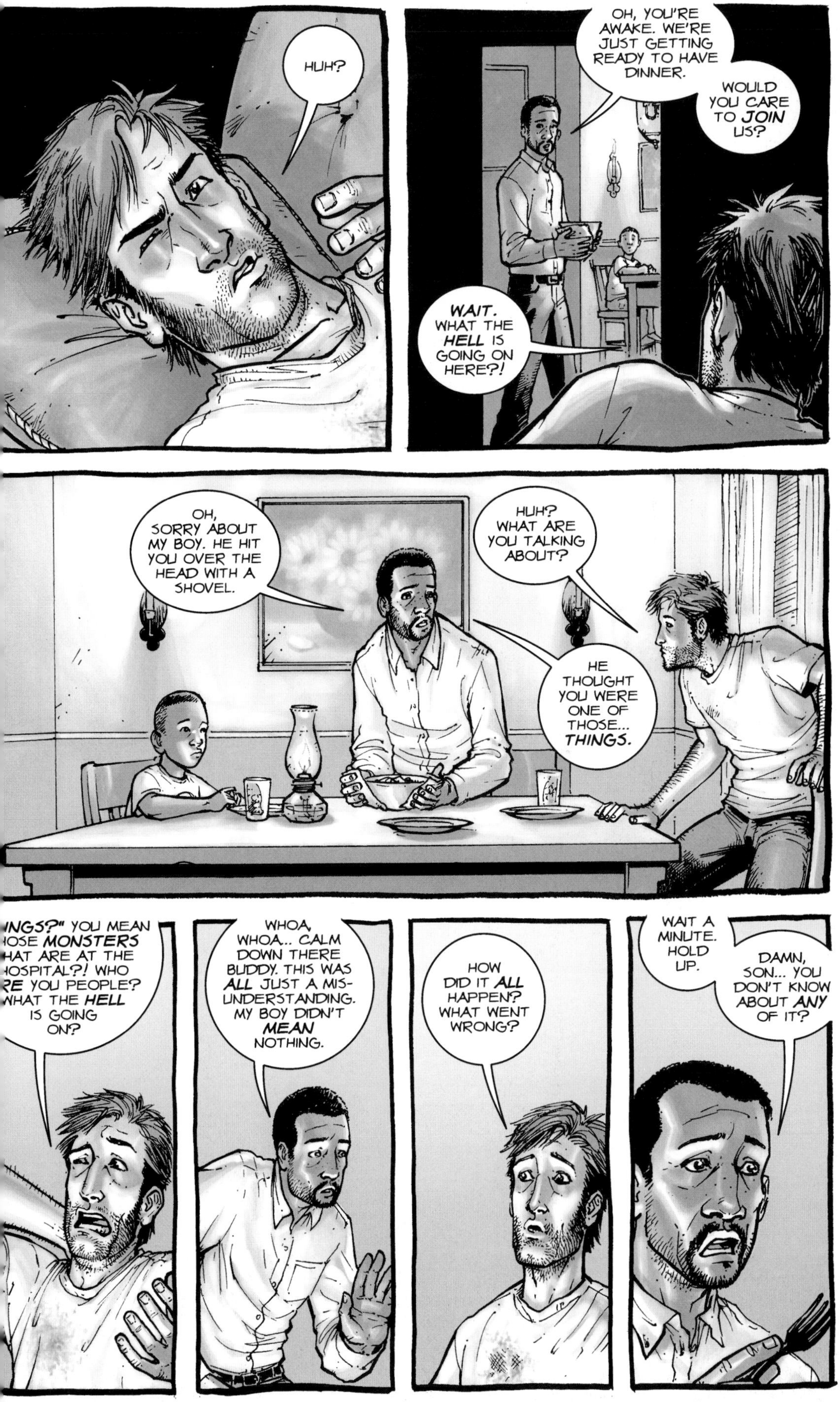
HUH?
OH, YOU'RE AWAKE. WE'RE JUST GETTING READY TO HAVE DINNER.
WOULD YOU CARE TO JOIN US?
WAIT. WHAT THE HELL IS GOING ON HERE?!
OH, SORRY ABOUT MY BOY. HE HIT YOU OVER THE HEAD WITH A SHOVEL.
HUH? WHAT ARE YOU TALKING ABOUT?
HE THOUGHT YOU WERE ONE OF THOSE... THINGS.
INGS?" YOU MEAN HOSE MONSTERS HAT ARE AT THE HOSPITAL?! WHO RE YOU PEOPLE? WHAT THE HELL IS GOING ON?
WHOA, WHOA... CALM DOWN THERE BUDDY. THIS WAS ALL JUST A MIS-UNDERSTANDING. MY BOY DIDN'T MEAN NOTHING.
HOW DID IT ALL HAPPEN? WHAT WENT WRONG?
WAIT A MINUTE. HOLD UP.
DAMN, SON... YOU DON'T KNOW ABOUT ANY OF IT?

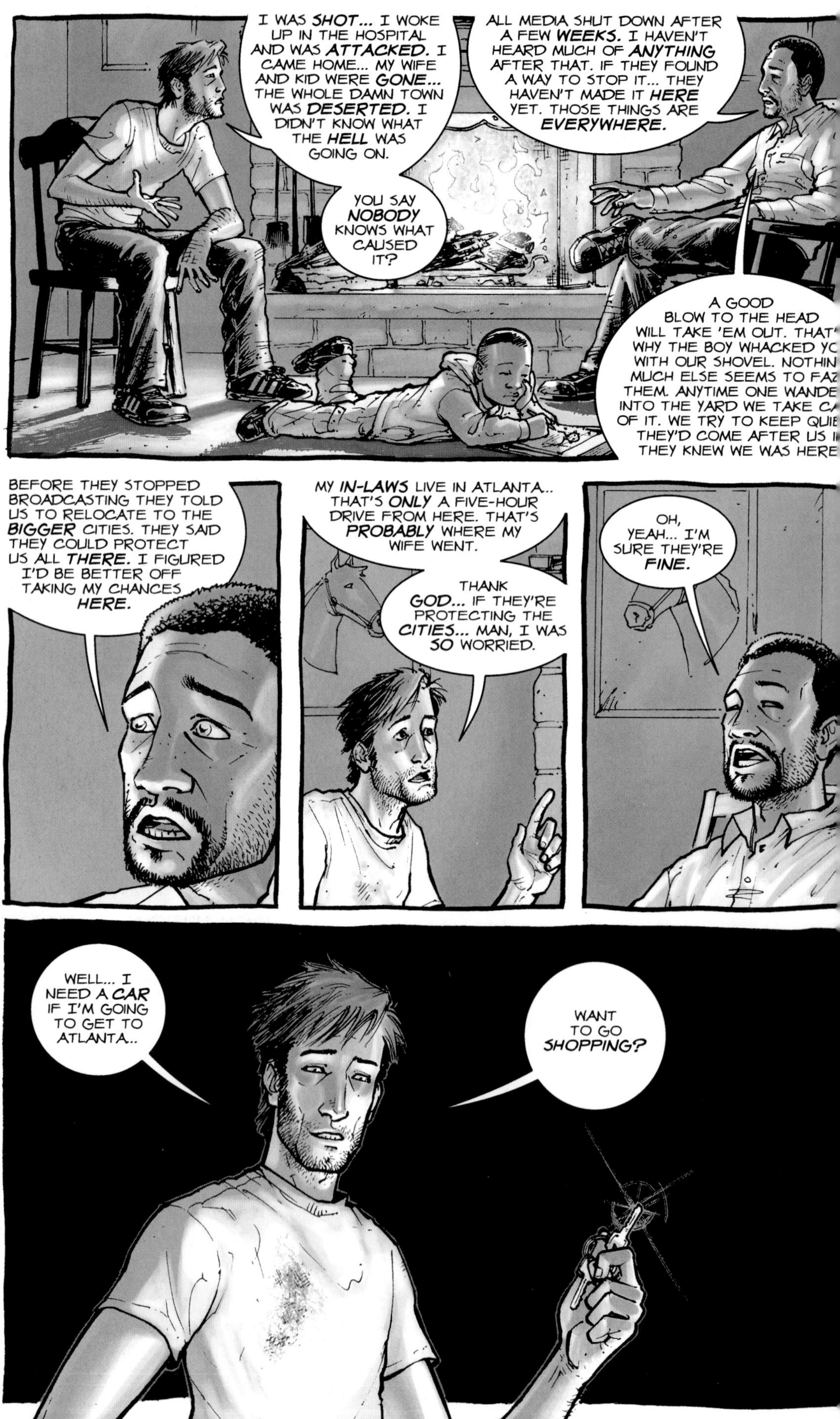
I WAS SHOT... I WOKE UP IN THE HOSPITAL AND WAS ATTACKED. I CAME HOME... MY WIFE AND KID WERE GONE... THE WHOLE DAMN TOWN WAS DESERTED. I DIDN'T KNOW WHAT THE HELL WAS GOING ON.
ALL MEDIA SHUT DOWN AFTER A FEW WEEKS. I HAVEN'T HEARD MUCH OF ANYTHING AFTER THAT. IF THEY FOUND A WAY TO STOP IT... THEY HAVEN'T MADE IT HERE YET. THOSE THINGS ARE EVERYWHERE.
YOU SAY NOBODY KNOWS WHAT CAUSED IT?
A GOOD BLOW TO THE HEAD WILL TAKE 'EM OUT. THAT' WHY THE BOY WHACKED YO WITH OUR SHOVEL. NOTHIN MUCH ELSE SEEMS TO FAZ THEM. ANYTIME ONE WANDE INTO THE YARD WE TAKE CA OF IT. WE TRY TO KEEP QUIE THEY'D COME AFTER US I THEY KNEW WE WAS HERE
BEFORE THEY STOPPED BROADCASTING THEY TOLD US TO RELOCATE TO THE BIGGER CITIES. THEY SAID THEY COULD PROTECT US ALL THERE. I FIGURED I'D BE BETTER OFF TAKING MY CHANCES HERE.
MY IN-LAWS LIVE IN ATLANTA.. THAT'S ONLY A FIVE-HOUR DRIVE FROM HERE. THAT'S PROBABLY WHERE MY WIFE WENT.
THANK GOD... IF THEY'RE PROTECTING THE CITIES... MAN, I WAS SO WORRIED.
OH, YEAH... I'M SURE THEY'RE FINE.
WELL... I NEED A CAR IF I'M GOING TO GET TO ATLANTA..
WANT TO GO SHOPPING?

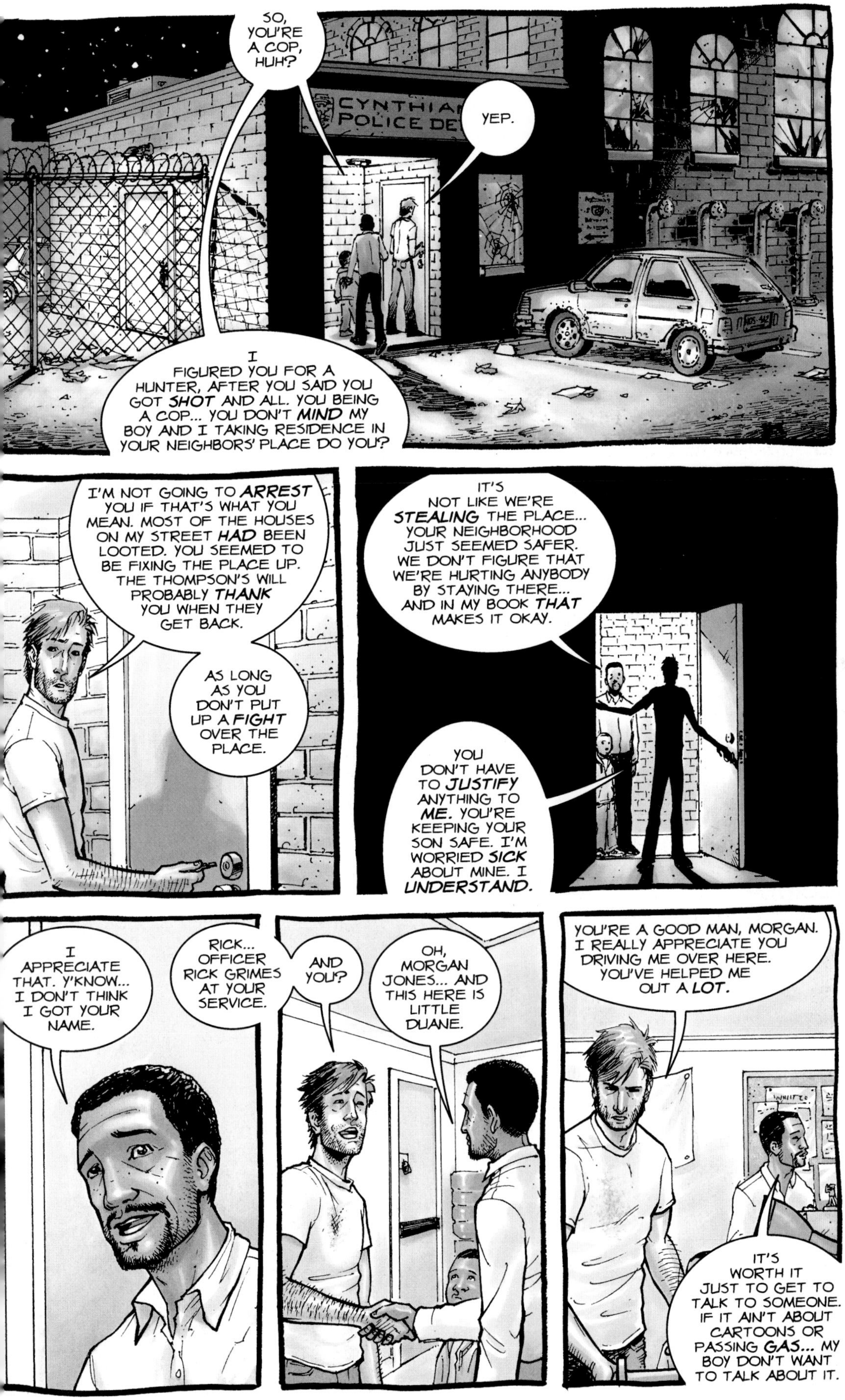
SO, YOU'RE A COP, HUH?
CYNTHIA POLICE DE
YEP.
I FIGURED YOU FOR A HUNTER, AFTER YOU SAID YOU GOT SHOT AND ALL. YOU BEING A COP... YOU DON'T MIND MY BOY AND I TAKING RESIDENCE IN YOUR NEIGHBORS' PLACE DO YOU?
I'M NOT GOING TO ARREST YOU IF THAT'S WHAT YOU MEAN. MOST OF THE HOUSES ON MY STREET HAD BEEN LOOTED. YOU SEEMED TO BE FIXING THE PLACE UP. THE THOMPSON'S WILL PROBABLY THANK YOU WHEN THEY GET BACK.
AS LONG AS YOU DON'T PUT UP A FIGHT OVER THE PLACE.
IT'S NOT LIKE WE'RE STEALING THE PLACE... YOUR NEIGHBORHOOD JUST SEEMED SAFER. WE DON'T FIGURE THAT WE'RE HURTING ANYBODY BY STAYING THERE... AND IN MY BOOK THAT MAKES IT OKAY.
YOU DON'T HAVE TO JUSTIFY ANYTHING TO ME. YOU'RE KEEPING YOUR SON SAFE. I'M WORRIED SICK ABOUT MINE. I UNDERSTAND.
I APPRECIATE THAT. Y'KNOW... I DON'T THINK I GOT YOUR NAME.
RICK... OFFICER RICK GRIMES AT YOUR SERVICE.
AND YOU?
OH, MORGAN JONES... AND THIS HERE IS LITTLE DUANE.
YOU'RE A GOOD MAN, MORGAN. I REALLY APPRECIATE YOU DRIVING ME OVER HERE. YOU'VE HELPED ME OUT A LOT.
IT'S WORTH IT JUST TO GET TO TALK TO SOMEONE. IF IT AIN'T ABOUT CARTOONS OR PASSING GAS... MY BOY DON'T WANT TO TALK ABOUT IT.

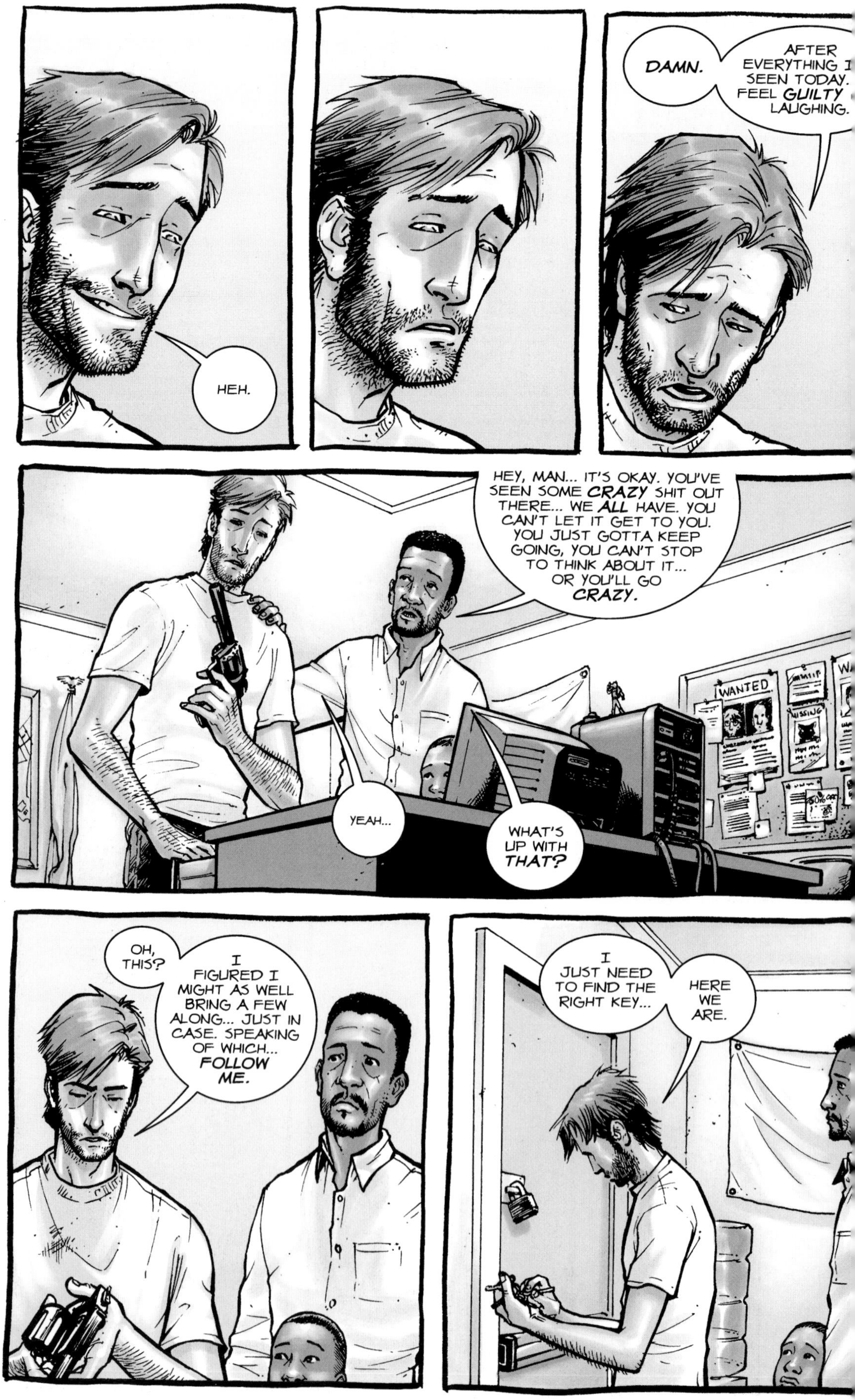
HEH.
DAMN.
AFTER EVERYTHING I SEEN TODAY. FEEL GUILTY LAUGHING.
HEY, MAN... IT'S OKAY. YOU'VE SEEN SOME CRAZY SHIT OUT THERE... WE ALL HAVE. YOU CAN'T LET IT GET TO YOU. YOU JUST GOTTA KEEP GOING, YOU CAN'T STOP TO THINK ABOUT IT... OR YOU'LL GO CRAZY.
YEAH...
WHAT'S UP WITH THAT?
WANTED
MISSING
OH, THIS?
I FIGURED I MIGHT AS WELL BRING A FEW ALONG... JUST IN CASE. SPEAKING OF WHICH... FOLLOW ME.
I JUST NEED TO FIND THE RIGHT KEY...
HERE WE ARE.

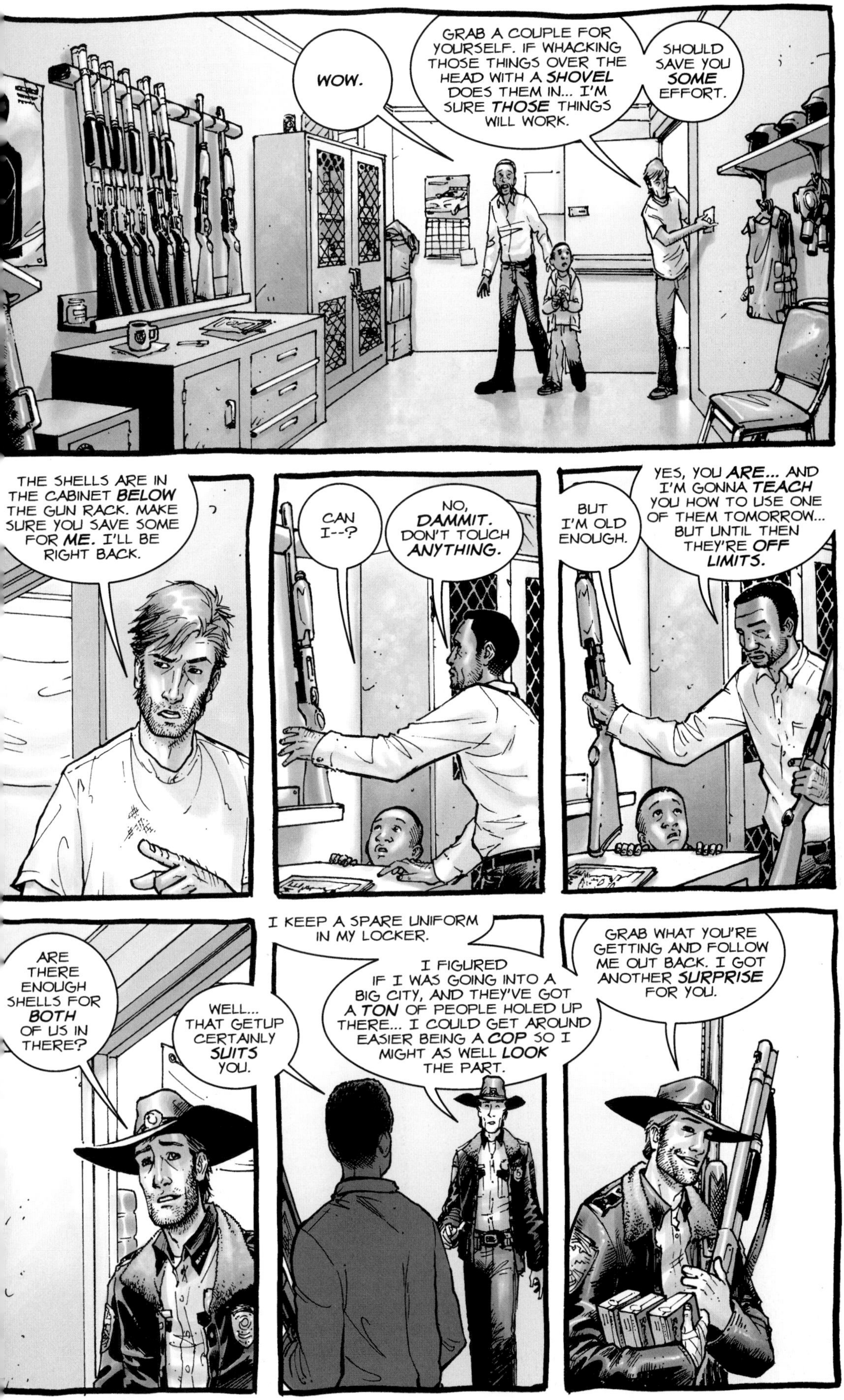
WOW.
GRAB A COUPLE FOR YOURSELF. IF WHACKING THOSE THINGS OVER THE HEAD WITH A SHOVEL DOES THEM IN... I'M SURE THOSE THINGS WILL WORK.
SHOULD SAVE YOU SOME EFFORT.
THE SHELLS ARE IN THE CABINET BELOW THE GUN RACK. MAKE SURE YOU SAVE SOME FOR ME. I'LL BE RIGHT BACK.
CAN I--?
NO, DAMMIT. DON'T TOUCH ANYTHING.
BUT I'M OLD ENOUGH.
YES, YOU ARE... AND I'M GONNA TEACH YOU HOW TO USE ONE OF THEM TOMORROW... BUT UNTIL THEN THEY'RE OFF LIMITS.
ARE THERE ENOUGH SHELLS FOR BOTH OF US IN THERE?
WELL... THAT GETUP CERTAINLY SUITS YOU.
I KEEP A SPARE UNIFORM IN MY LOCKER.
I FIGURED IF I WAS GOING INTO A BIG CITY, AND THEY'VE GOT A TON OF PEOPLE HOLED UP THERE... I COULD GET AROUND EASIER BEING A COP SO I MIGHT AS WELL LOOK THE PART.
GRAB WHAT YOU'RE GETTING AND FOLLOW ME OUT BACK. I GOT ANOTHER SURPRISE FOR YOU.

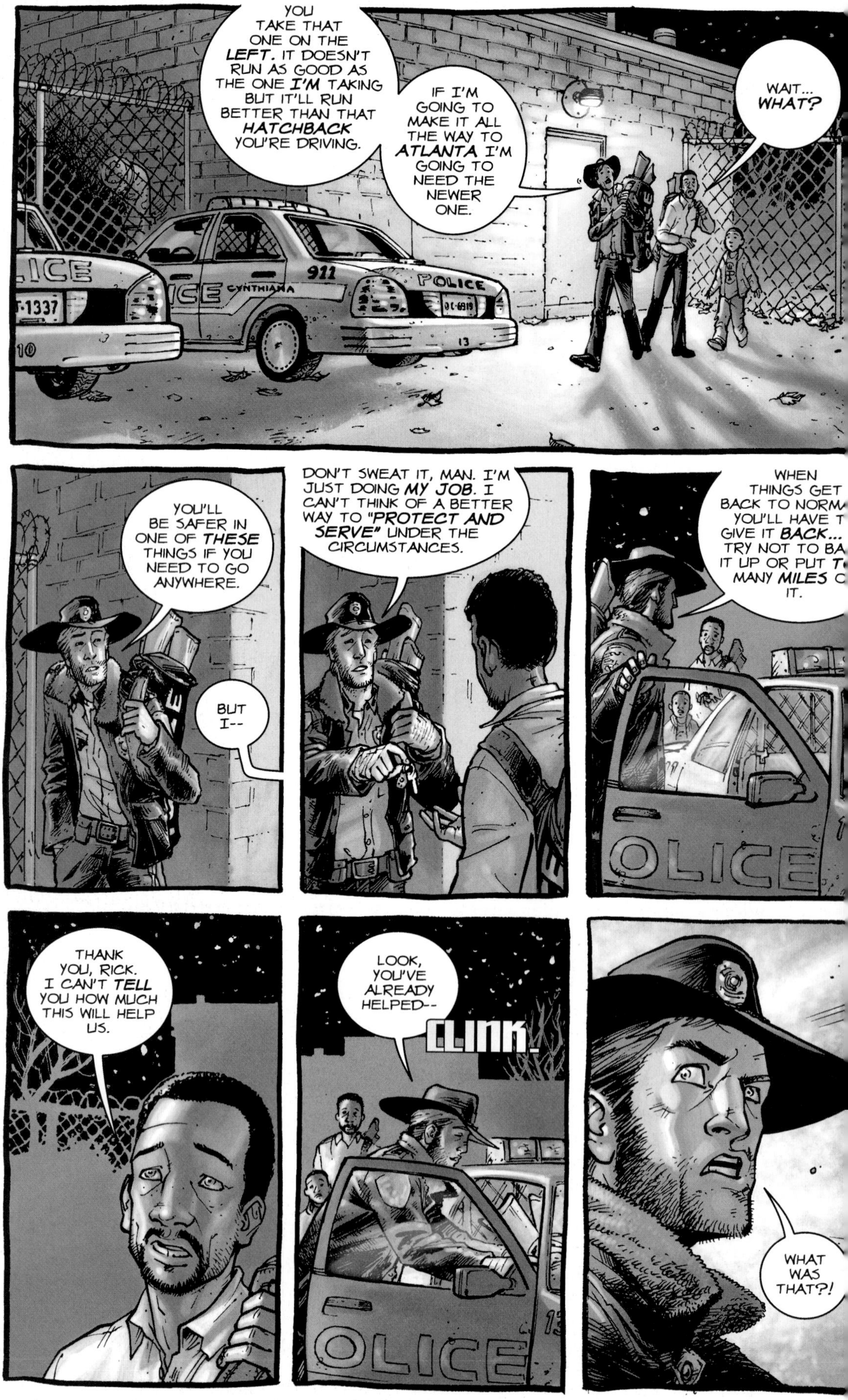
YOU TAKE THAT ONE ON THE LEFT. IT DOESN'T RUN AS GOOD AS THE ONE I'M TAKING BUT IT'LL RUN BETTER THAN THAT HATCHBACK YOU'RE DRIVING.
IF I'M GOING TO MAKE IT ALL THE WAY TO ATLANTA I'M GOING TO NEED THE NEWER ONE.
WAIT... WHAT?
YOU'LL BE SAFER IN ONE OF THESE THINGS IF YOU NEED TO GO ANYWHERE.
BUT I--
DON'T SWEAT IT, MAN. I'M JUST DOING MY JOB. I CAN'T THINK OF A BETTER WAY TO "PROTECT AND SERVE" UNDER THE CIRCUMSTANCES.
WHEN THINGS GET BACK TO NORMA YOU'LL HAVE T GIVE IT BACK... TRY NOT TO BA IT UP OR PUT T MANY MILES C IT.
THANK YOU, RICK. I CAN'T TELL YOU HOW MUCH THIS WILL HELP US.
LOOK, YOU'VE ALREADY HELPED--
CLINK.
WHAT WAS THAT?!

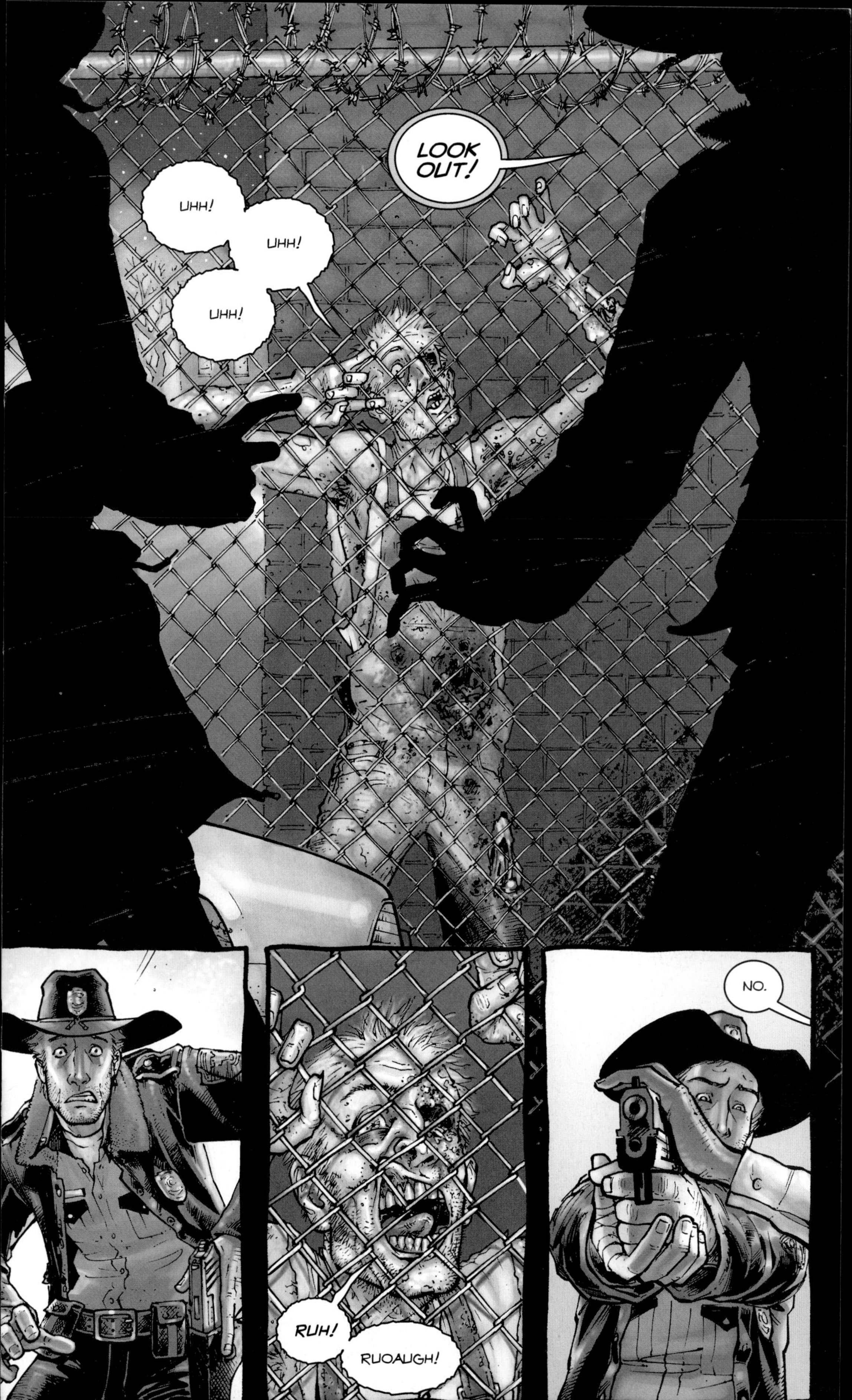
LOOK OUT!
UHH!
UHH!
UHH!
RUH!
RUOAUGH!
NO.

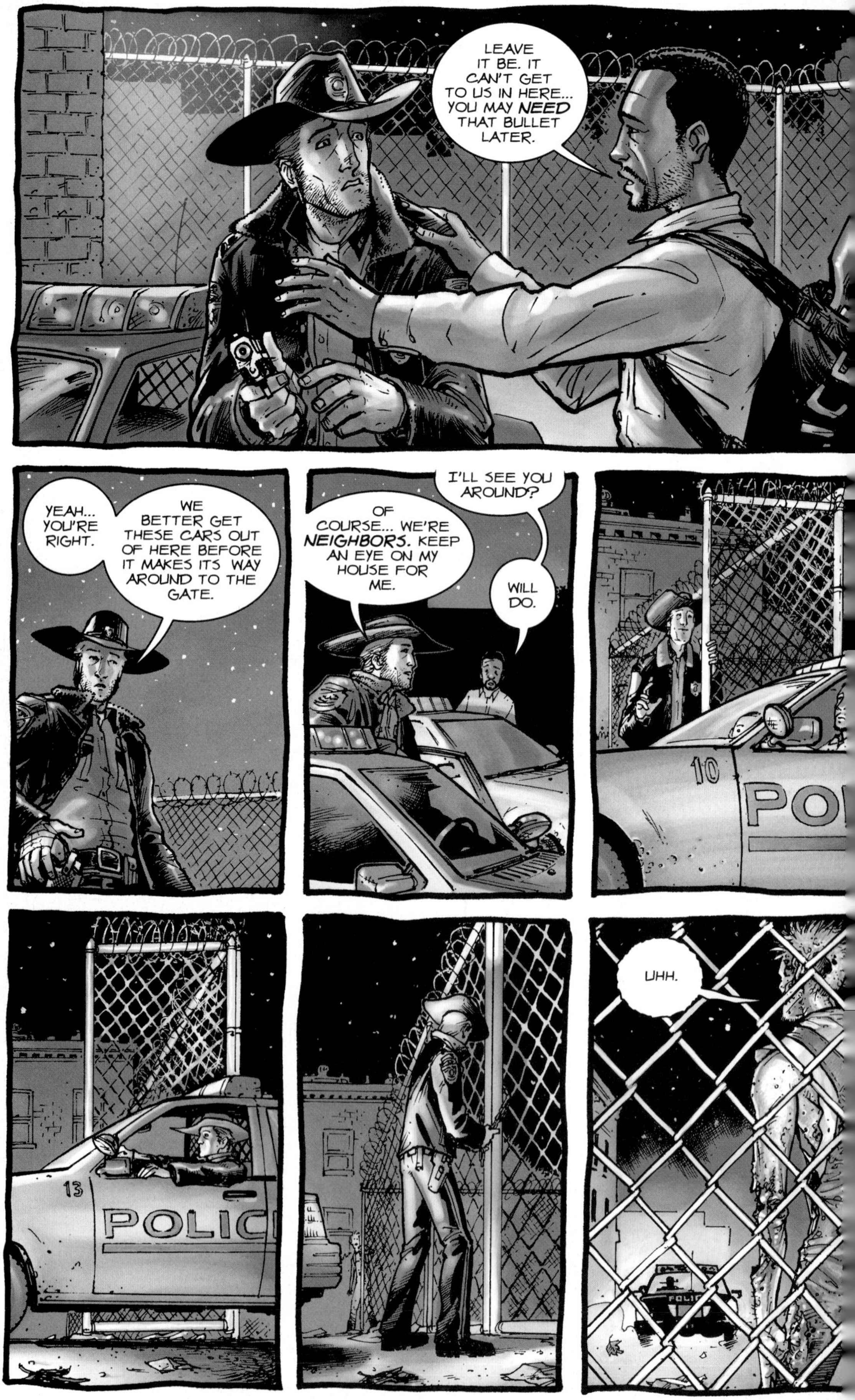
LEAVE IT BE. IT CAN'T GET TO US IN HERE... YOU MAY NEED THAT BULLET LATER.
YEAH... YOU'RE RIGHT.
WE BETTER GET THESE CARS OUT OF HERE BEFORE IT MAKES ITS WAY AROUND TO THE GATE.
I'LL SEE YOU AROUND?
OF COURSE... WE'RE NEIGHBORS. KEEP AN EYE ON MY HOUSE FOR ME.
WILL DO.
10
POLI
13
POLIC
UHH.

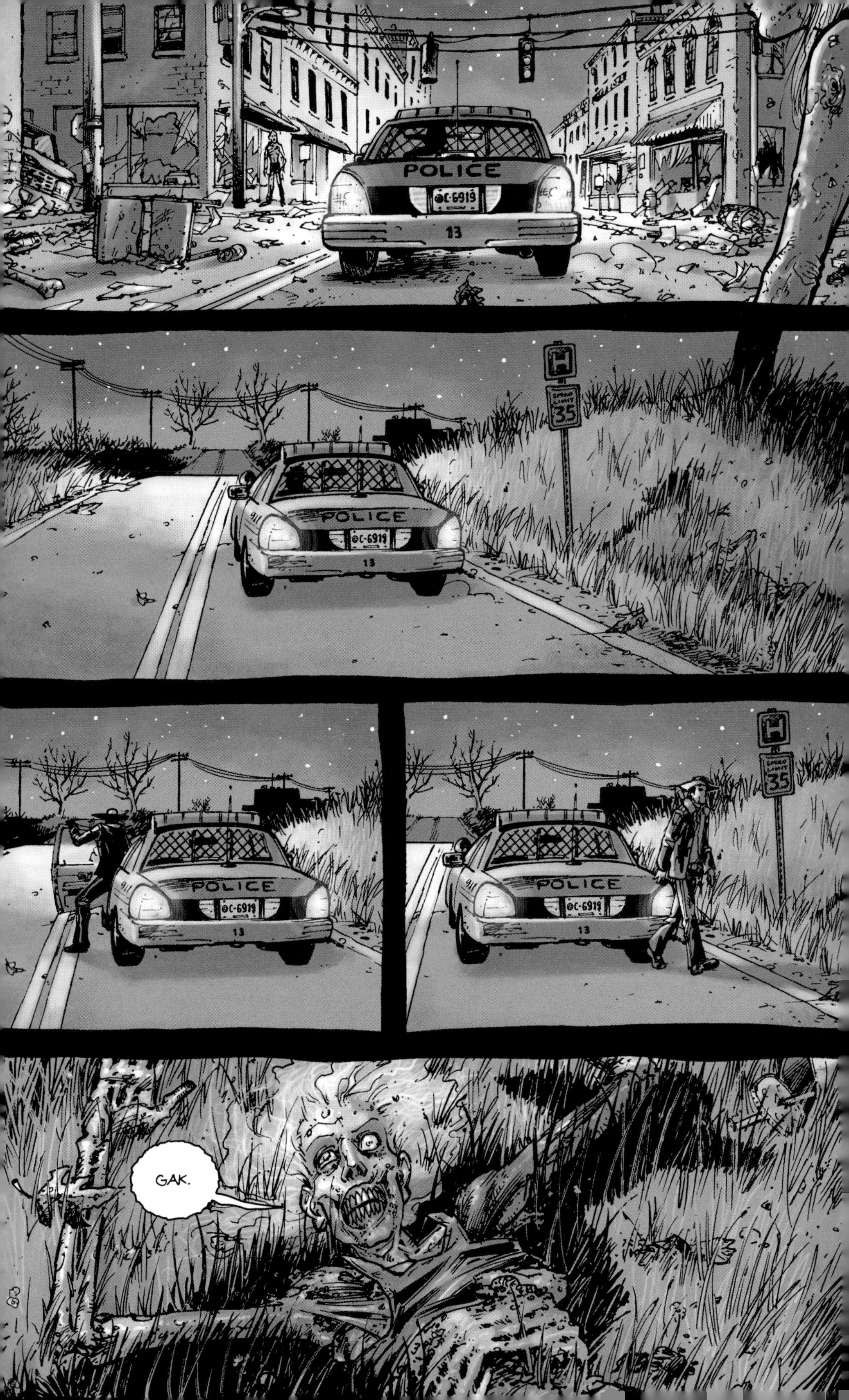

POLICE
POLICE
POLICE
POLICE
GAK.

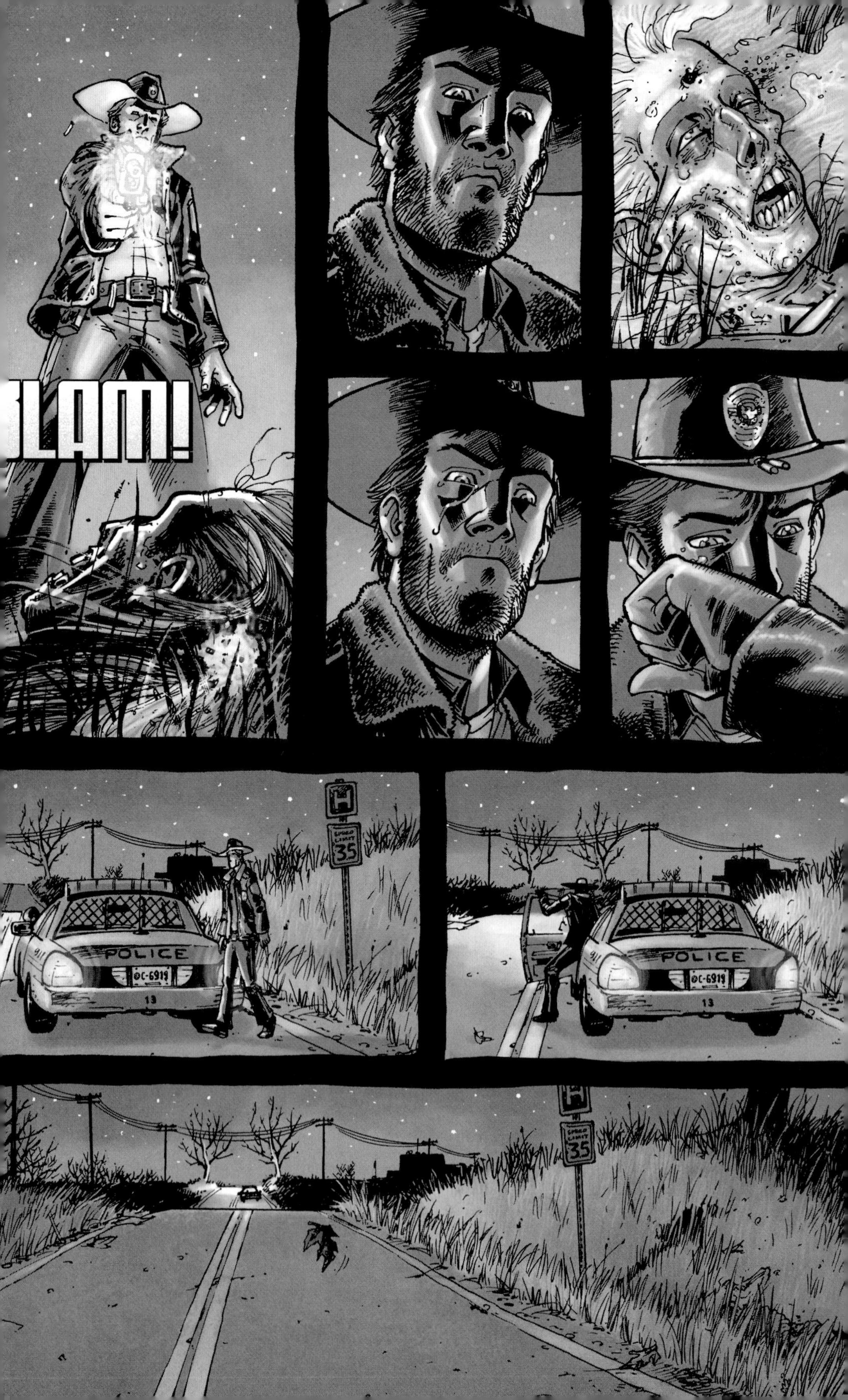
BLAM!
POLICE
C-6919
35
POLICE
C-6919

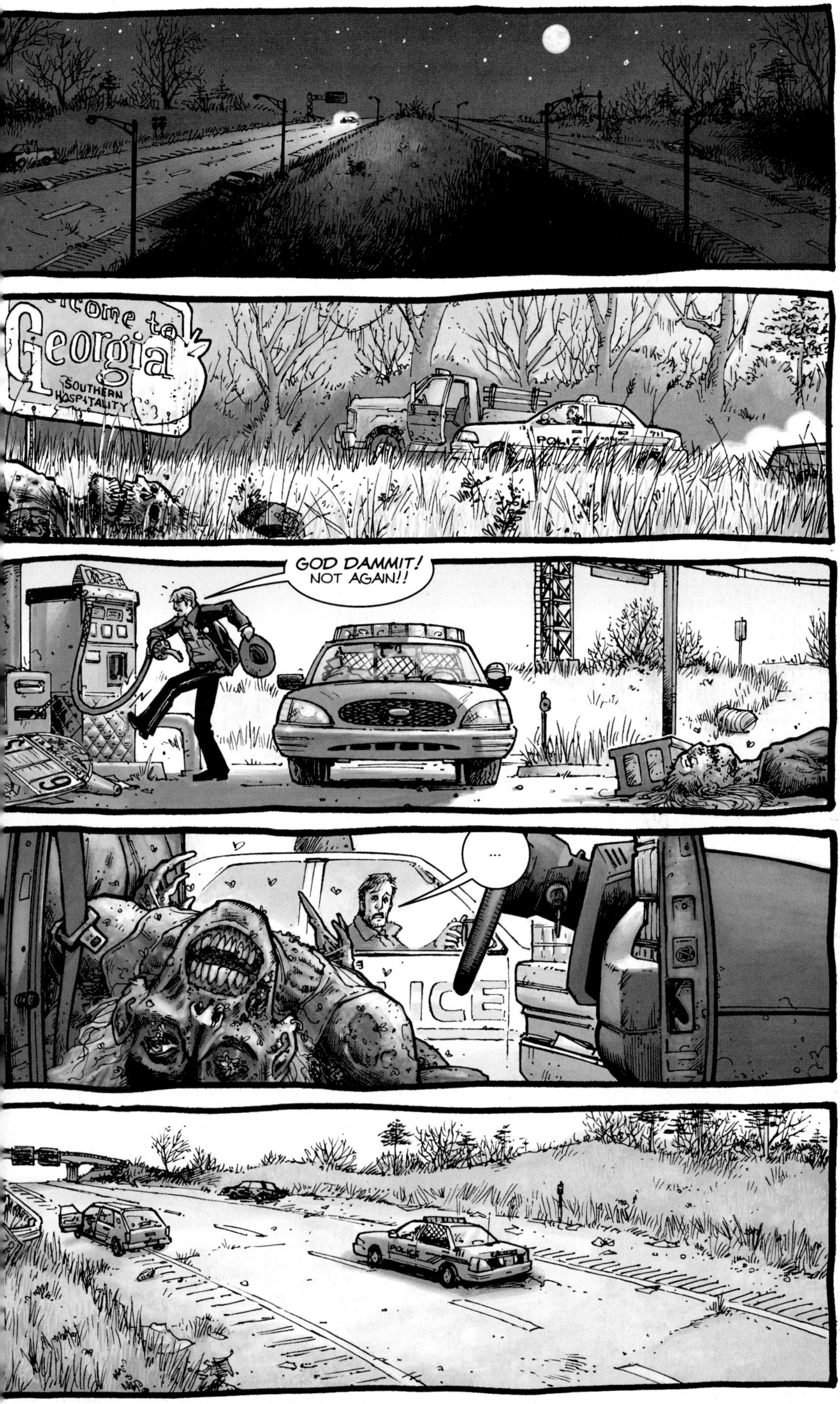
Welcome to Georgia
SOUTHERN HOSPITALITY
POLICE
GOD DAMMIT! NOT AGAIN!!
...
POLICE

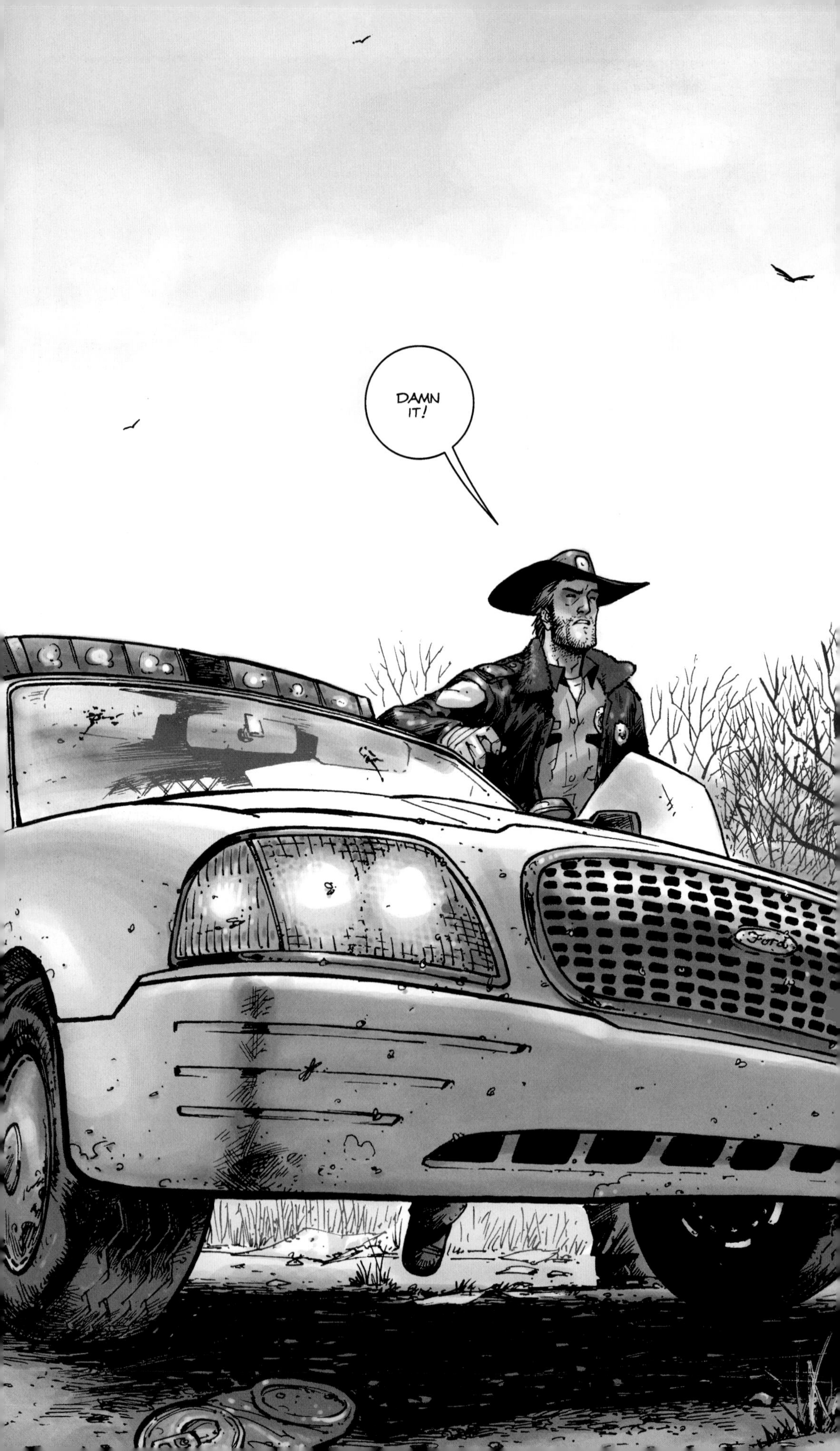
DAMN IT!

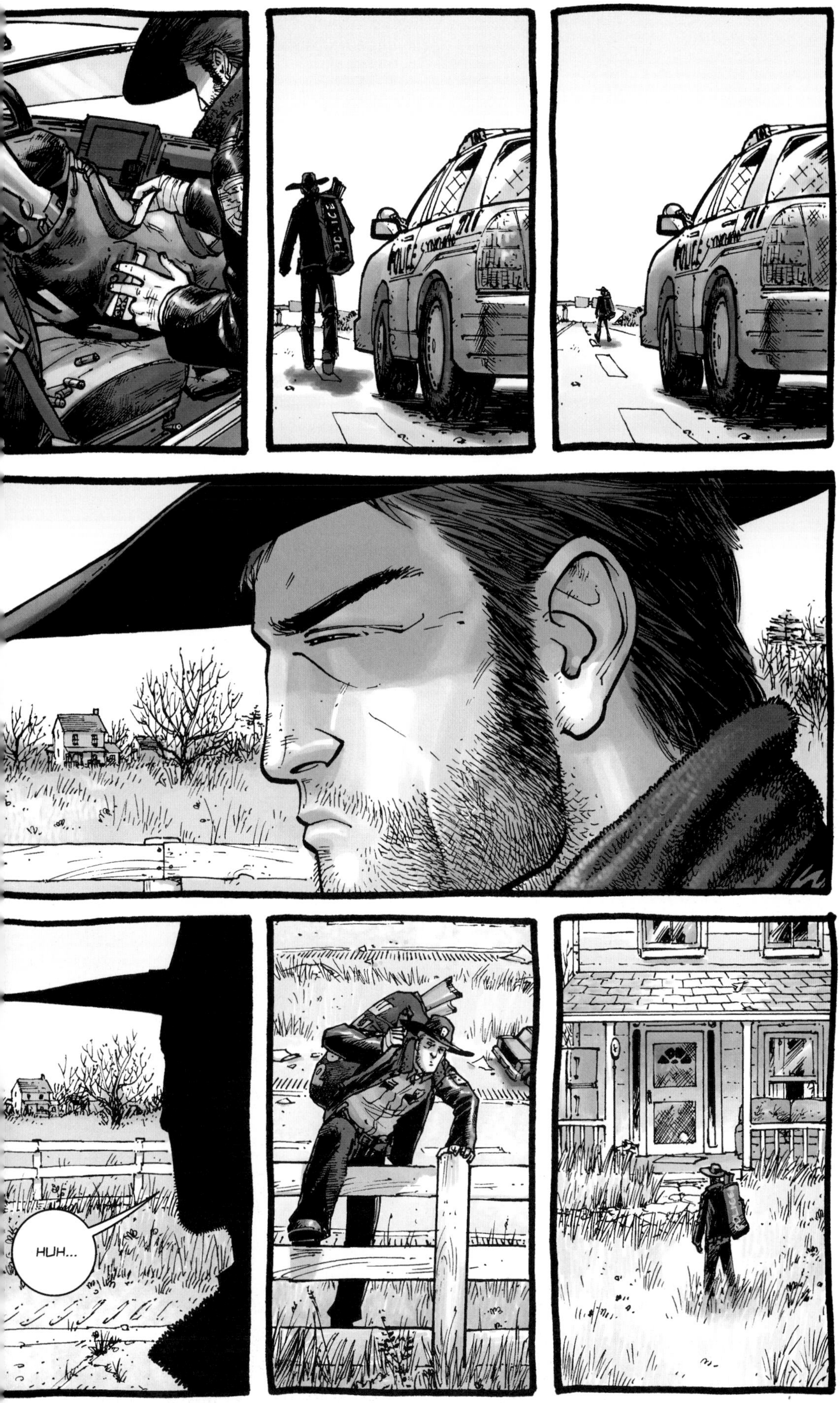
HUH...

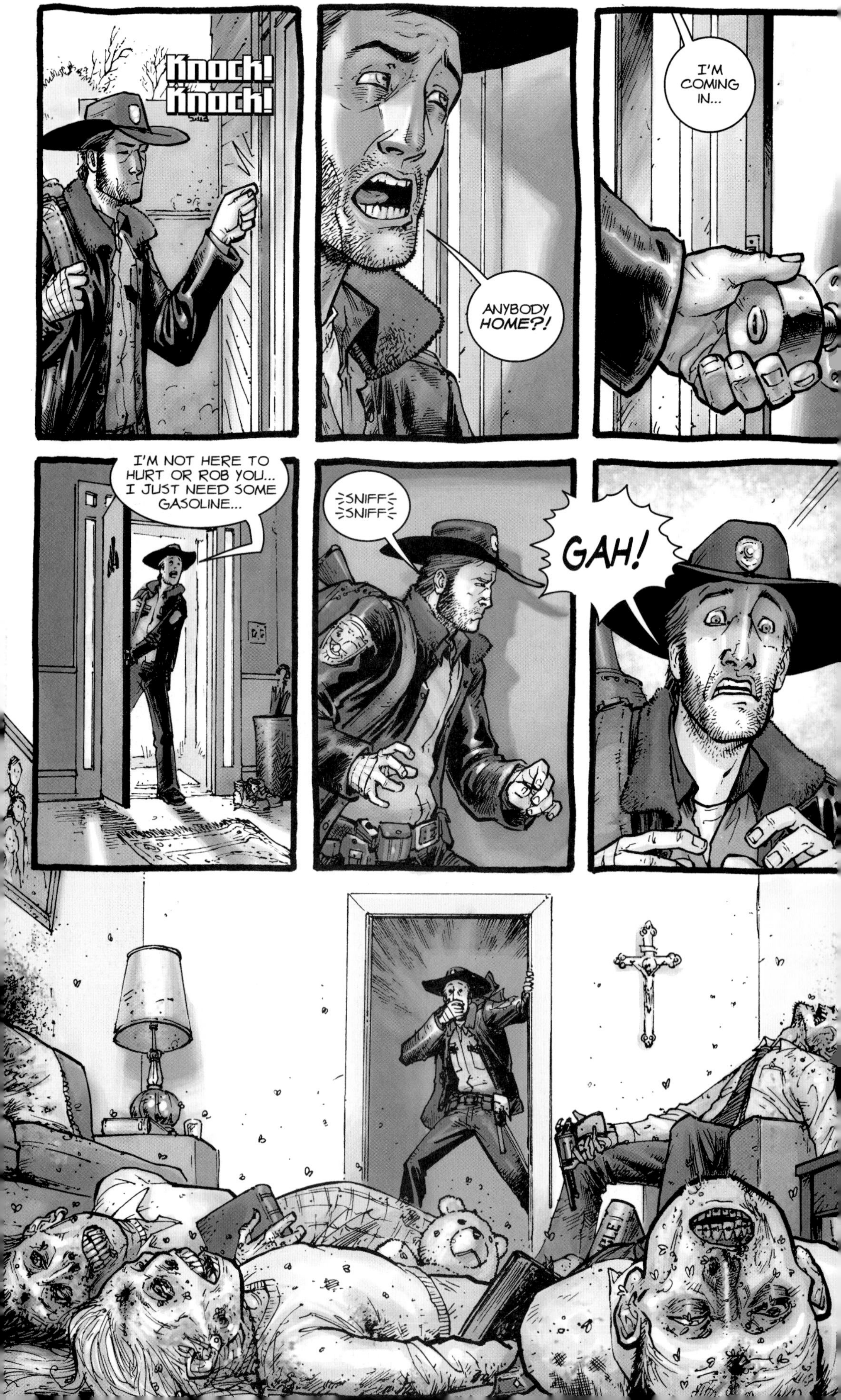
KNOCK! KNOCK!
ANYBODY HOME?!
I'M COMING IN...
I'M NOT HERE TO HURT OR ROB YOU... I JUST NEED SOME GASOLINE...
SNIFF SNIFF
GAH!

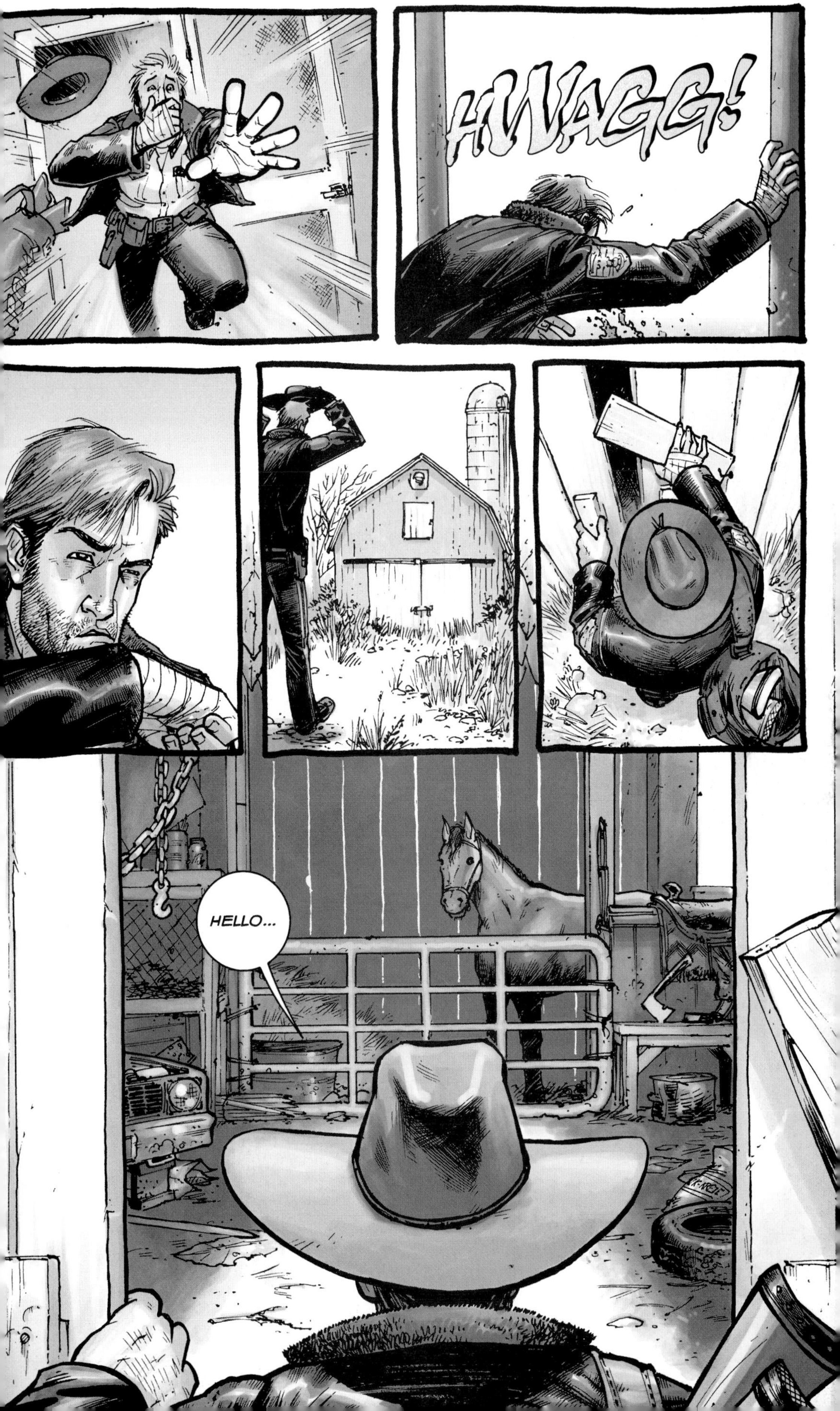
HWAGG!
HELLO...

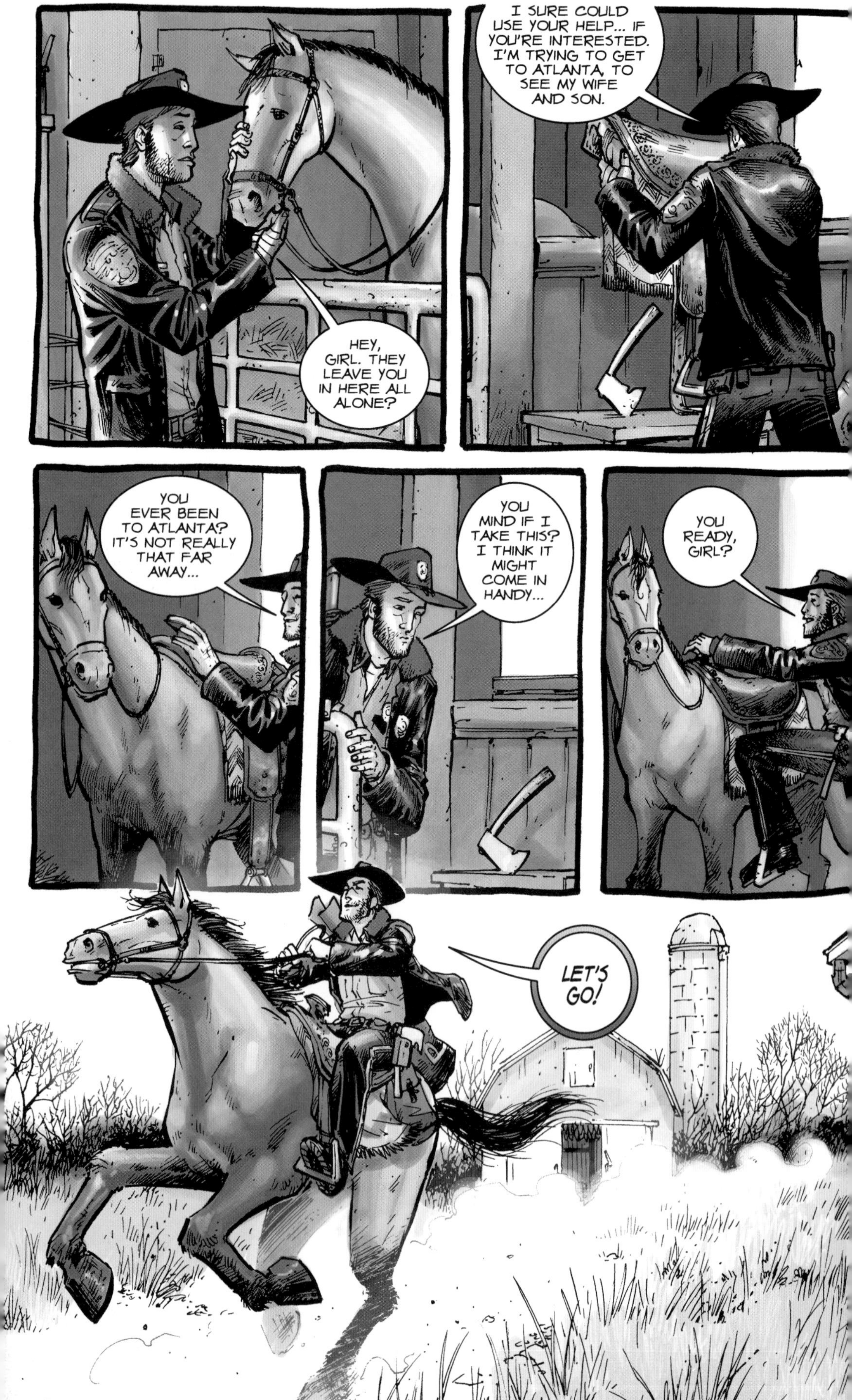
HEY, GIRL. THEY LEAVE YOU IN HERE ALL ALONE?
I SURE COULD USE YOUR HELP... IF YOU'RE INTERESTED. I'M TRYING TO GET TO ATLANTA, TO SEE MY WIFE AND SON.
YOU EVER BEEN TO ATLANTA? IT'S NOT REALLY THAT FAR AWAY...
YOU MIND IF I TAKE THIS? I THINK IT MIGHT COME IN HANDY...
YOU READY, GIRL?
LET'S GO!

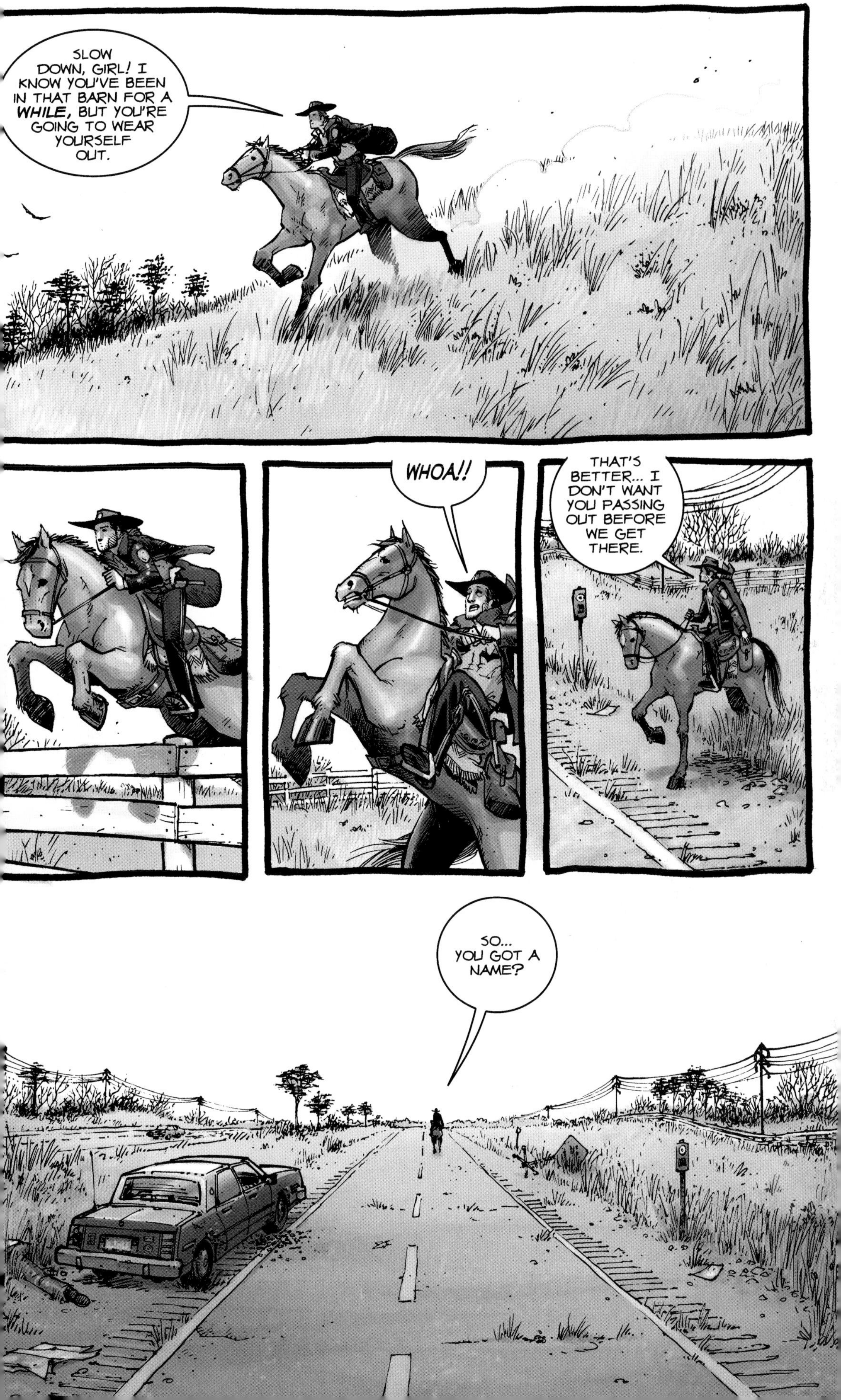
SLOW DOWN, GIRL! I KNOW YOU'VE BEEN IN THAT BARN FOR A *WHILE,* BUT YOU'RE GOING TO WEAR YOURSELF OUT.
WHOA!!
THAT'S BETTER... I DON'T WANT YOU PASSING OUT BEFORE WE GET THERE.
SO... YOU GOT A NAME?

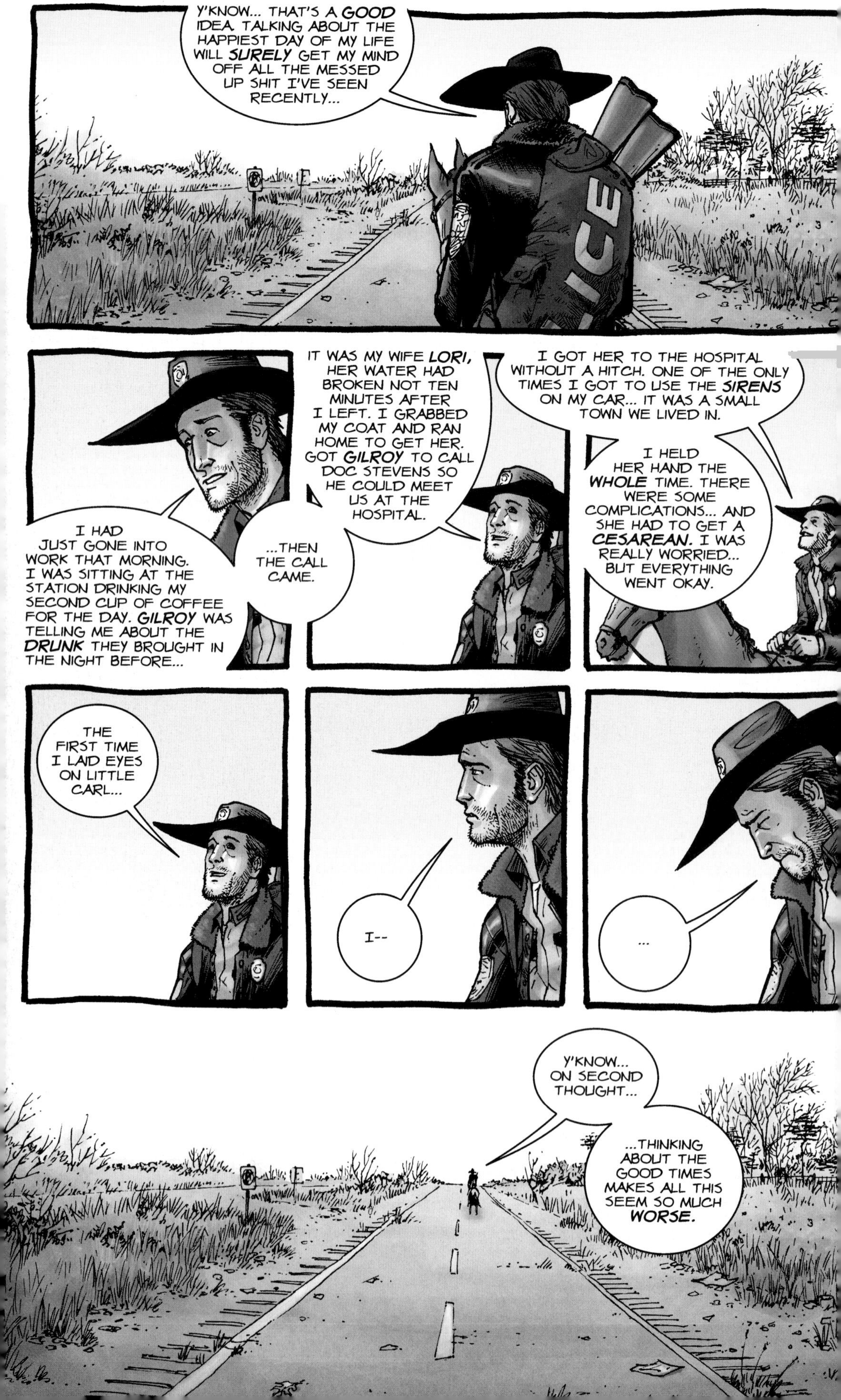

Y'KNOW... THAT'S A GOOD IDEA. TALKING ABOUT THE HAPPIEST DAY OF MY LIFE WILL SURELY GET MY MIND OFF ALL THE MESSED UP SHIT I'VE SEEN RECENTLY...
I HAD JUST GONE INTO WORK THAT MORNING. I WAS SITTING AT THE STATION DRINKING MY SECOND CUP OF COFFEE FOR THE DAY. GILROY WAS TELLING ME ABOUT THE DRUNK THEY BROUGHT IN THE NIGHT BEFORE...
...THEN THE CALL CAME.
IT WAS MY WIFE LORI, HER WATER HAD BROKEN NOT TEN MINUTES AFTER I LEFT. I GRABBED MY COAT AND RAN HOME TO GET HER. GOT GILROY TO CALL DOC STEVENS SO HE COULD MEET US AT THE HOSPITAL.
I GOT HER TO THE HOSPITAL WITHOUT A HITCH. ONE OF THE ONLY TIMES I GOT TO USE THE SIRENS ON MY CAR... IT WAS A SMALL TOWN WE LIVED IN.
I HELD HER HAND THE WHOLE TIME. THERE WERE SOME COMPLICATIONS... AND SHE HAD TO GET A CESAREAN. I WAS REALLY WORRIED... BUT EVERYTHING WENT OKAY.
THE FIRST TIME I LAID EYES ON LITTLE CARL...
I--
...
Y'KNOW... ON SECOND THOUGHT...
...THINKING ABOUT THE GOOD TIMES MAKES ALL THIS SEEM SO MUCH WORSE.

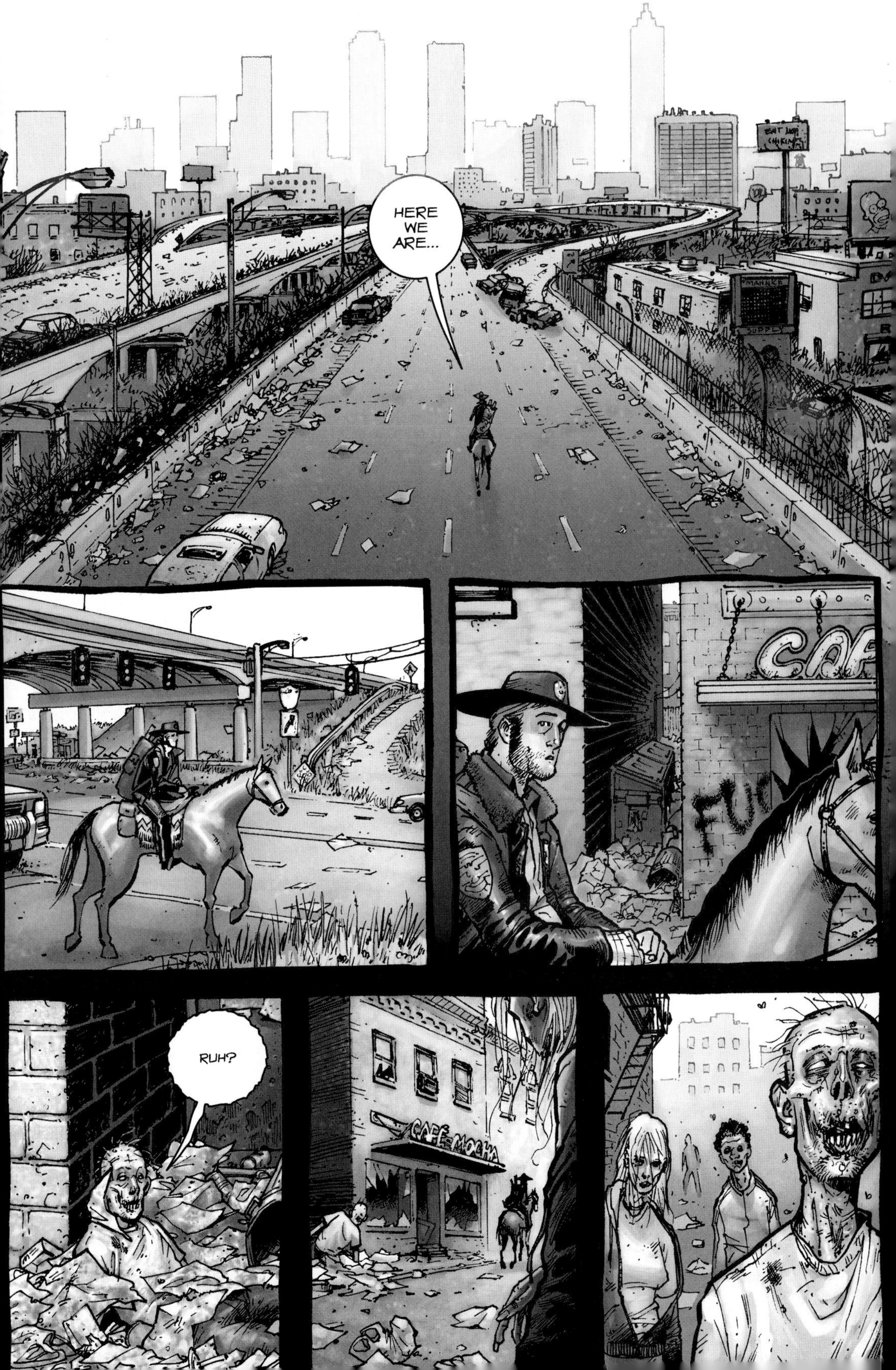
HERE WE ARE...
RUH?
CAFE MOCHA

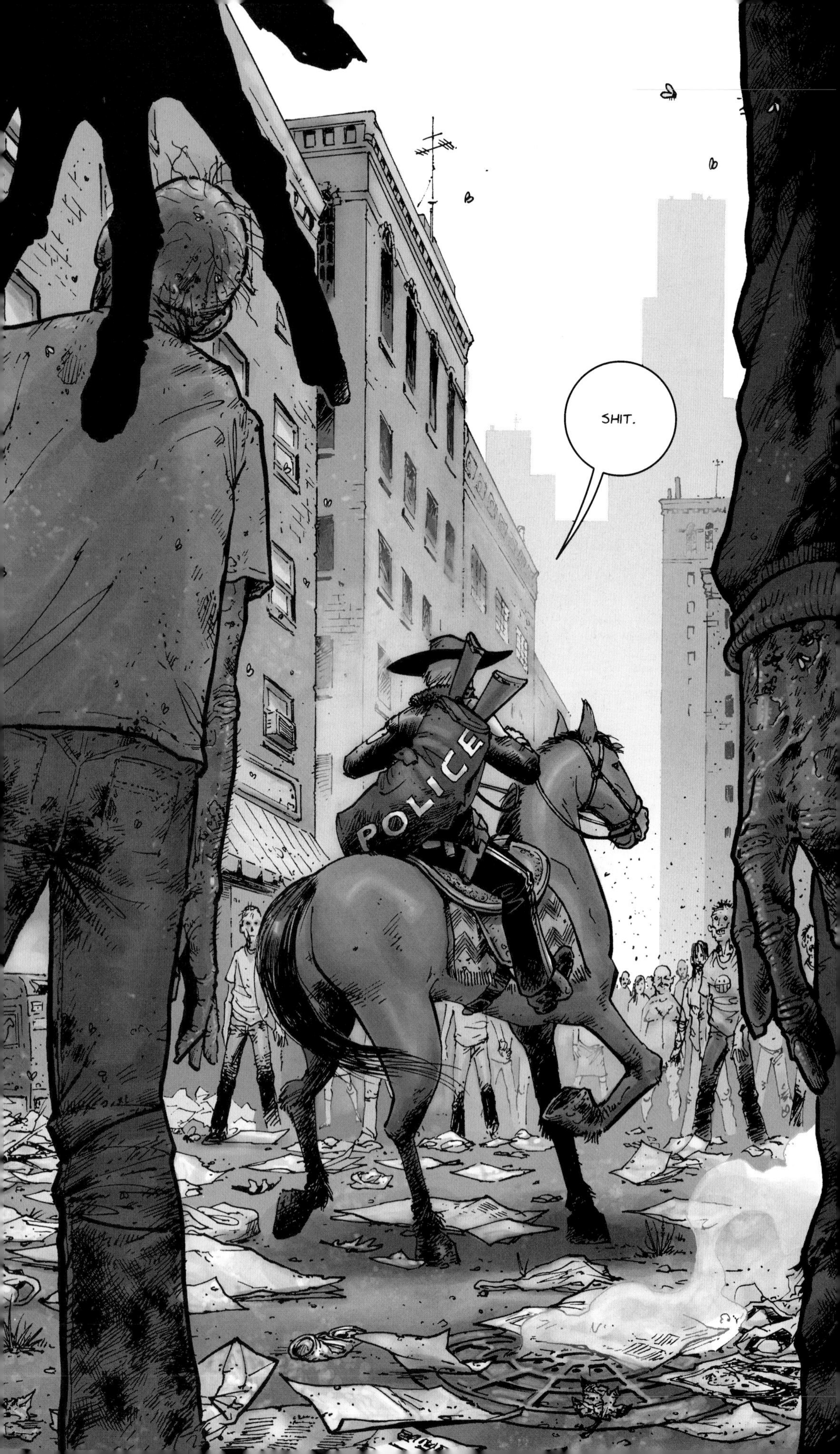
SHIT.
POLICE

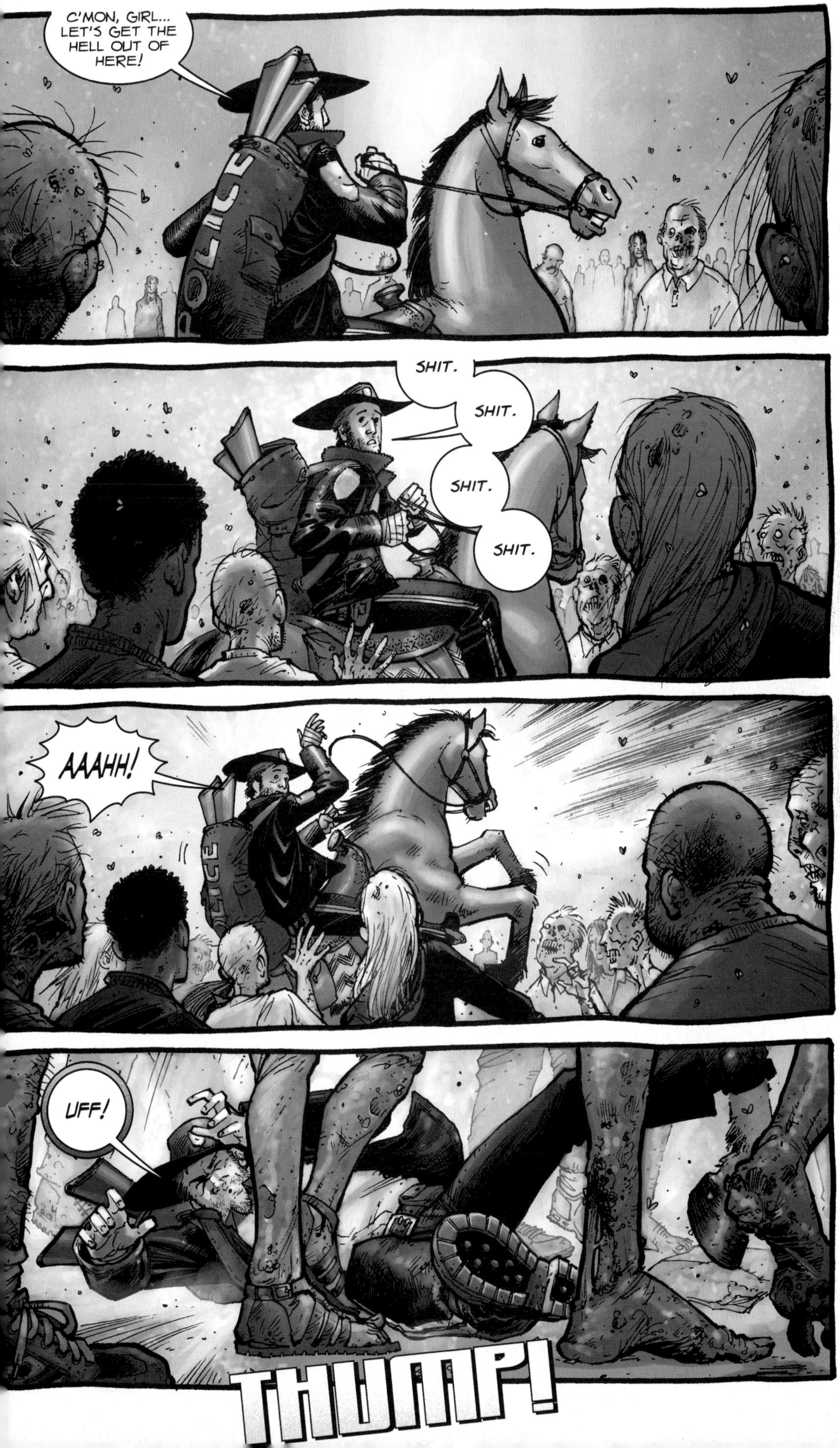

C'MON, GIRL... LET'S GET THE HELL OUT OF HERE!
SHIT.
SHIT.
SHIT.
SHIT.
AAAHH!
UFF!
THUMP!

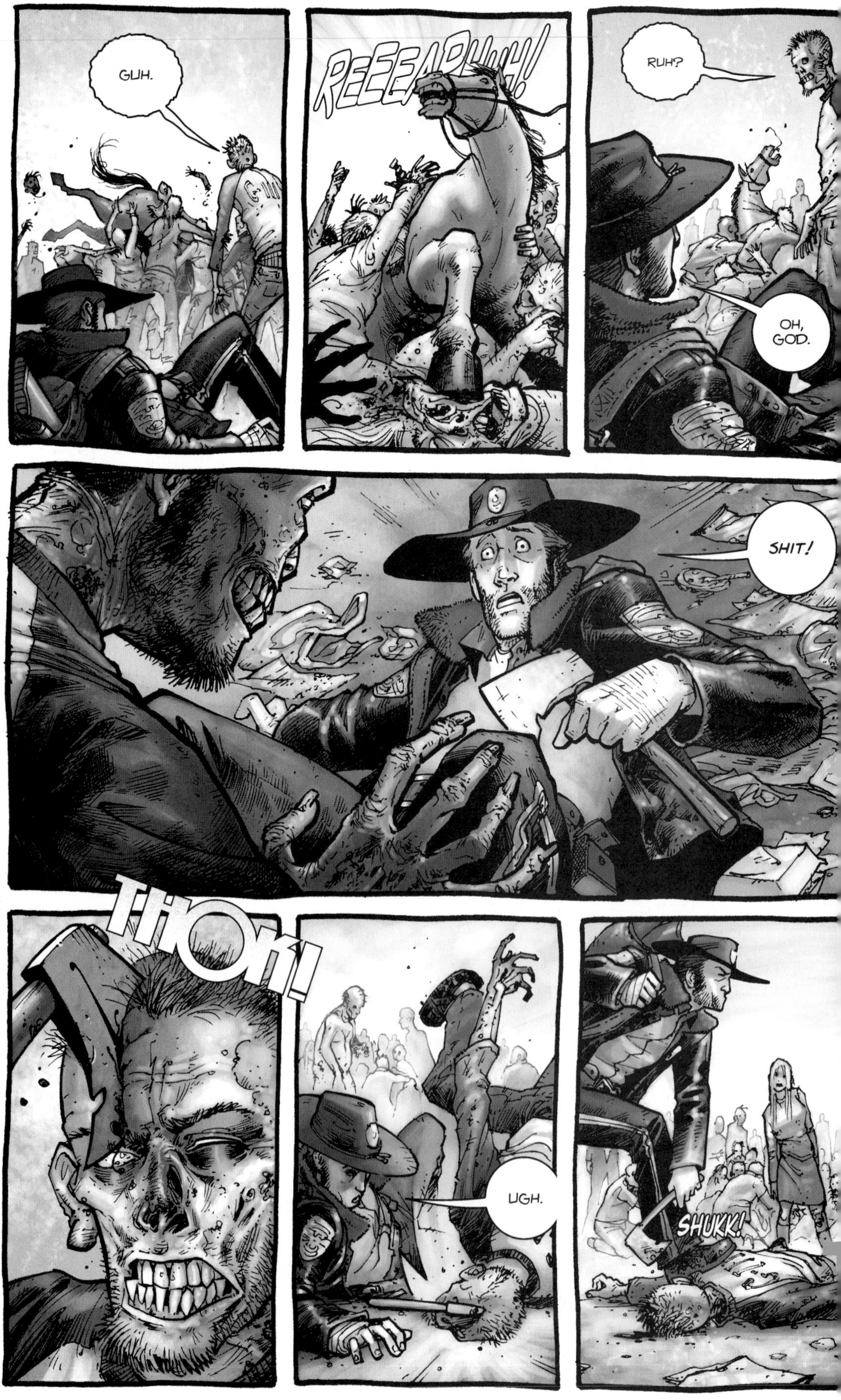
GUH.
REEEEARHHH!
RUH?
OH, GOD.
SHIT!
THOK!
UGH.
SHUKK!

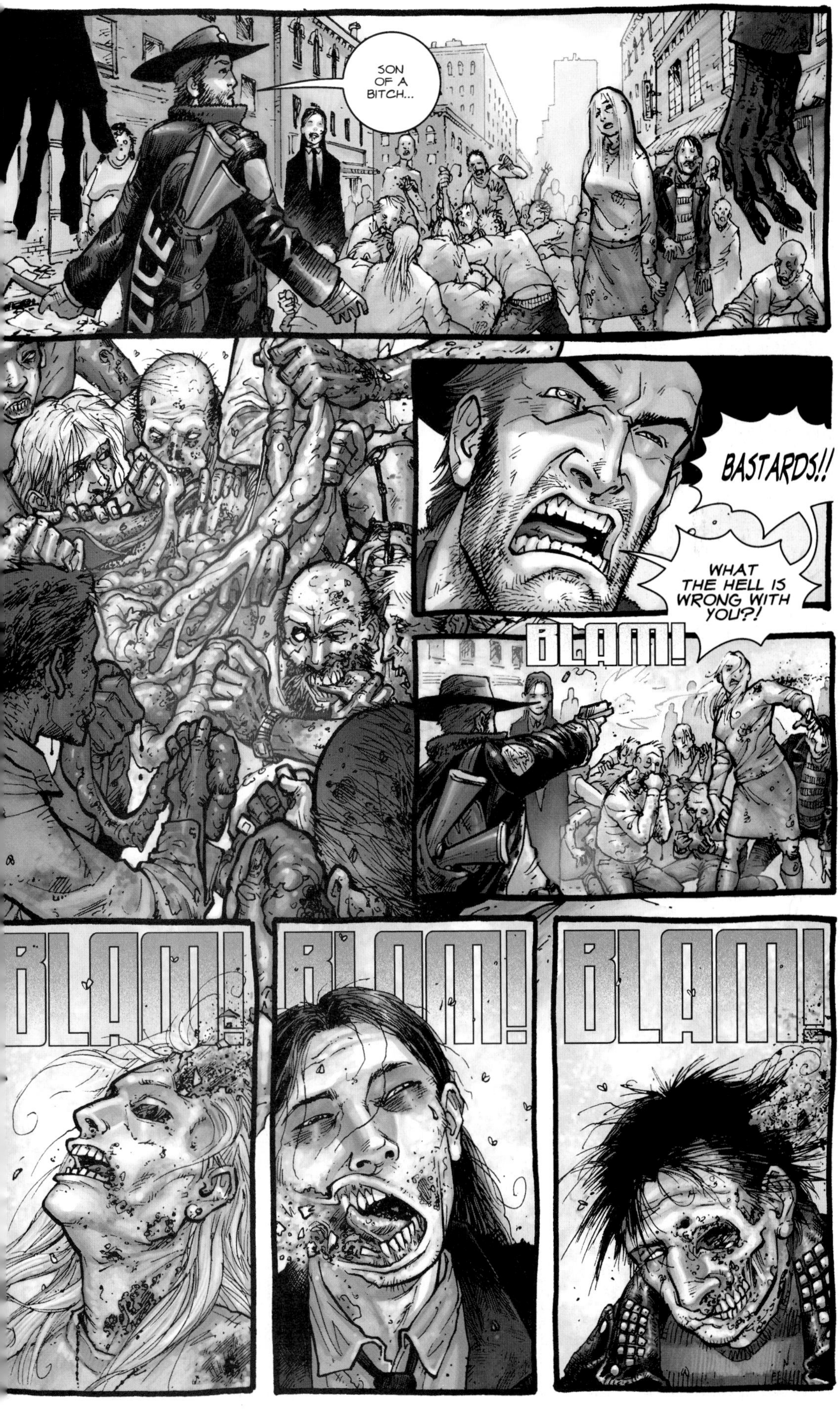
SON OF A BITCH...
BASTARDS!!
WHAT THE HELL IS WRONG WITH YOU?!
BLAM!
BLAM!
BLAM!
BLAM!

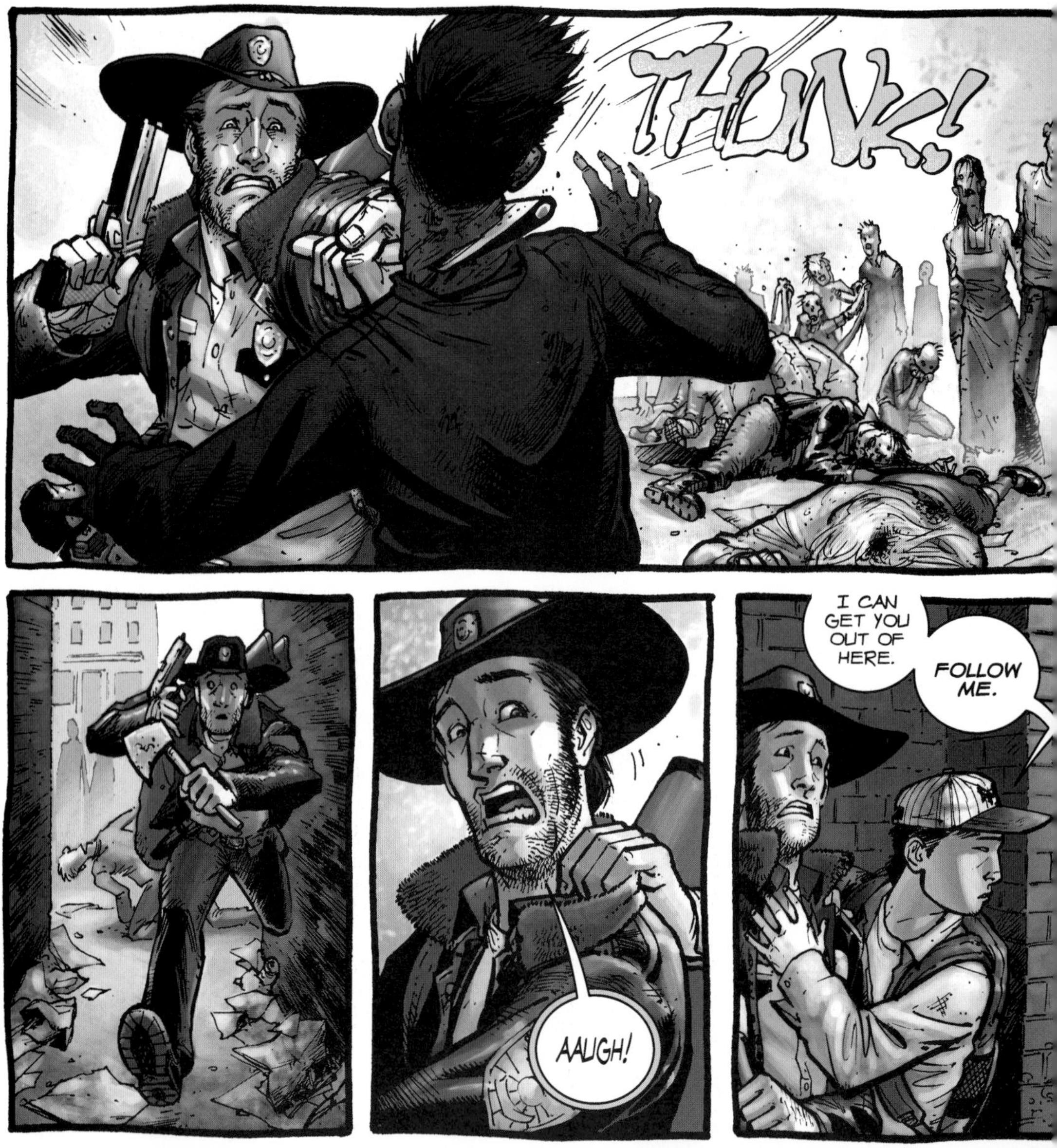
THUNK!
I CAN GET YOU OUT OF HERE.
FOLLOW ME.
AAUGH!
AND STOP USING THAT GUN!
YOU'LL HAVE THE WHOLE CITY ON US!

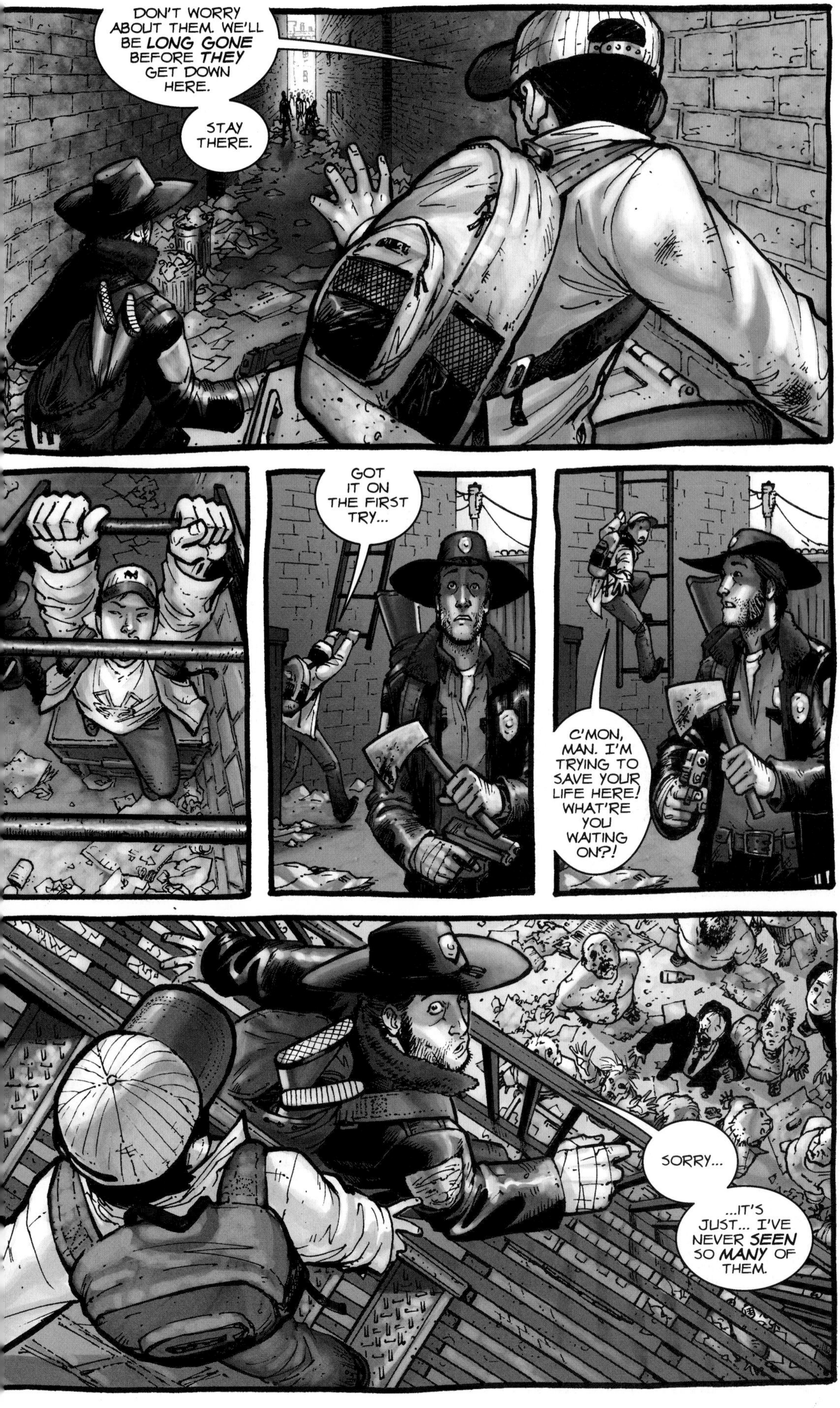
DON'T WORRY ABOUT THEM. WE'LL BE LONG GONE BEFORE THEY GET DOWN HERE.
STAY THERE.
GOT IT ON THE FIRST TRY...
C'MON, MAN. I'M TRYING TO SAVE YOUR LIFE HERE! WHAT'RE YOU WAITING ON?!
SORRY...
...IT'S JUST... I'VE NEVER SEEN SO MANY OF THEM.

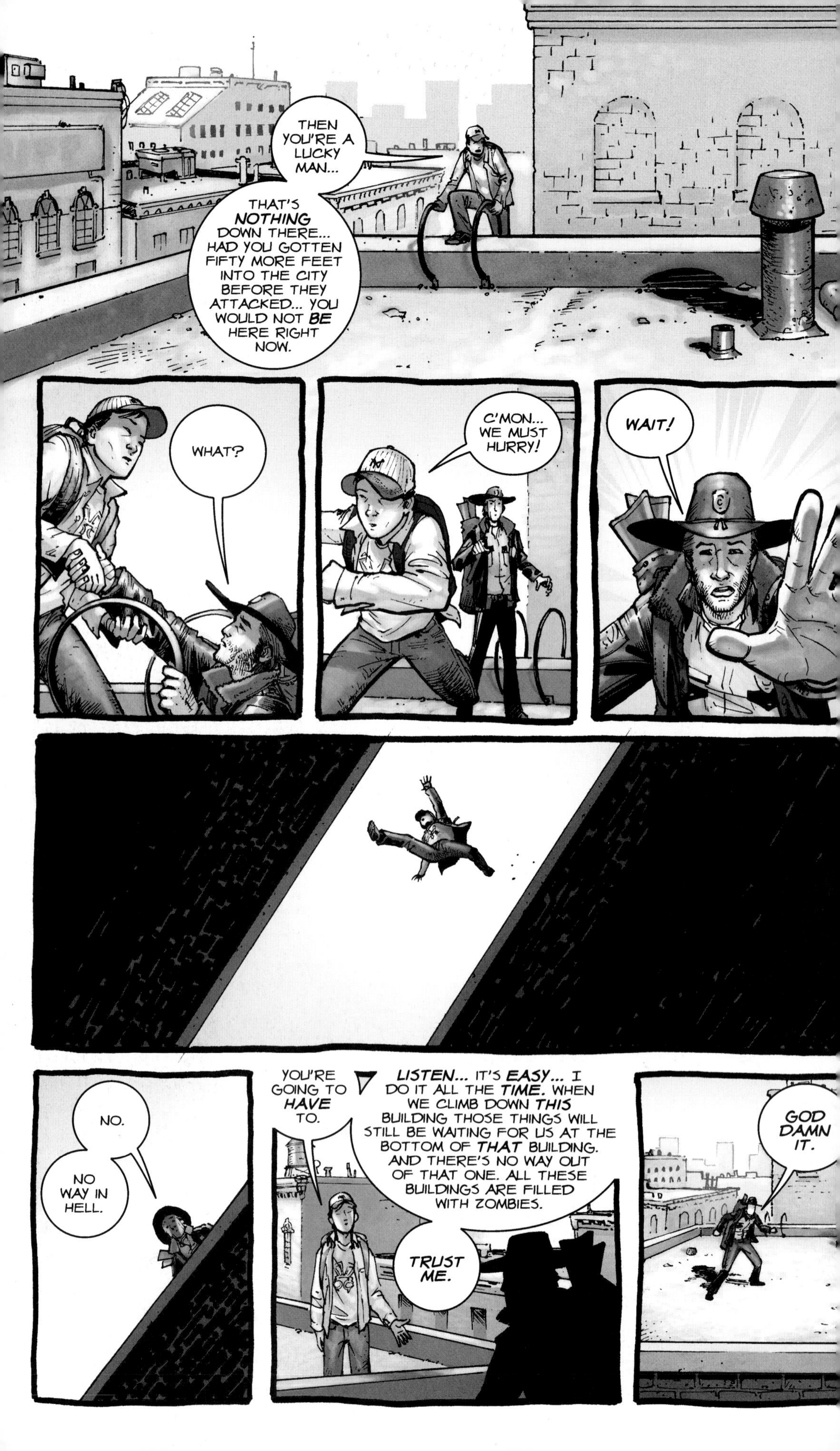
THEN YOU'RE A LUCKY MAN...
THAT'S NOTHING DOWN THERE... HAD YOU GOTTEN FIFTY MORE FEET INTO THE CITY BEFORE THEY ATTACKED... YOU WOULD NOT BE HERE RIGHT NOW.
WHAT?
C'MON... WE MUST HURRY!
WAIT!
NO.
NO WAY IN HELL.
YOU'RE GOING TO HAVE TO.
LISTEN... IT'S EASY... I DO IT ALL THE TIME. WHEN WE CLIMB DOWN THIS BUILDING THOSE THINGS WILL STILL BE WAITING FOR US AT THE BOTTOM OF THAT BUILDING. AND THERE'S NO WAY OUT OF THAT ONE. ALL THESE BUILDINGS ARE FILLED WITH ZOMBIES.
TRUST ME.
GOD DAMN IT.

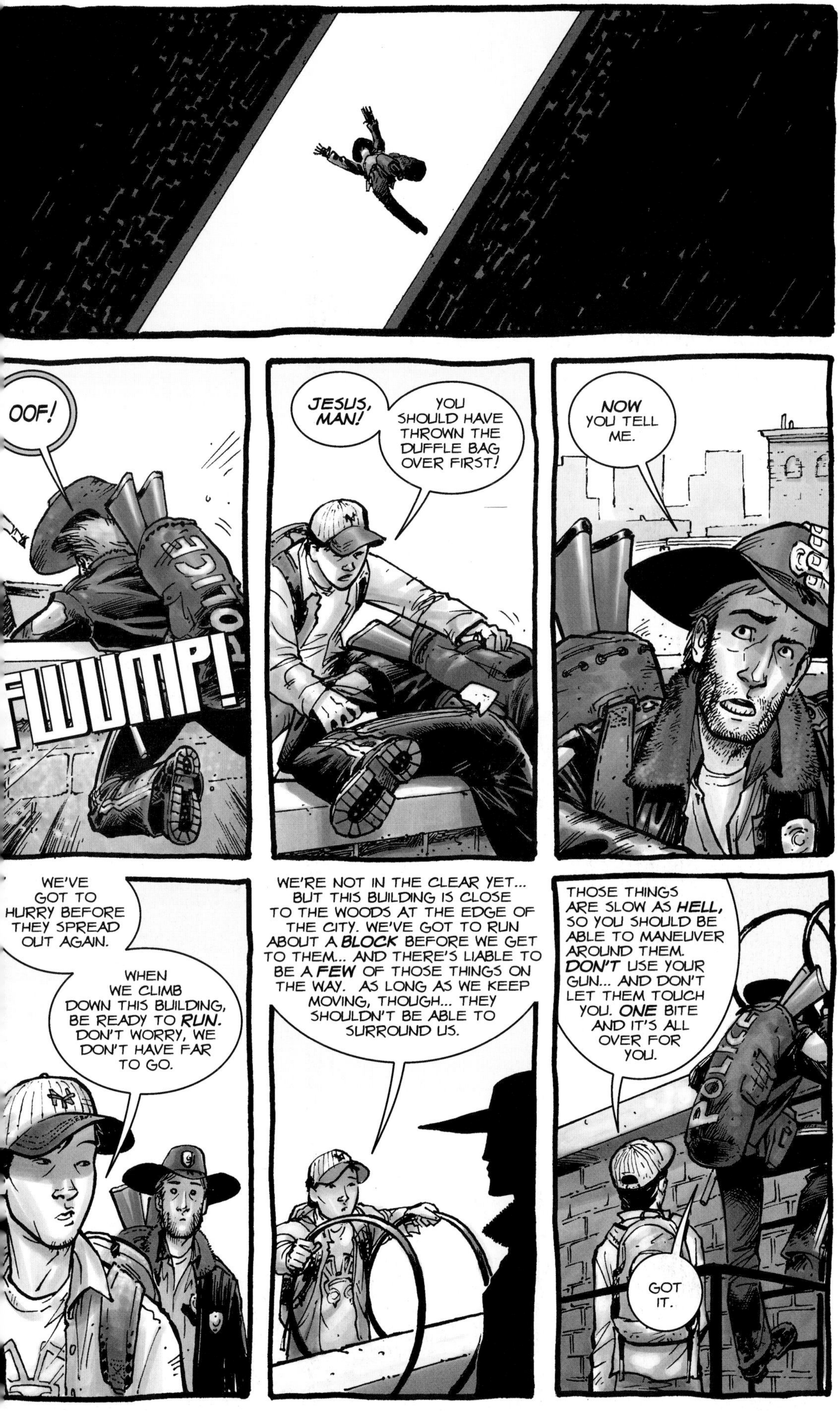
OOF!
FWUMP!
JESUS, MAN!
YOU SHOULD HAVE THROWN THE DUFFLE BAG OVER FIRST!
NOW YOU TELL ME.
WE'VE GOT TO HURRY BEFORE THEY SPREAD OUT AGAIN.
WHEN WE CLIMB DOWN THIS BUILDING, BE READY TO RUN. DON'T WORRY, WE DON'T HAVE FAR TO GO.
WE'RE NOT IN THE CLEAR YET... BUT THIS BUILDING IS CLOSE TO THE WOODS AT THE EDGE OF THE CITY. WE'VE GOT TO RUN ABOUT A BLOCK BEFORE WE GET TO THEM... AND THERE'S LIABLE TO BE A FEW OF THOSE THINGS ON THE WAY. AS LONG AS WE KEEP MOVING, THOUGH... THEY SHOULDN'T BE ABLE TO SURROUND US.
THOSE THINGS ARE SLOW AS HELL, SO YOU SHOULD BE ABLE TO MANEUVER AROUND THEM. DON'T USE YOUR GUN... AND DON'T LET THEM TOUCH YOU. ONE BITE AND IT'S ALL OVER FOR YOU.
GOT IT.

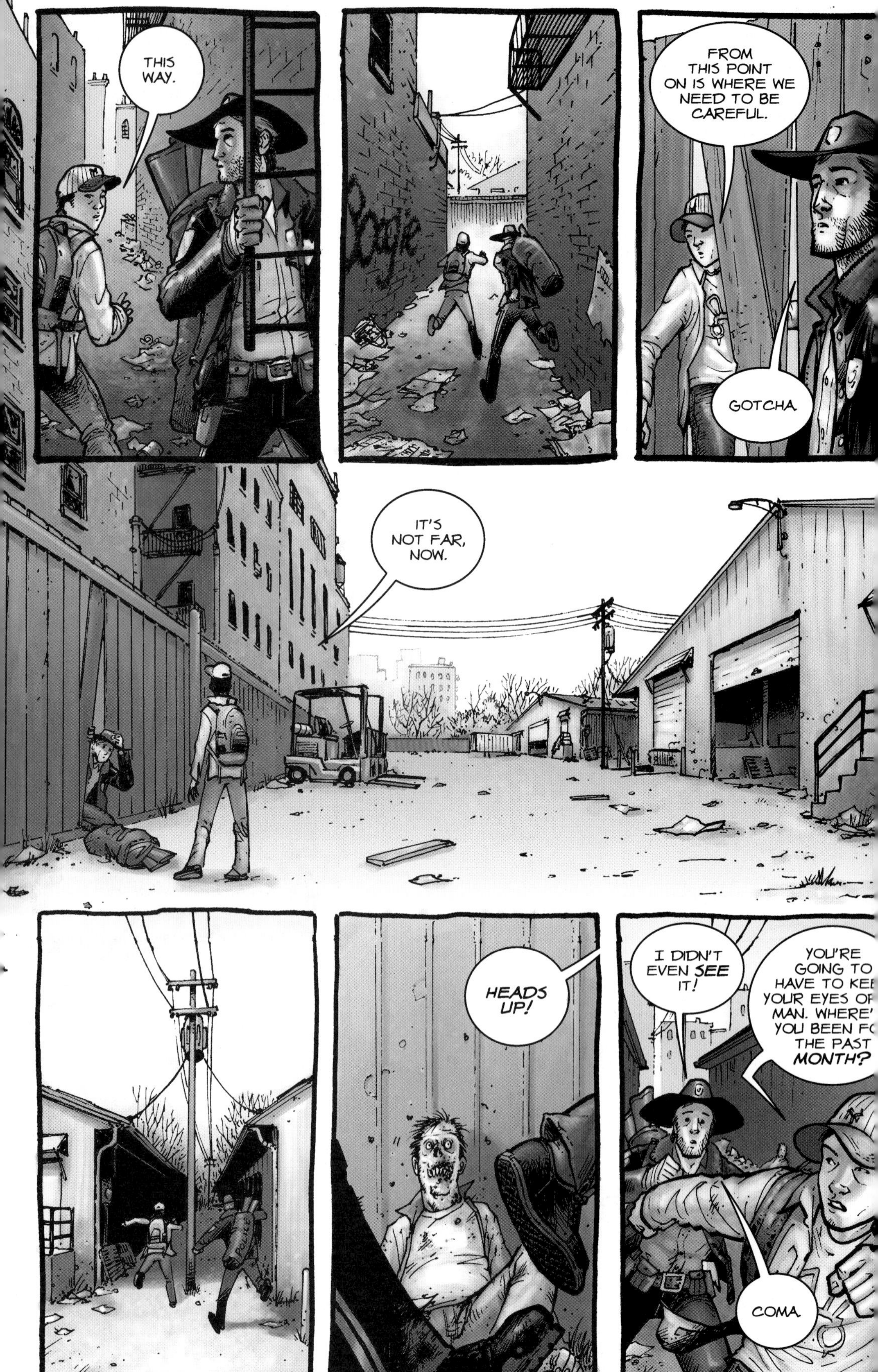
THIS WAY.
FROM THIS POINT ON IS WHERE WE NEED TO BE CAREFUL.
GOTCHA
IT'S NOT FAR, NOW.
HEADS UP!
I DIDN'T EVEN SEE IT!
YOU'RE GOING TO HAVE TO KEE YOUR EYES OF MAN. WHERE' YOU BEEN FO THE PAST MONTH?
COMA

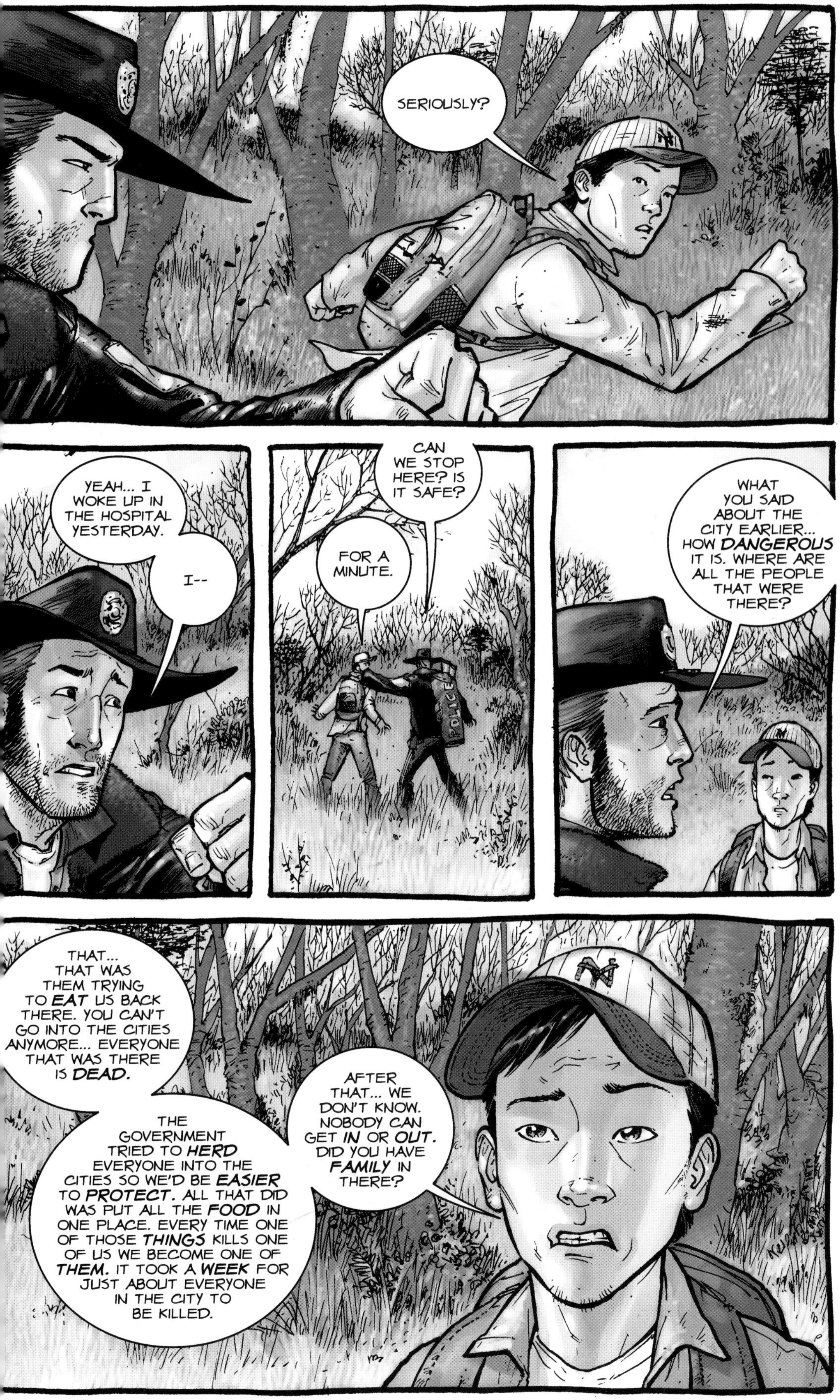
SERIOUSLY?
YEAH... I WOKE UP IN THE HOSPITAL YESTERDAY.
I--
CAN WE STOP HERE? IS IT SAFE?
FOR A MINUTE.
POLICE
WHAT YOU SAID ABOUT THE CITY EARLIER... HOW DANGEROUS IT IS. WHERE ARE ALL THE PEOPLE THAT WERE THERE?
THAT... THAT WAS THEM TRYING TO EAT US BACK THERE. YOU CAN'T GO INTO THE CITIES ANYMORE... EVERYONE THAT WAS THERE IS DEAD.
THE GOVERNMENT TRIED TO HERD EVERYONE INTO THE CITIES SO WE'D BE EASIER TO PROTECT. ALL THAT DID WAS PUT ALL THE FOOD IN ONE PLACE. EVERY TIME ONE OF THOSE THINGS KILLS ONE OF US WE BECOME ONE OF THEM. IT TOOK A WEEK FOR JUST ABOUT EVERYONE IN THE CITY TO BE KILLED.
AFTER THAT... WE DON'T KNOW. NOBODY CAN GET IN OR OUT. DID YOU HAVE FAMILY IN THERE?

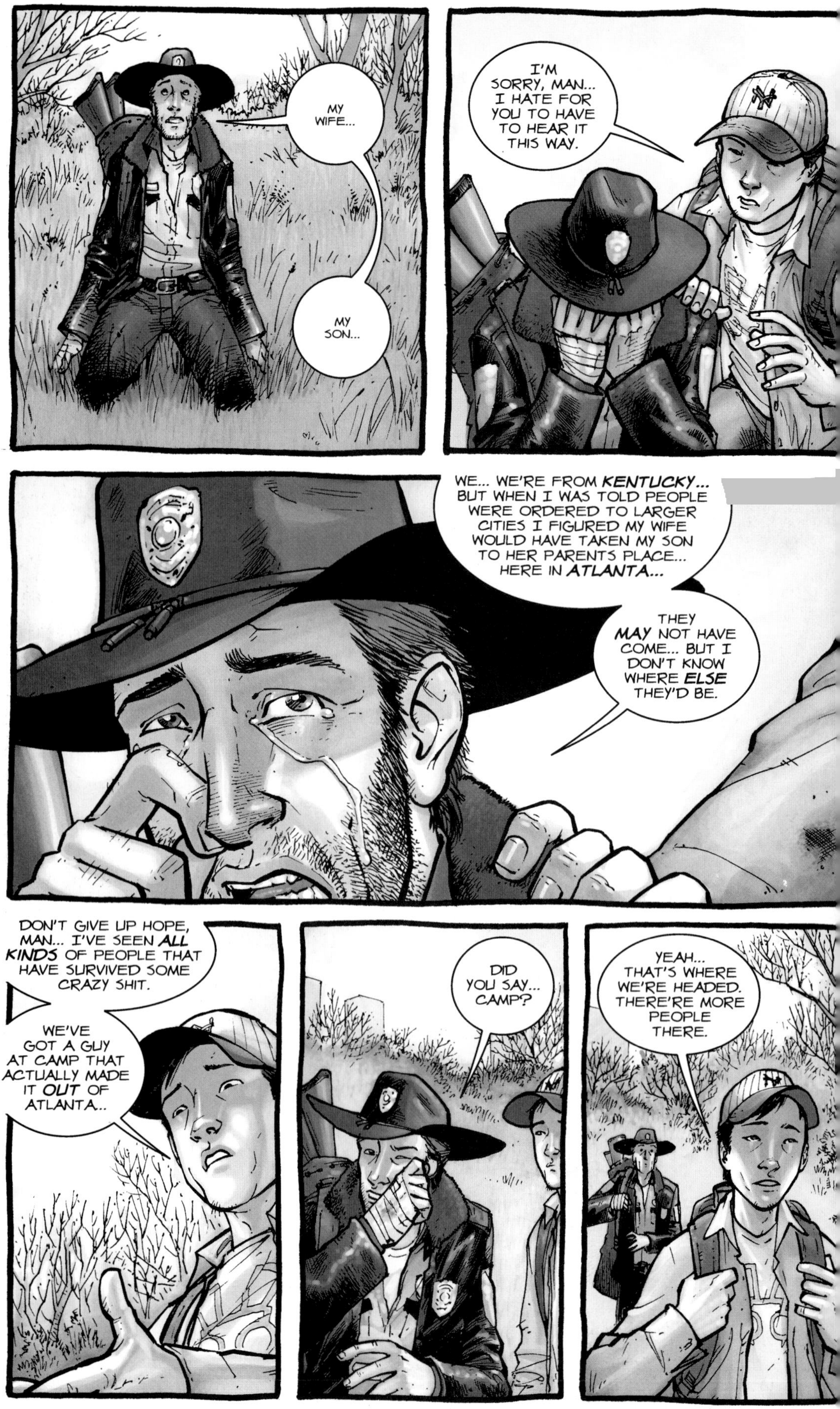
MY WIFE...
MY SON...
I'M SORRY, MAN... I HATE FOR YOU TO HAVE TO HEAR IT THIS WAY.
WE... WE'RE FROM KENTUCKY... BUT WHEN I WAS TOLD PEOPLE WERE ORDERED TO LARGER CITIES I FIGURED MY WIFE WOULD HAVE TAKEN MY SON TO HER PARENTS PLACE... HERE IN ATLANTA...
THEY MAY NOT HAVE COME... BUT I DON'T KNOW WHERE ELSE THEY'D BE.
DON'T GIVE UP HOPE, MAN... I'VE SEEN ALL KINDS OF PEOPLE THAT HAVE SURVIVED SOME CRAZY SHIT.
WE'VE GOT A GUY AT CAMP THAT ACTUALLY MADE IT OUT OF ATLANTA...
DID YOU SAY... CAMP?
YEAH... THAT'S WHERE WE'RE HEADED. THERE'RE MORE PEOPLE THERE.

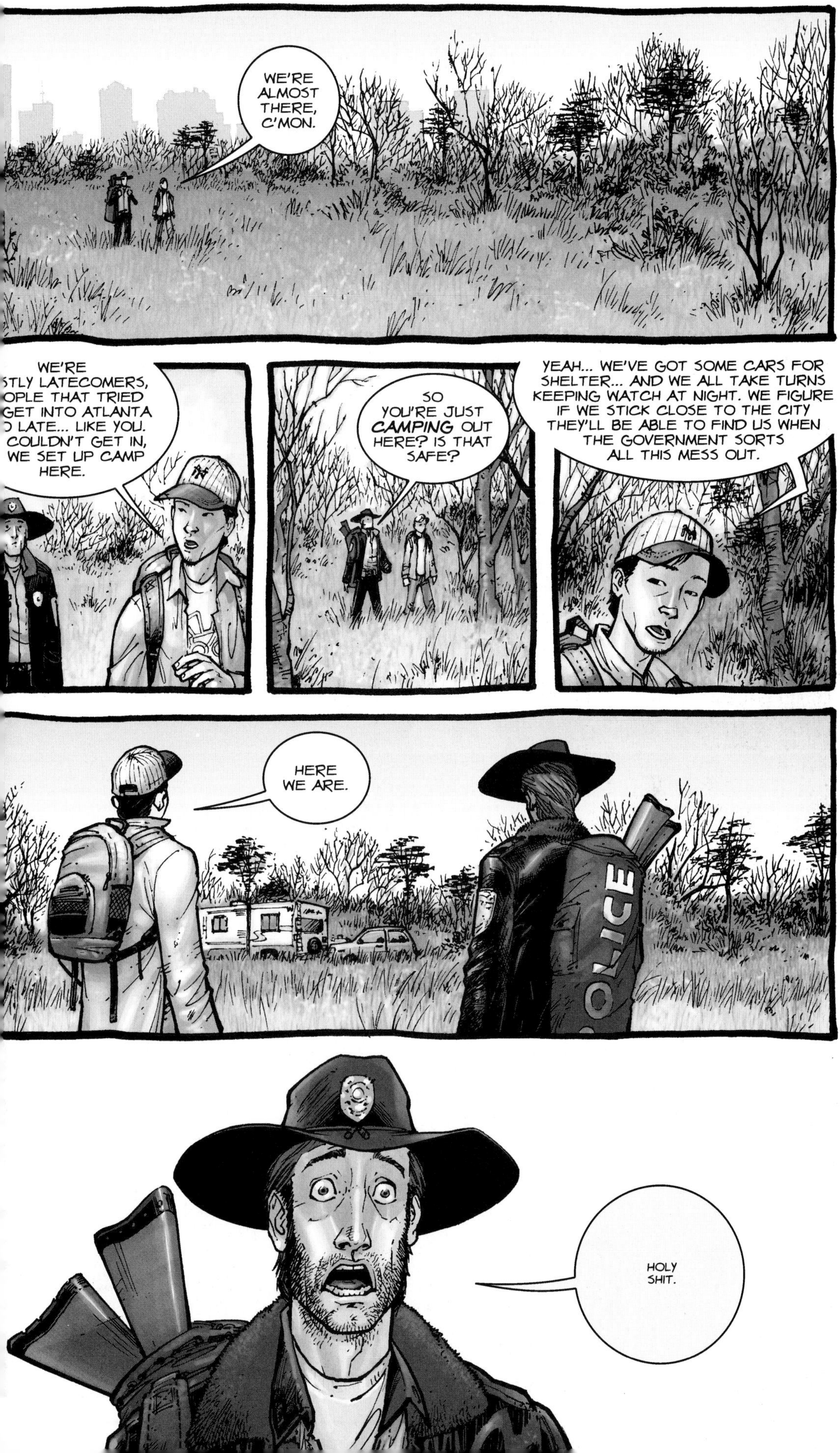
WE'RE ALMOST THERE, C'MON.
WE'RE STLY LATECOMERS, OPLE THAT TRIED GET INTO ATLANTA LATE... LIKE YOU. COULDN'T GET IN, WE SET UP CAMP HERE.
SO YOU'RE JUST CAMPING OUT HERE? IS THAT SAFE?
YEAH... WE'VE GOT SOME CARS FOR SHELTER... AND WE ALL TAKE TURNS KEEPING WATCH AT NIGHT. WE FIGURE IF WE STICK CLOSE TO THE CITY THEY'LL BE ABLE TO FIND US WHEN THE GOVERNMENT SORTS ALL THIS MESS OUT.
HERE WE ARE.
POLICE
HOLY SHIT.

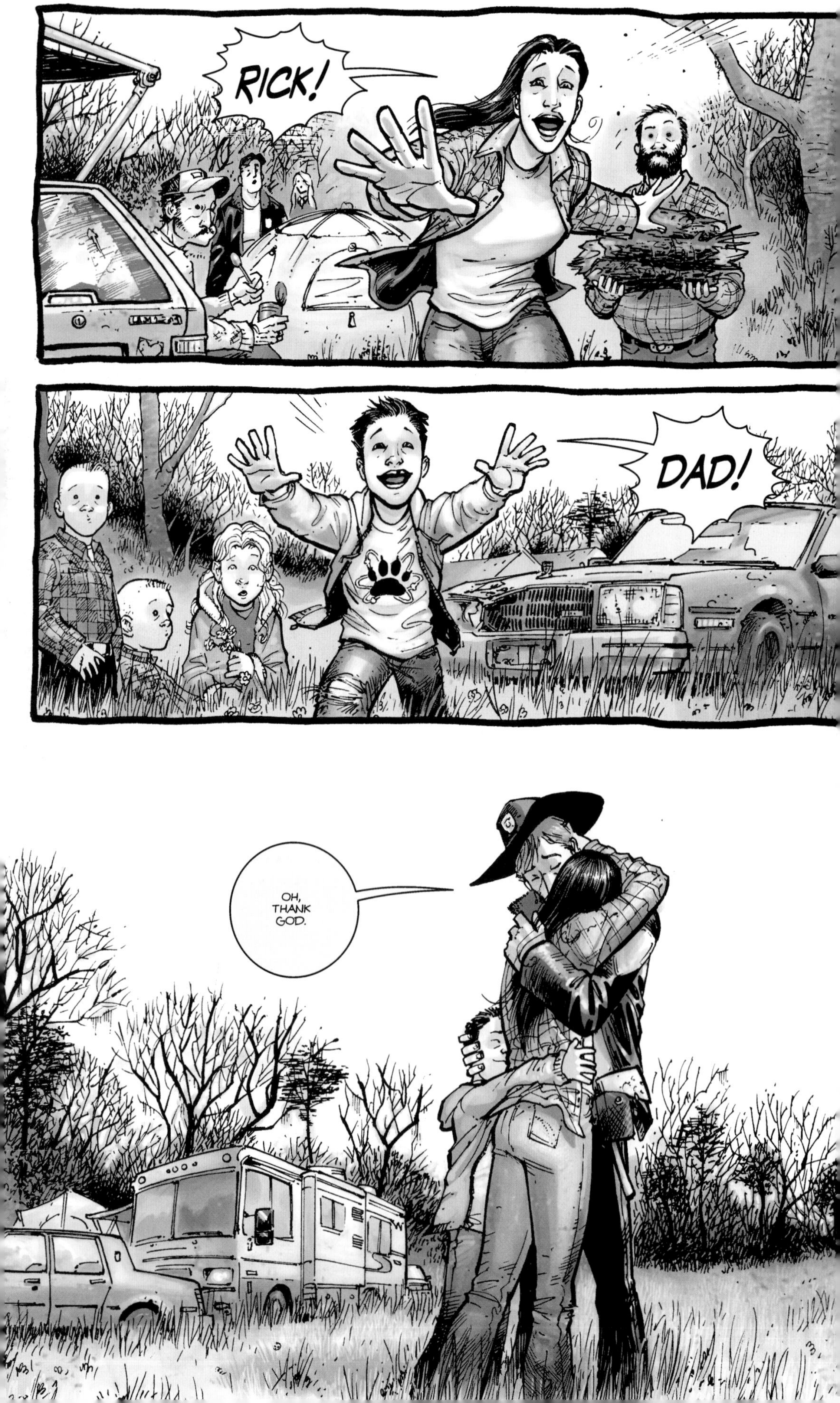
RICK!
DAD!
OH, THANK GOD.

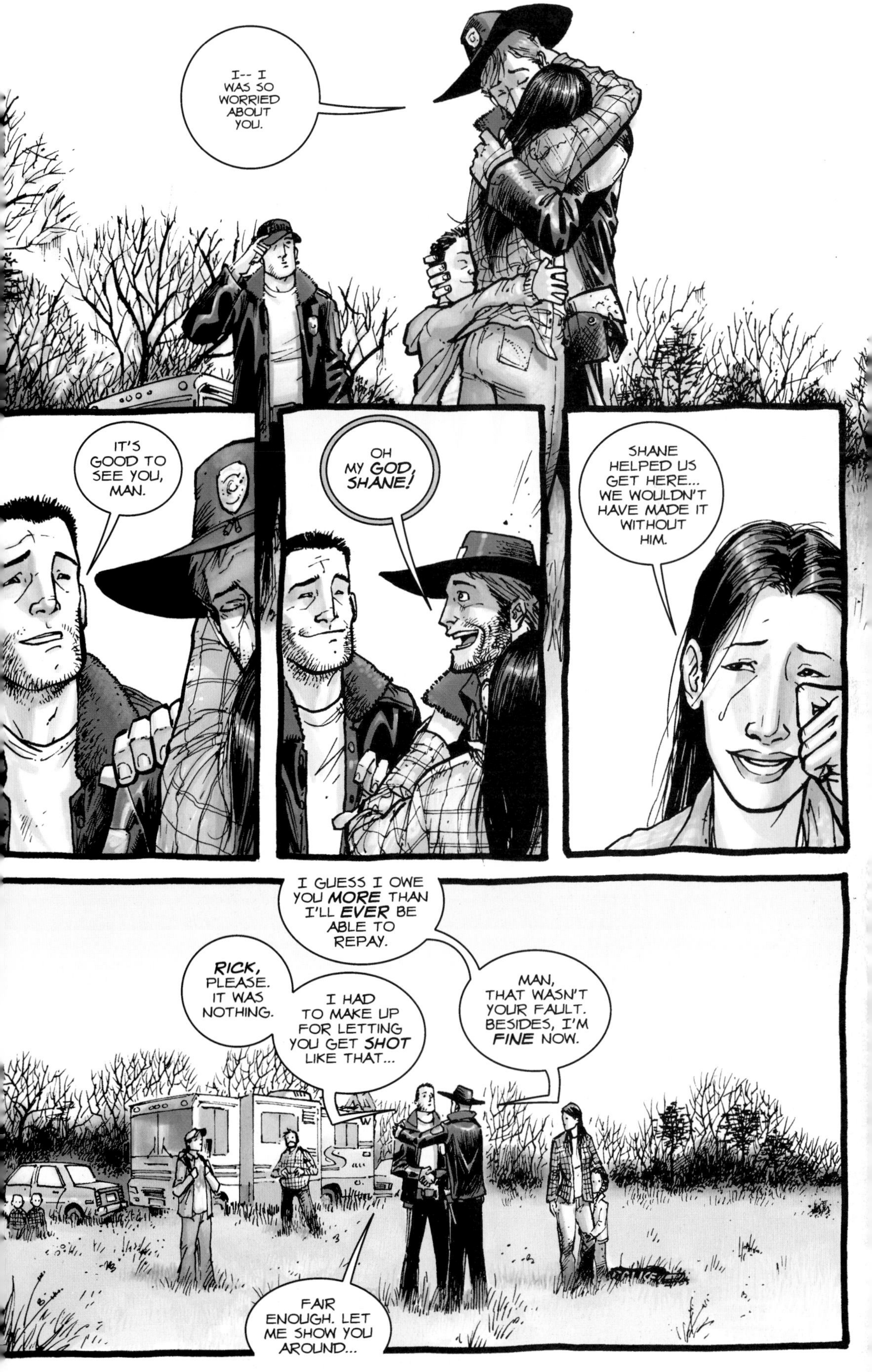

I-- I WAS SO WORRIED ABOUT YOU.
IT'S GOOD TO SEE YOU, MAN.
OH MY **GOD, SHANE!**
SHANE HELPED US GET HERE... WE WOULDN'T HAVE MADE IT WITHOUT HIM.
I GUESS I OWE YOU **MORE** THAN I'LL **EVER** BE ABLE TO REPAY.
RICK, PLEASE. IT WAS NOTHING.
I HAD TO MAKE UP FOR LETTING YOU GET **SHOT** LIKE THAT...
MAN, THAT WASN'T YOUR FAULT. BESIDES, I'M **FINE** NOW.
FAIR ENOUGH. LET ME SHOW YOU AROUND...

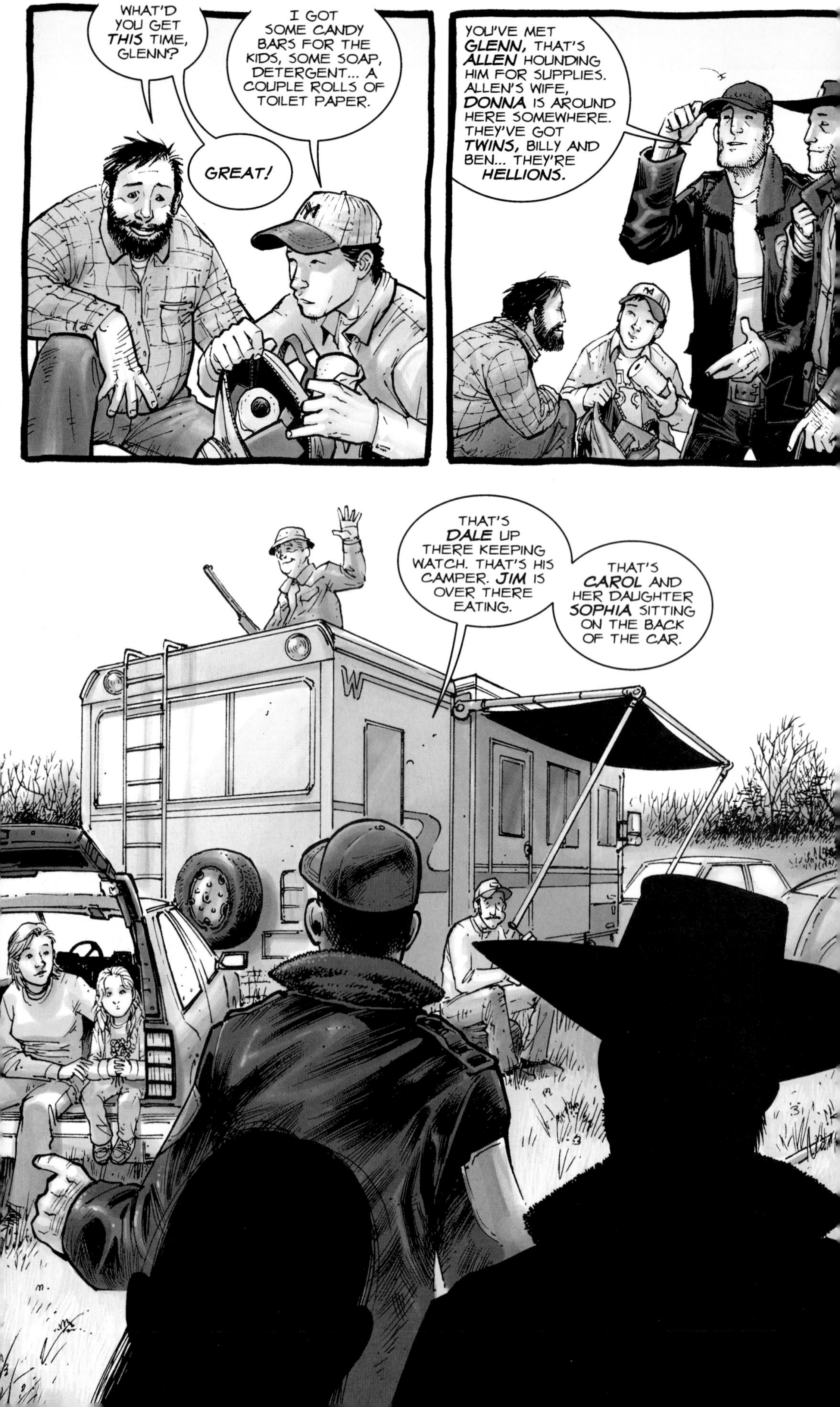
WHAT'D YOU GET THIS TIME, GLENN?
I GOT SOME CANDY BARS FOR THE KIDS, SOME SOAP, DETERGENT... A COUPLE ROLLS OF TOILET PAPER.
GREAT!
YOU'VE MET GLENN, THAT'S ALLEN HOUNDING HIM FOR SUPPLIES. ALLEN'S WIFE, DONNA IS AROUND HERE SOMEWHERE. THEY'VE GOT TWINS, BILLY AND BEN... THEY'RE HELLIONS.
THAT'S DALE UP THERE KEEPING WATCH. THAT'S HIS CAMPER. JIM IS OVER THERE EATING.
THAT'S CAROL AND HER DAUGHTER SOPHIA SITTING ON THE BACK OF THE CAR.

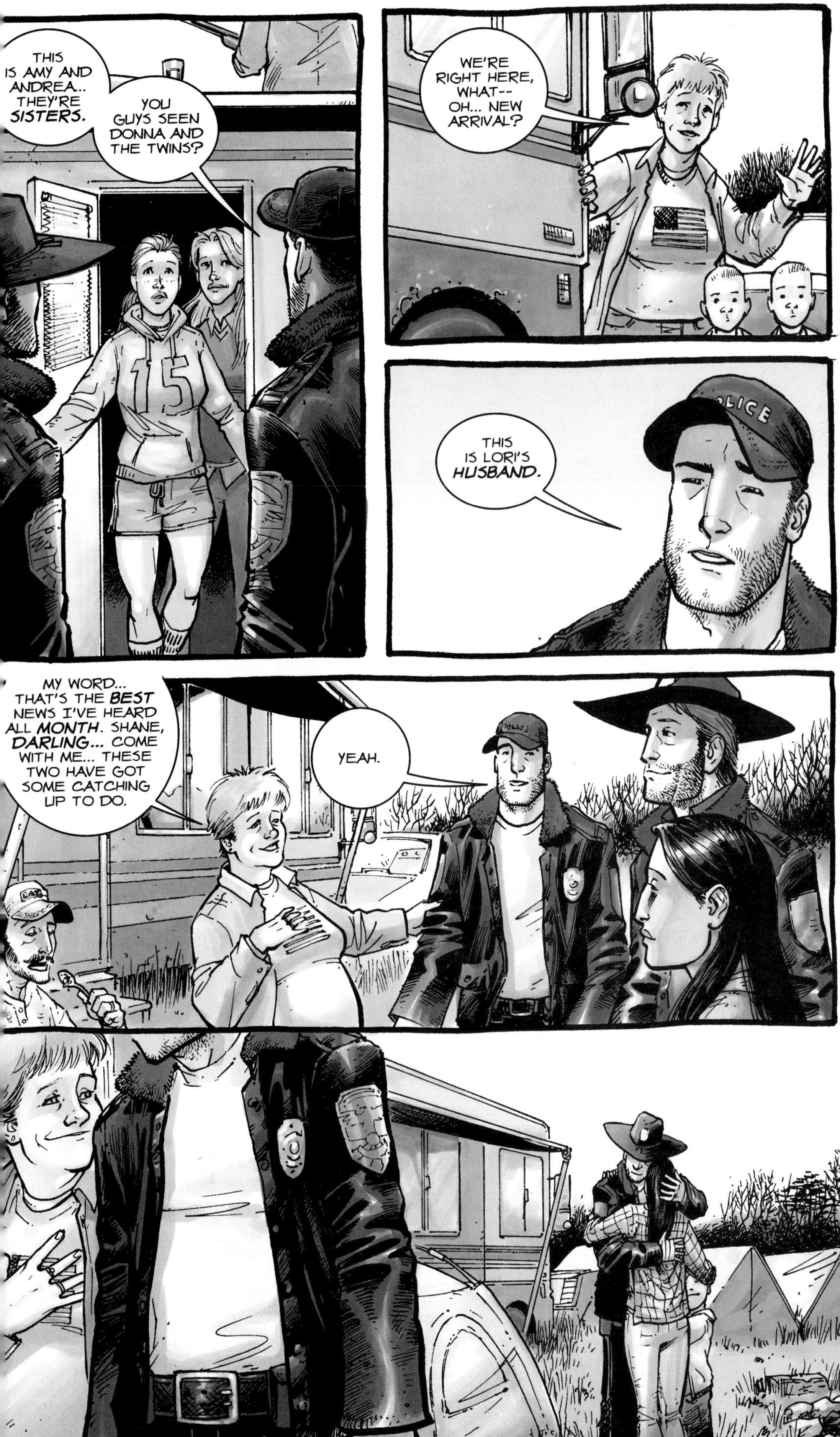
THIS IS AMY AND ANDREA... THEY'RE **SISTERS.**
YOU GUYS SEEN DONNA AND THE TWINS?
WE'RE RIGHT HERE, WHAT-- OH... NEW ARRIVAL?
POLICE
THIS IS LORI'S **HUSBAND.**
MY WORD... THAT'S THE **BEST** NEWS I'VE HEARD ALL **MONTH**. SHANE, **DARLING...** COME WITH ME... THESE TWO HAVE GOT SOME CATCHING UP TO DO.
YEAH.

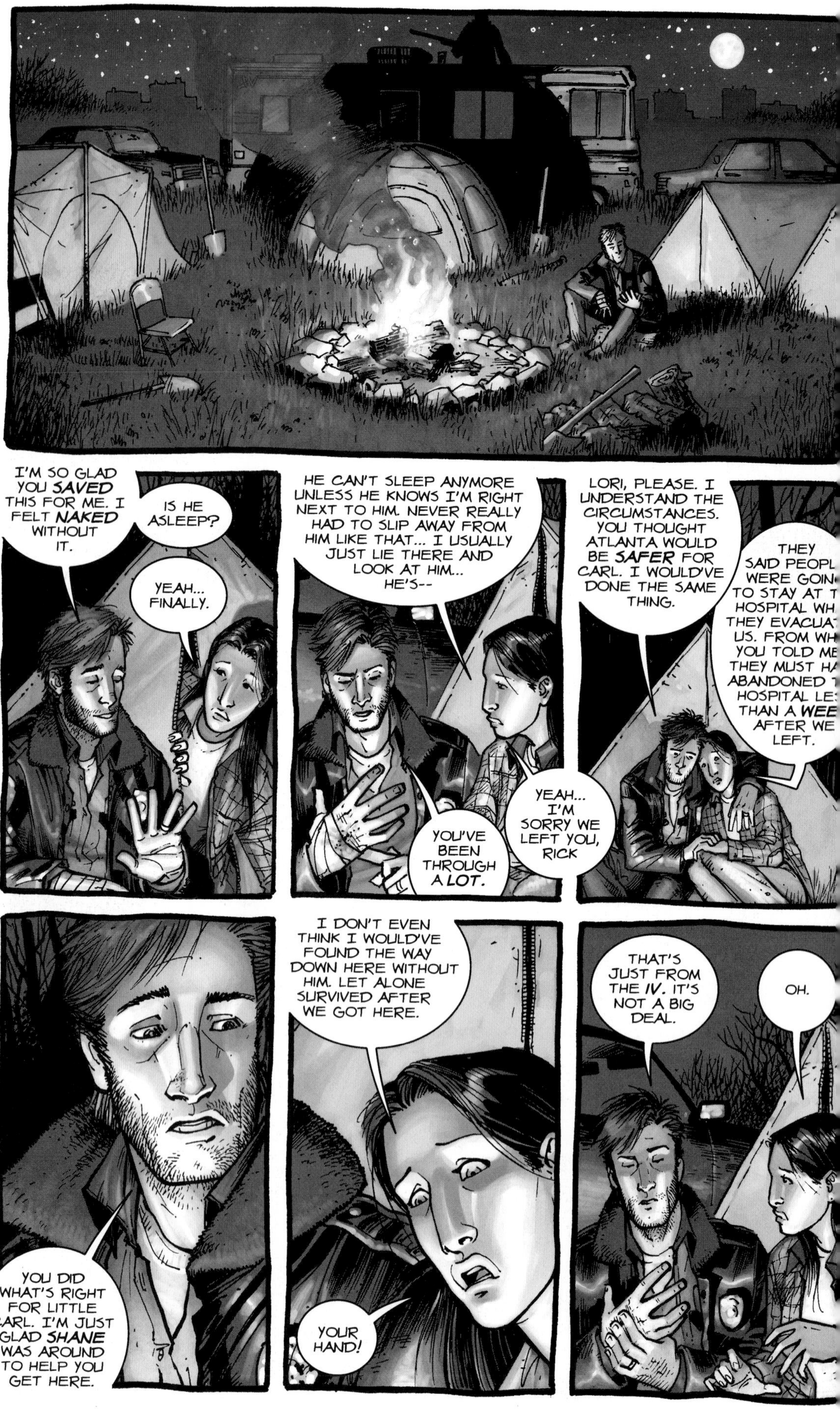
I'M SO GLAD YOU SAVED THIS FOR ME. I FELT NAKED WITHOUT IT.
IS HE ASLEEP?
YEAH... FINALLY.
HE CAN'T SLEEP ANYMORE UNLESS HE KNOWS I'M RIGHT NEXT TO HIM. NEVER REALLY HAD TO SLIP AWAY FROM HIM LIKE THAT... I USUALLY JUST LIE THERE AND LOOK AT HIM... HE'S--
YOU'VE BEEN THROUGH A LOT.
YEAH... I'M SORRY WE LEFT YOU, RICK
LORI, PLEASE. I UNDERSTAND THE CIRCUMSTANCES. YOU THOUGHT ATLANTA WOULD BE SAFER FOR CARL. I WOULD'VE DONE THE SAME THING.
YOU DID WHAT'S RIGHT FOR LITTLE CARL. I'M JUST GLAD SHANE WAS AROUND TO HELP YOU GET HERE.
I DON'T EVEN THINK I WOULD'VE FOUND THE WAY DOWN HERE WITHOUT HIM. LET ALONE SURVIVED AFTER WE GOT HERE.
YOUR HAND!
THAT'S JUST FROM THE IV. IT'S NOT A BIG DEAL.
OH.

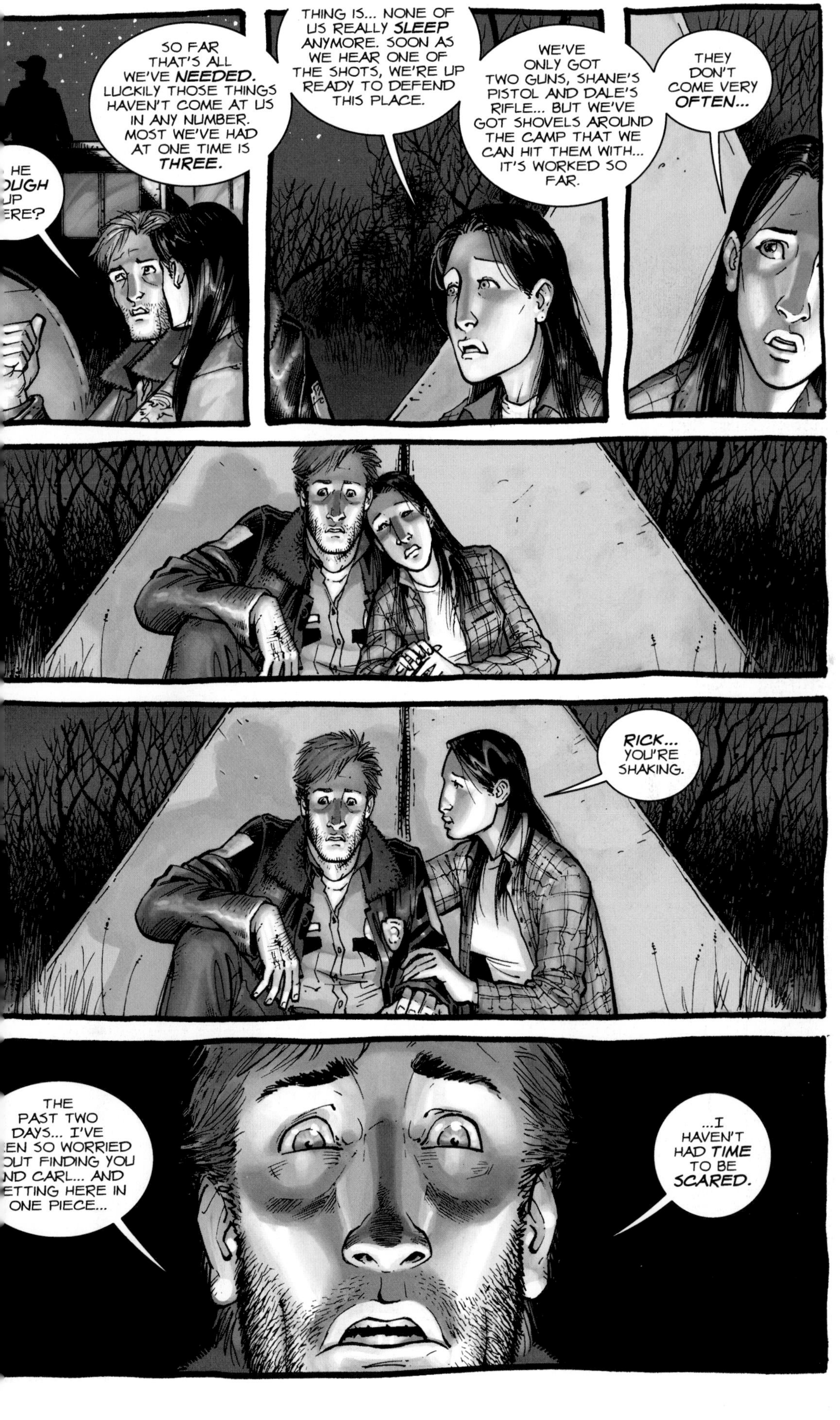

HE OUGH UP ERE?
SO FAR THAT'S ALL WE'VE NEEDED. LUCKILY THOSE THINGS HAVEN'T COME AT US IN ANY NUMBER. MOST WE'VE HAD AT ONE TIME IS THREE.
THING IS... NONE OF US REALLY SLEEP ANYMORE. SOON AS WE HEAR ONE OF THE SHOTS, WE'RE UP READY TO DEFEND THIS PLACE.
WE'VE ONLY GOT TWO GUNS, SHANE'S PISTOL AND DALE'S RIFLE... BUT WE'VE GOT SHOVELS AROUND THE CAMP THAT WE CAN HIT THEM WITH... IT'S WORKED SO FAR.
THEY DON'T COME VERY OFTEN...
RICK... YOU'RE SHAKING.
THE PAST TWO DAYS... I'VE EN SO WORRIED OUT FINDING YOU ND CARL... AND ETTING HERE IN ONE PIECE...
...I HAVEN'T HAD TIME TO BE SCARED.

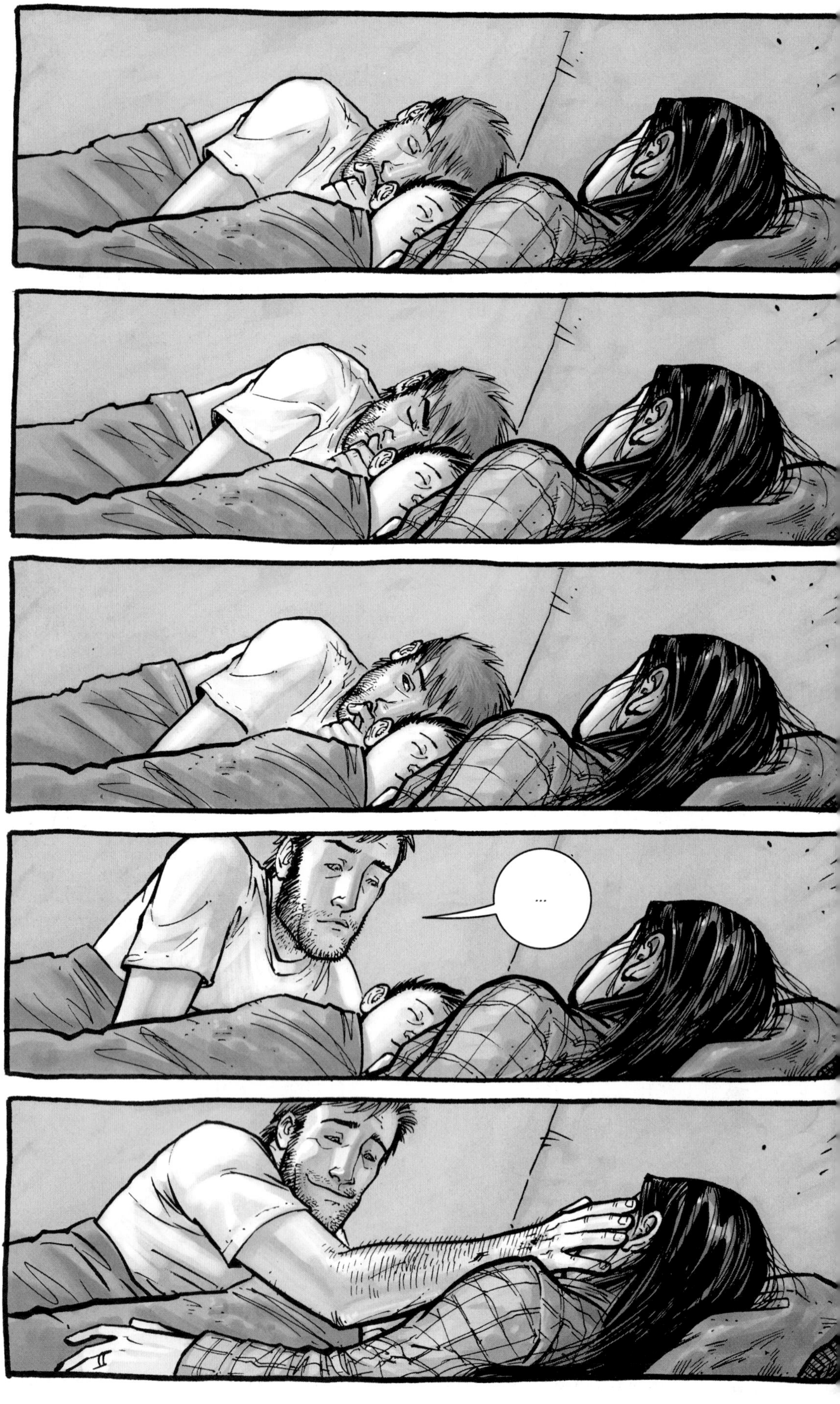
...

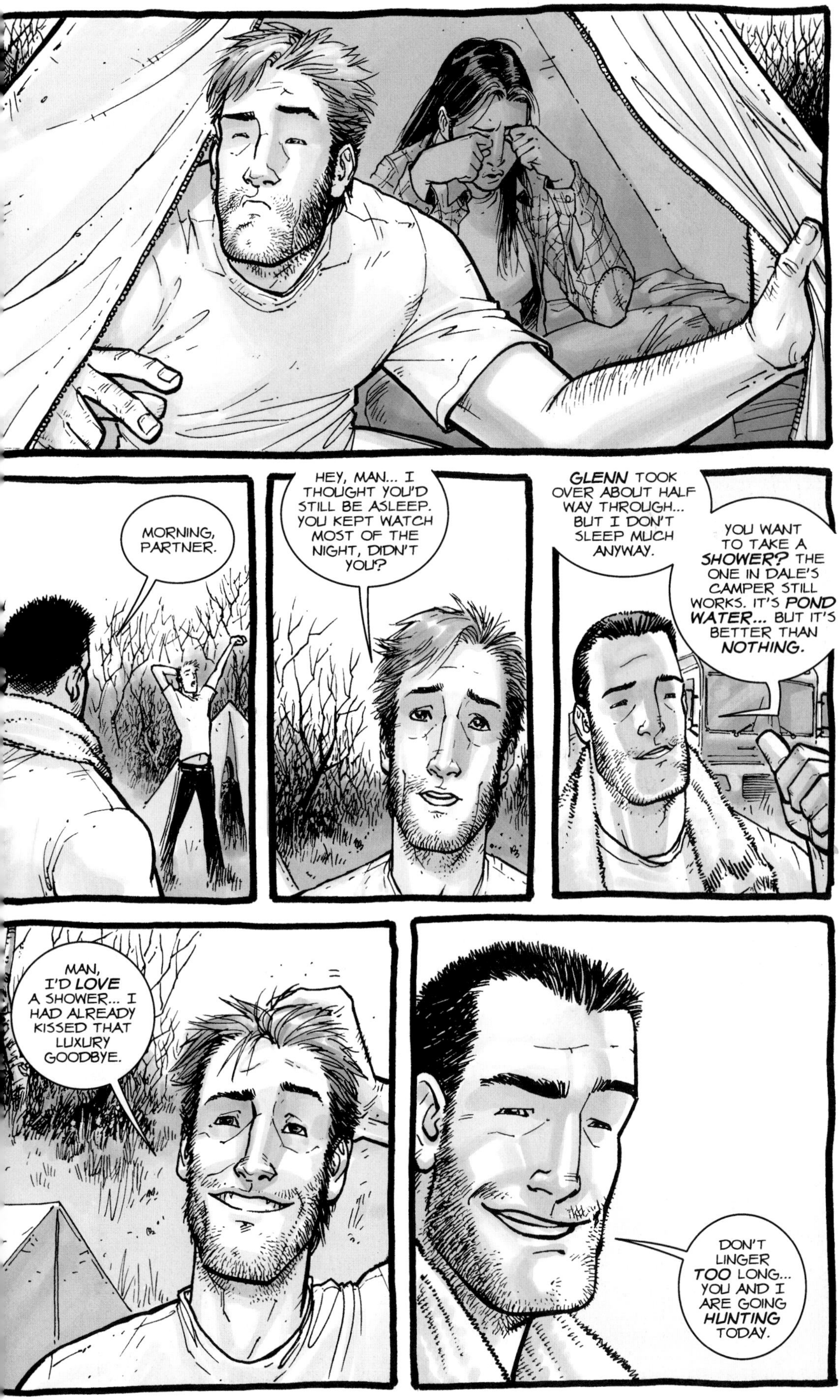
MORNING, PARTNER.
HEY, MAN... I THOUGHT YOU'D STILL BE ASLEEP. YOU KEPT WATCH MOST OF THE NIGHT, DIDN'T YOU?
GLENN TOOK OVER ABOUT HALF WAY THROUGH... BUT I DON'T SLEEP MUCH ANYWAY.
YOU WANT TO TAKE A SHOWER? THE ONE IN DALE'S CAMPER STILL WORKS. IT'S POND WATER... BUT IT'S BETTER THAN NOTHING.
MAN, I'D LOVE A SHOWER... I HAD ALREADY KISSED THAT LUXURY GOODBYE.
DON'T LINGER TOO LONG... YOU AND I ARE GOING HUNTING TODAY.

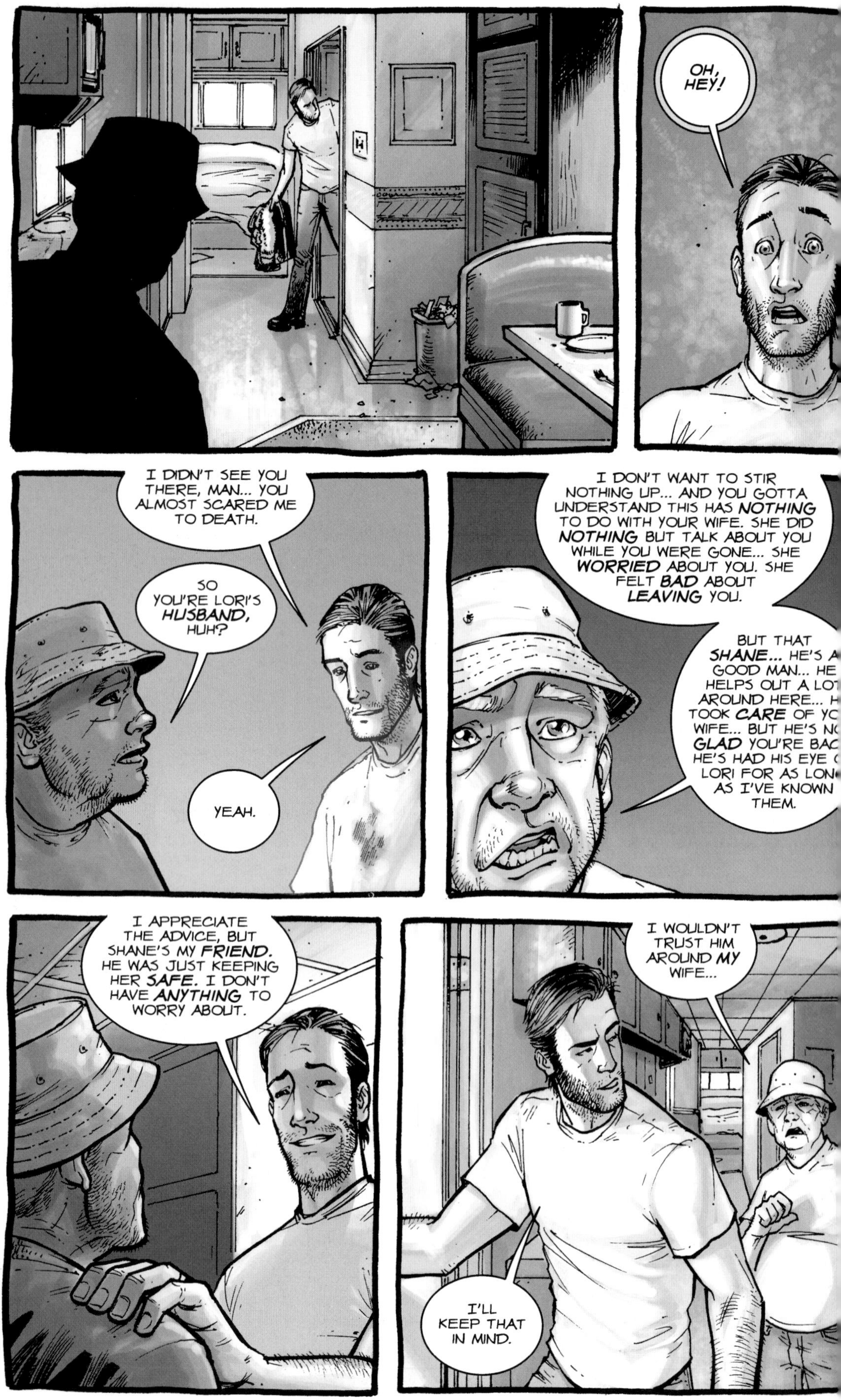

OH, HEY!
I DIDN'T SEE YOU THERE, MAN... YOU ALMOST SCARED ME TO DEATH.
SO YOU'RE LORI'S HUSBAND, HUH?
YEAH.
I DON'T WANT TO STIR NOTHING UP... AND YOU GOTTA UNDERSTAND THIS HAS NOTHING TO DO WITH YOUR WIFE. SHE DID NOTHING BUT TALK ABOUT YOU WHILE YOU WERE GONE... SHE WORRIED ABOUT YOU. SHE FELT BAD ABOUT LEAVING YOU.
BUT THAT SHANE... HE'S A GOOD MAN... HE HELPS OUT A LOT AROUND HERE... H TOOK CARE OF YO WIFE... BUT HE'S NO GLAD YOU'RE BAC HE'S HAD HIS EYE LORI FOR AS LON AS I'VE KNOWN THEM.
I APPRECIATE THE ADVICE, BUT SHANE'S MY FRIEND. HE WAS JUST KEEPING HER SAFE. I DON'T HAVE ANYTHING TO WORRY ABOUT.
I WOULDN'T TRUST HIM AROUND MY WIFE...
I'LL KEEP THAT IN MIND.

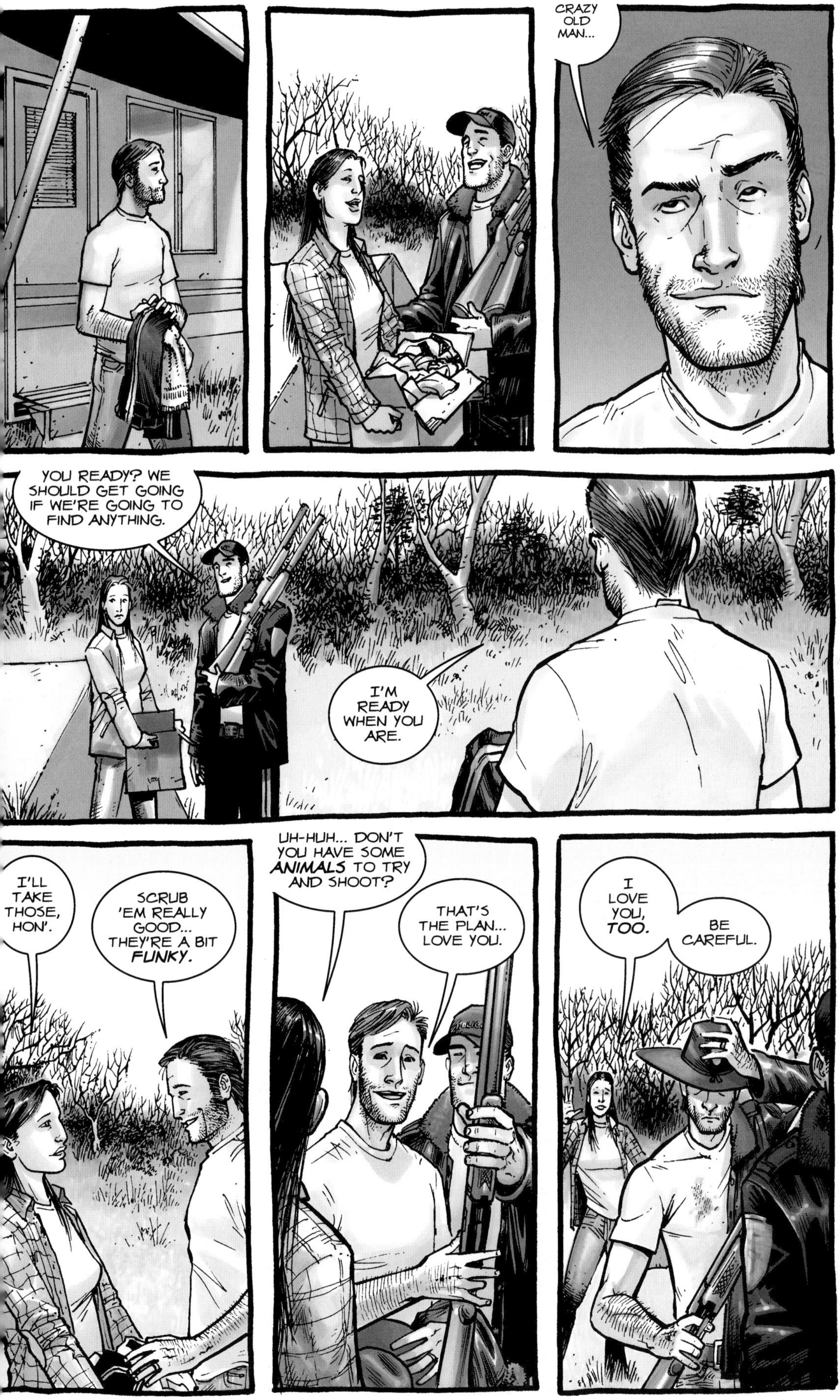
CRAZY OLD MAN...
YOU READY? WE SHOULD GET GOING IF WE'RE GOING TO FIND ANYTHING.
I'M READY WHEN YOU ARE.
I'LL TAKE THOSE, HON'.
SCRUB 'EM REALLY GOOD... THEY'RE A BIT *FUNKY*.
UH-HUH... DON'T YOU HAVE SOME *ANIMALS* TO TRY AND SHOOT?
THAT'S THE PLAN... LOVE YOU.
I LOVE YOU, *TOO*.
BE CAREFUL.

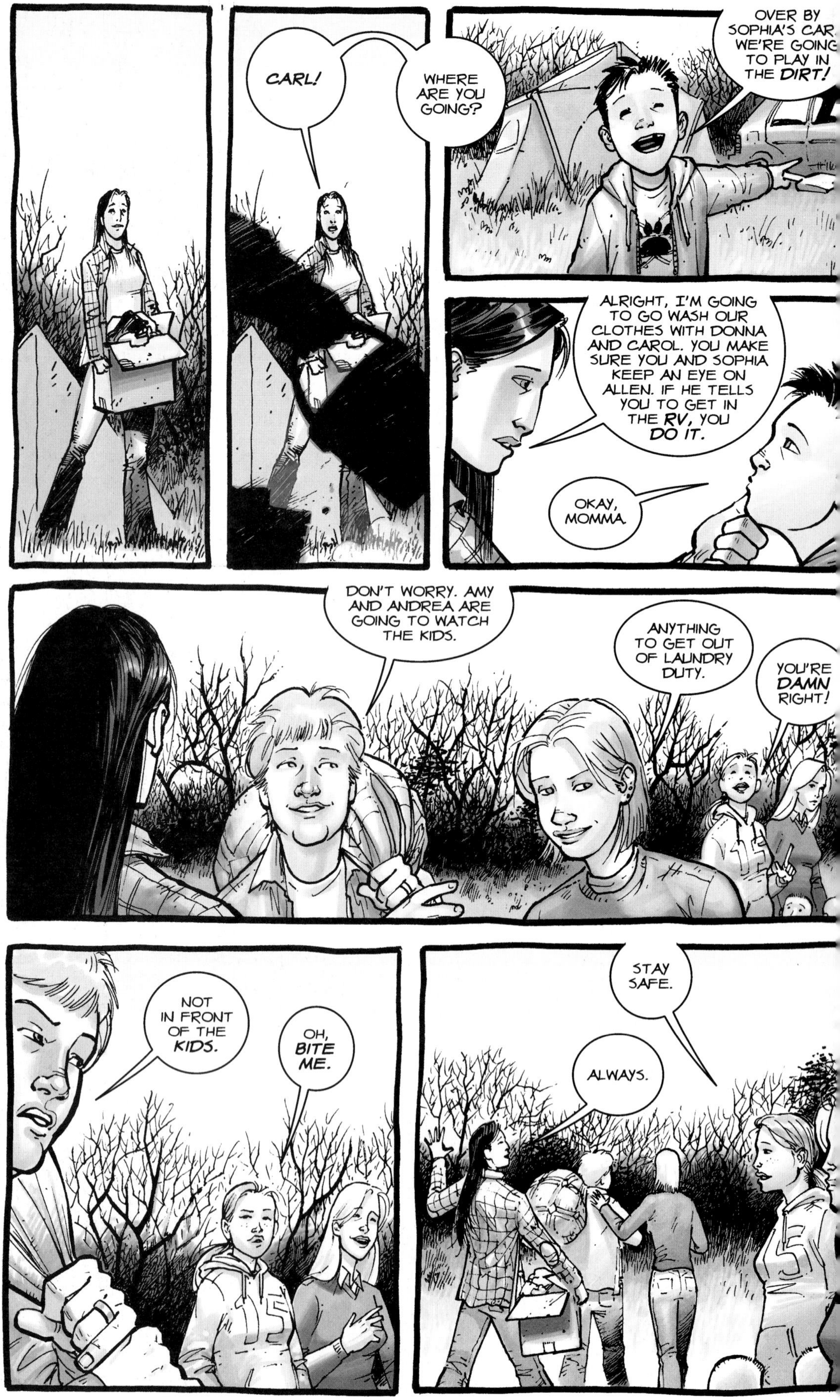
CARL!
WHERE ARE YOU GOING?
OVER BY SOPHIA'S CAR. WE'RE GOING TO PLAY IN THE DIRT!
ALRIGHT, I'M GOING TO GO WASH OUR CLOTHES WITH DONNA AND CAROL. YOU MAKE SURE YOU AND SOPHIA KEEP AN EYE ON ALLEN. IF HE TELLS YOU TO GET IN THE RV, YOU DO IT.
OKAY, MOMMA.
DON'T WORRY. AMY AND ANDREA ARE GOING TO WATCH THE KIDS.
ANYTHING TO GET OUT OF LAUNDRY DUTY.
YOU'RE DAMN RIGHT!
NOT IN FRONT OF THE KIDS.
OH, BITE ME.
STAY SAFE.
ALWAYS.

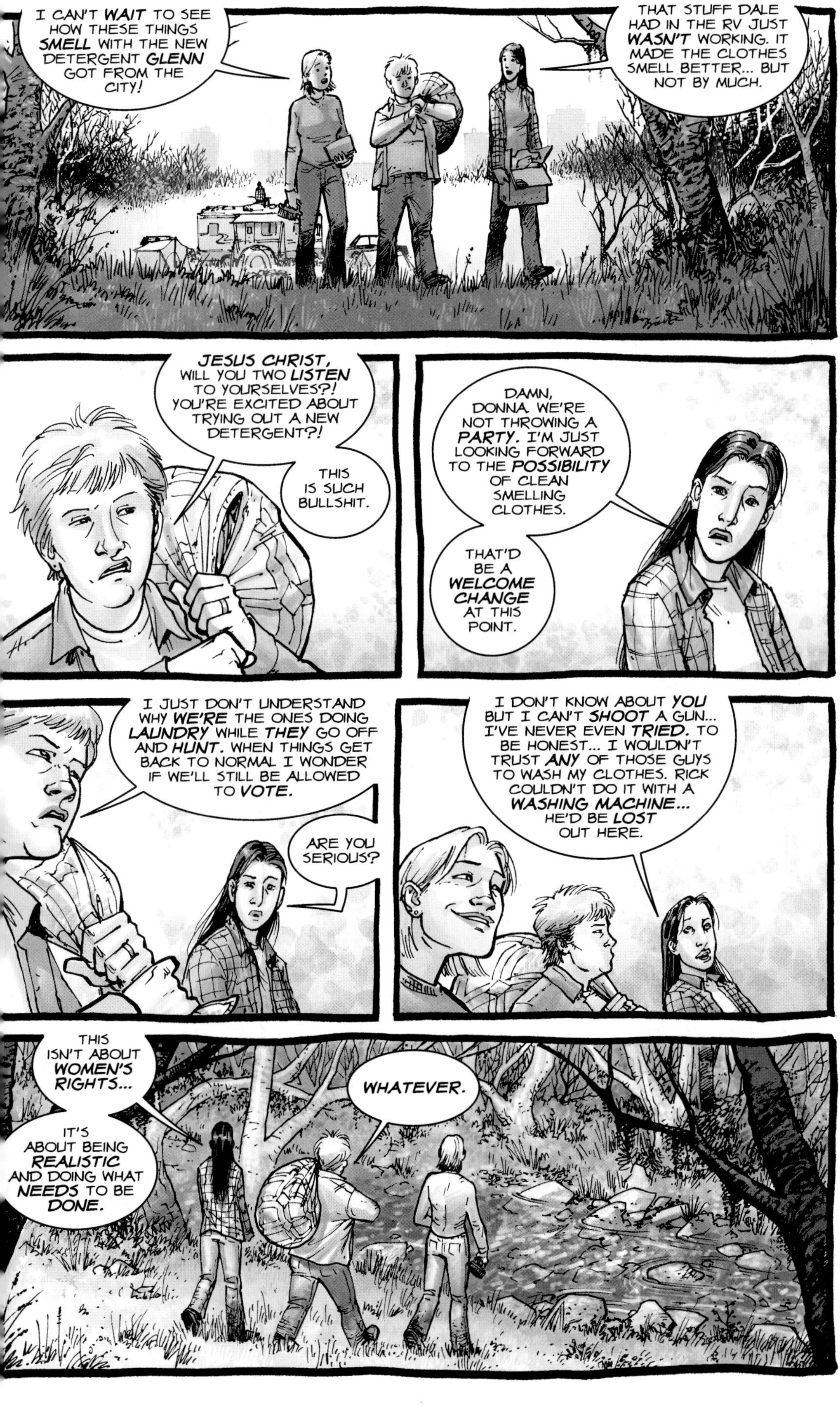
I CAN'T WAIT TO SEE HOW THESE THINGS SMELL WITH THE NEW DETERGENT GLENN GOT FROM THE CITY!
THAT STUFF DALE HAD IN THE RV JUST WASN'T WORKING. IT MADE THE CLOTHES SMELL BETTER... BUT NOT BY MUCH.
JESUS CHRIST, WILL YOU TWO LISTEN TO YOURSELVES?! YOU'RE EXCITED ABOUT TRYING OUT A NEW DETERGENT?!
THIS IS SUCH BULLSHIT.
DAMN, DONNA. WE'RE NOT THROWING A PARTY. I'M JUST LOOKING FORWARD TO THE POSSIBILITY OF CLEAN SMELLING CLOTHES.
THAT'D BE A WELCOME CHANGE AT THIS POINT.
I JUST DON'T UNDERSTAND WHY WE'RE THE ONES DOING LAUNDRY WHILE THEY GO OFF AND HUNT. WHEN THINGS GET BACK TO NORMAL I WONDER IF WE'LL STILL BE ALLOWED TO VOTE.
ARE YOU SERIOUS?
I DON'T KNOW ABOUT YOU BUT I CAN'T SHOOT A GUN... I'VE NEVER EVEN TRIED. TO BE HONEST... I WOULDN'T TRUST ANY OF THOSE GUYS TO WASH MY CLOTHES. RICK COULDN'T DO IT WITH A WASHING MACHINE... HE'D BE LOST OUT HERE.
THIS ISN'T ABOUT WOMEN'S RIGHTS...
IT'S ABOUT BEING REALISTIC AND DOING WHAT NEEDS TO BE DONE.
WHATEVER.

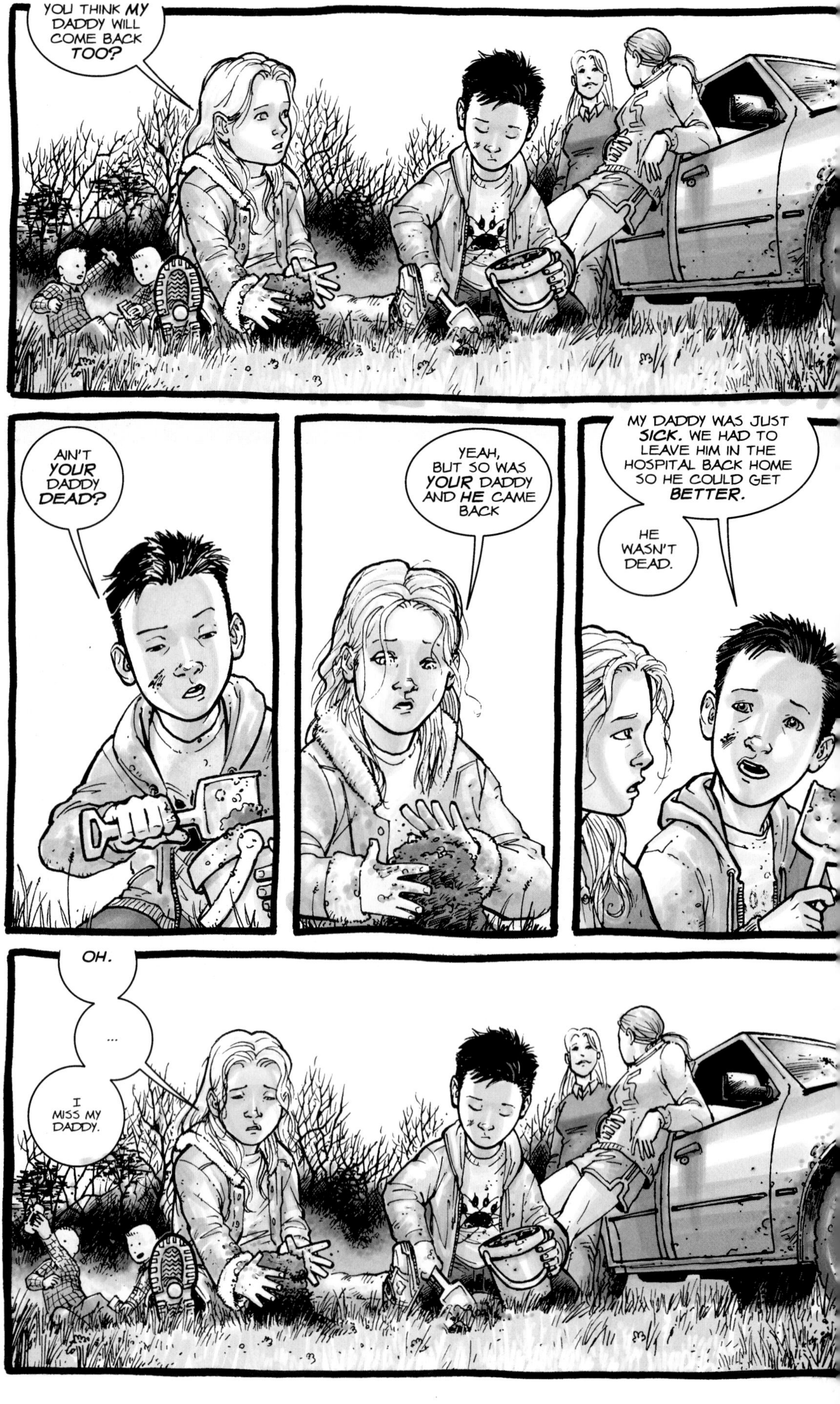
YOU THINK MY DADDY WILL COME BACK TOO?
AIN'T YOUR DADDY DEAD?
YEAH, BUT SO WAS YOUR DADDY AND HE CAME BACK
MY DADDY WAS JUST SICK. WE HAD TO LEAVE HIM IN THE HOSPITAL BACK HOME SO HE COULD GET BETTER.
HE WASN'T DEAD.
OH.
...
I MISS MY DADDY.

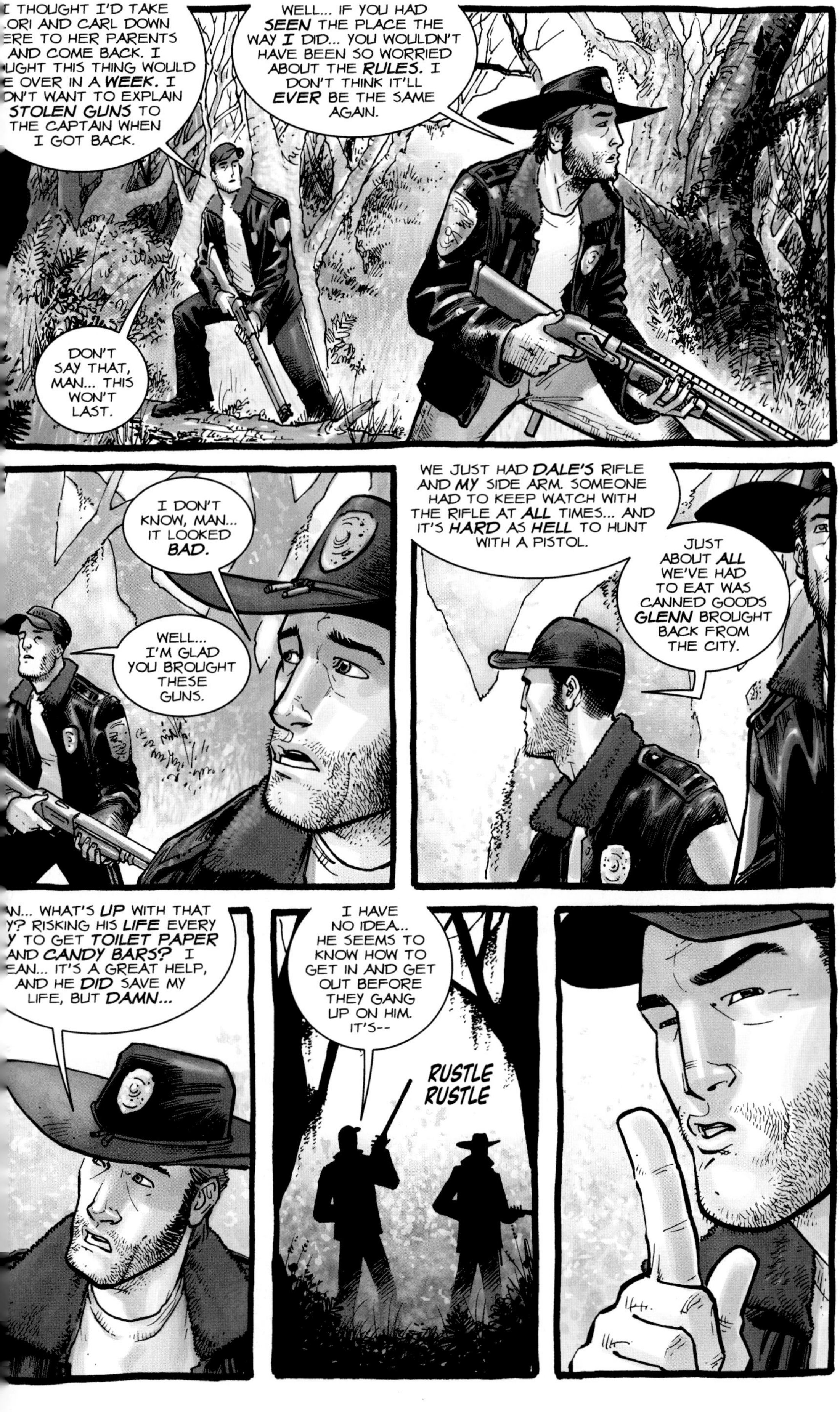
I THOUGHT I'D TAKE LORI AND CARL DOWN HERE TO HER PARENTS AND COME BACK. I THOUGHT THIS THING WOULD BE OVER IN A WEEK. I DIDN'T WANT TO EXPLAIN STOLEN GUNS TO THE CAPTAIN WHEN I GOT BACK.
WELL... IF YOU HAD SEEN THE PLACE THE WAY I DID... YOU WOULDN'T HAVE BEEN SO WORRIED ABOUT THE RULES. I DON'T THINK IT'LL EVER BE THE SAME AGAIN.
DON'T SAY THAT, MAN... THIS WON'T LAST.
I DON'T KNOW, MAN... IT LOOKED BAD.
WELL... I'M GLAD YOU BROUGHT THESE GUNS.
WE JUST HAD DALE'S RIFLE AND MY SIDE ARM. SOMEONE HAD TO KEEP WATCH WITH THE RIFLE AT ALL TIMES... AND IT'S HARD AS HELL TO HUNT WITH A PISTOL.
JUST ABOUT ALL WE'VE HAD TO EAT WAS CANNED GOODS GLENN BROUGHT BACK FROM THE CITY.
MAN... WHAT'S UP WITH THAT GUY? RISKING HIS LIFE EVERY DAY TO GET TOILET PAPER AND CANDY BARS? I MEAN... IT'S A GREAT HELP, AND HE DID SAVE MY LIFE, BUT DAMN...
I HAVE NO IDEA... HE SEEMS TO KNOW HOW TO GET IN AND GET OUT BEFORE THEY GANG UP ON HIM. IT'S--
RUSTLE RUSTLE

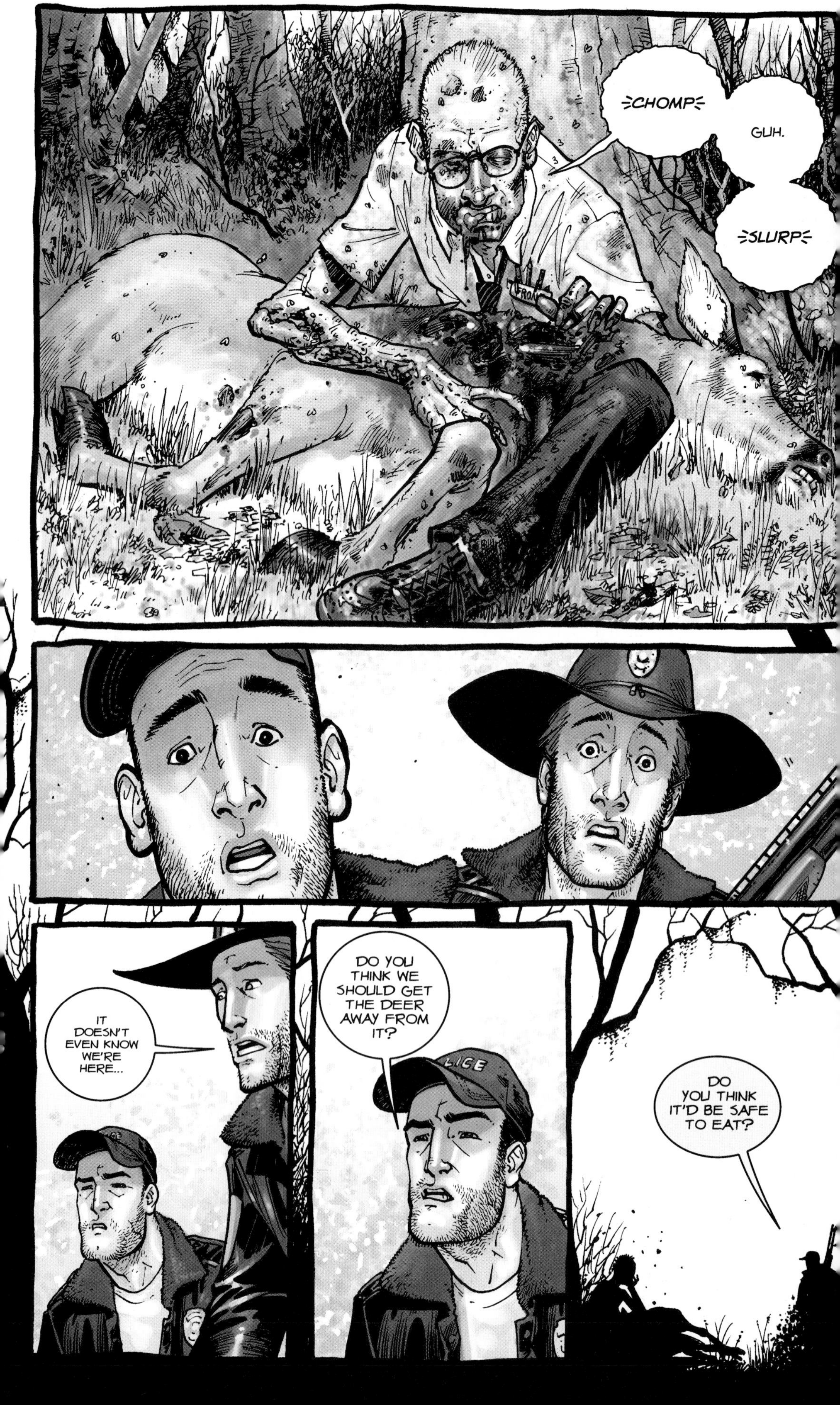
CHOMP
GUH.
SLURP
IT DOESN'T EVEN KNOW WE'RE HERE...
DO YOU THINK WE SHOULD GET THE DEER AWAY FROM IT?
LICE
DO YOU THINK IT'D BE SAFE TO EAT?

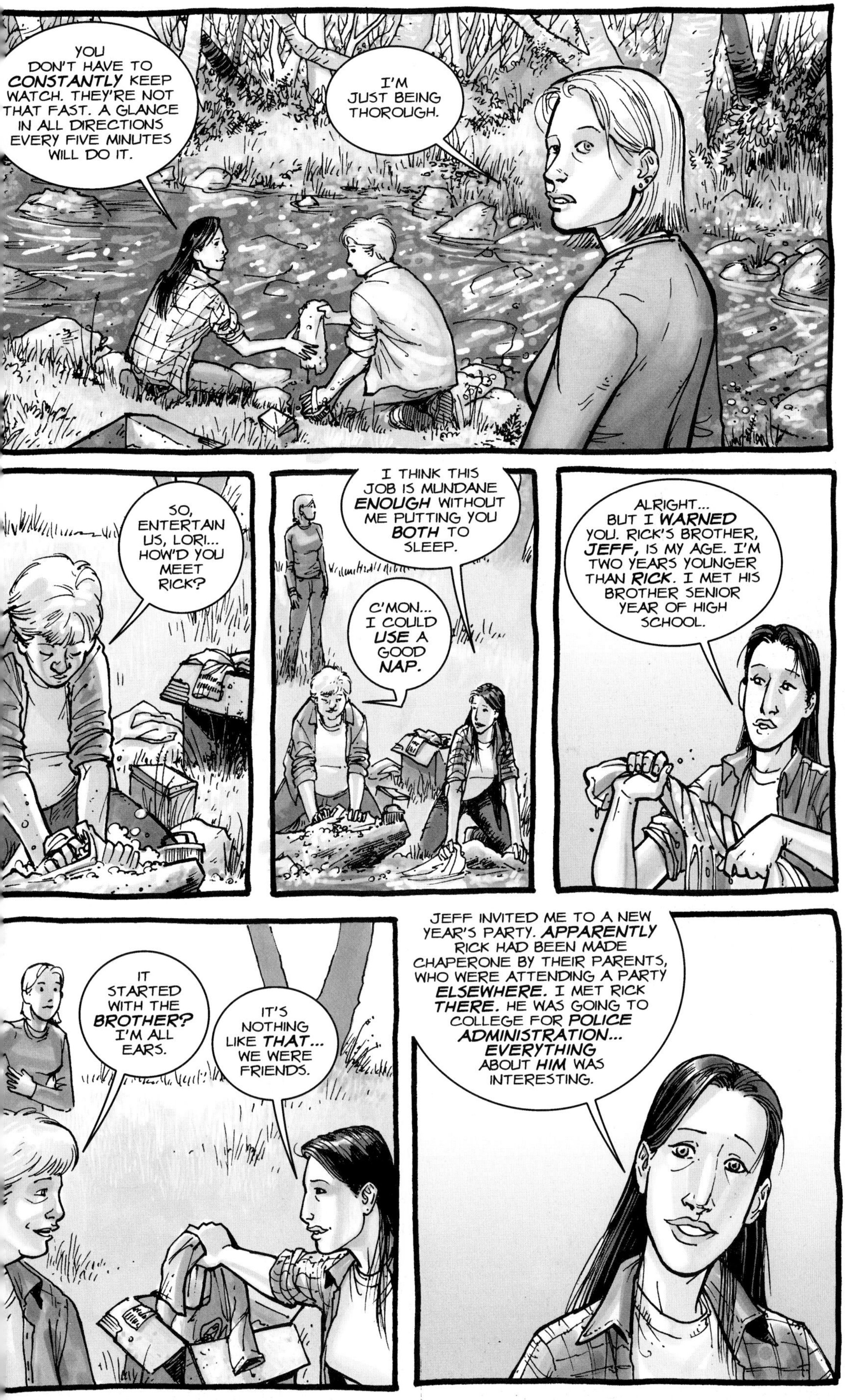
YOU DON'T HAVE TO CONSTANTLY KEEP WATCH. THEY'RE NOT THAT FAST. A GLANCE IN ALL DIRECTIONS EVERY FIVE MINUTES WILL DO IT.
I'M JUST BEING THOROUGH.
SO, ENTERTAIN US, LORI... HOW'D YOU MEET RICK?
I THINK THIS JOB IS MUNDANE ENOUGH WITHOUT ME PUTTING YOU BOTH TO SLEEP.
C'MON... I COULD USE A GOOD NAP.
ALRIGHT... BUT I WARNED YOU. RICK'S BROTHER, JEFF, IS MY AGE. I'M TWO YEARS YOUNGER THAN RICK. I MET HIS BROTHER SENIOR YEAR OF HIGH SCHOOL.
IT STARTED WITH THE BROTHER? I'M ALL EARS.
IT'S NOTHING LIKE THAT... WE WERE FRIENDS.
JEFF INVITED ME TO A NEW YEAR'S PARTY. APPARENTLY RICK HAD BEEN MADE CHAPERONE BY THEIR PARENTS, WHO WERE ATTENDING A PARTY ELSEWHERE. I MET RICK THERE. HE WAS GOING TO COLLEGE FOR POLICE ADMINISTRATION... EVERYTHING ABOUT HIM WAS INTERESTING.

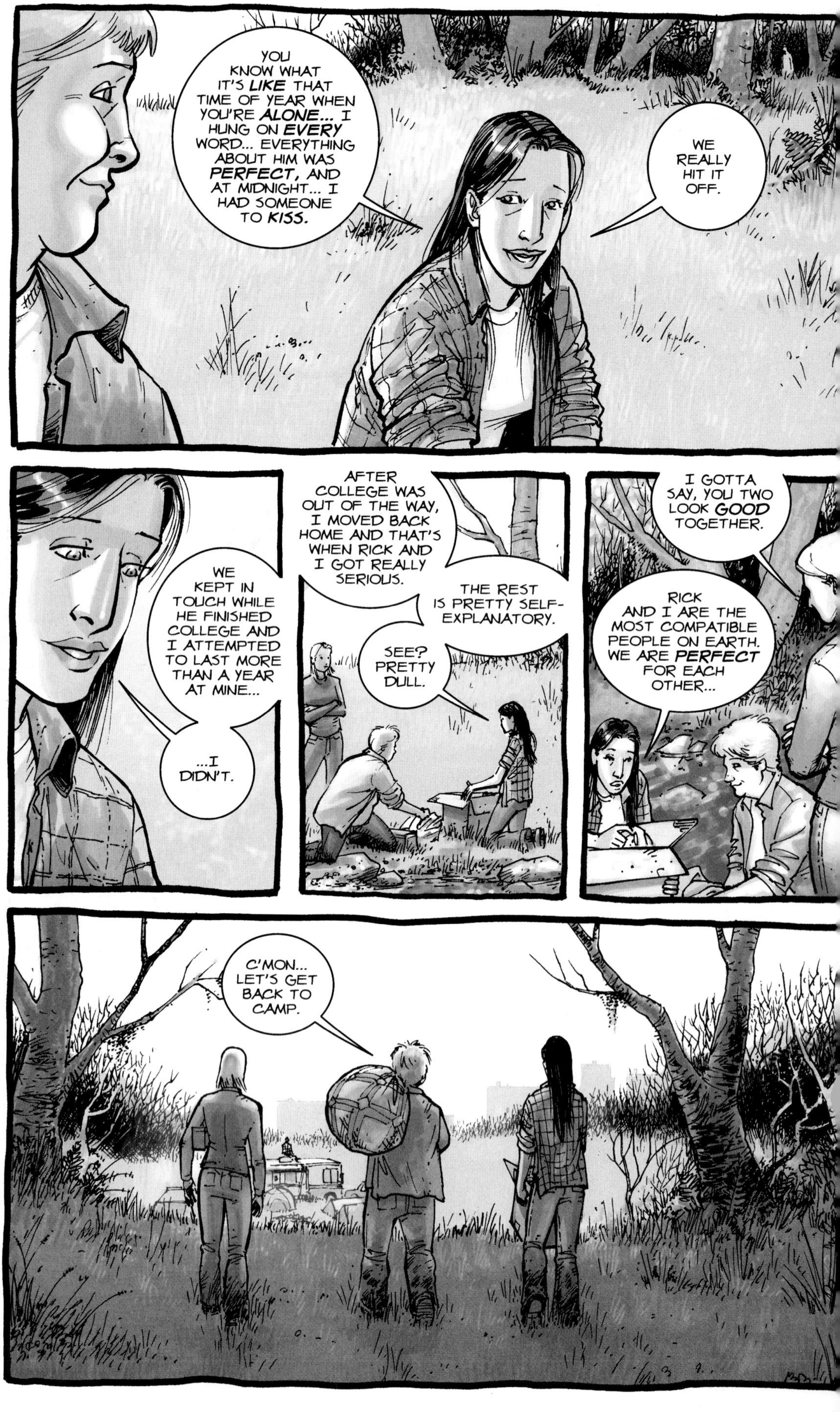
YOU KNOW WHAT IT'S LIKE THAT TIME OF YEAR WHEN YOU'RE ALONE... I HUNG ON EVERY WORD... EVERYTHING ABOUT HIM WAS PERFECT, AND AT MIDNIGHT... I HAD SOMEONE TO KISS.
WE REALLY HIT IT OFF.
WE KEPT IN TOUCH WHILE HE FINISHED COLLEGE AND I ATTEMPTED TO LAST MORE THAN A YEAR AT MINE...
...I DIDN'T.
AFTER COLLEGE WAS OUT OF THE WAY, I MOVED BACK HOME AND THAT'S WHEN RICK AND I GOT REALLY SERIOUS.
THE REST IS PRETTY SELF-EXPLANATORY.
SEE? PRETTY DULL.
I GOTTA SAY, YOU TWO LOOK GOOD TOGETHER.
RICK AND I ARE THE MOST COMPATIBLE PEOPLE ON EARTH. WE ARE PERFECT FOR EACH OTHER...
C'MON... LET'S GET BACK TO CAMP.

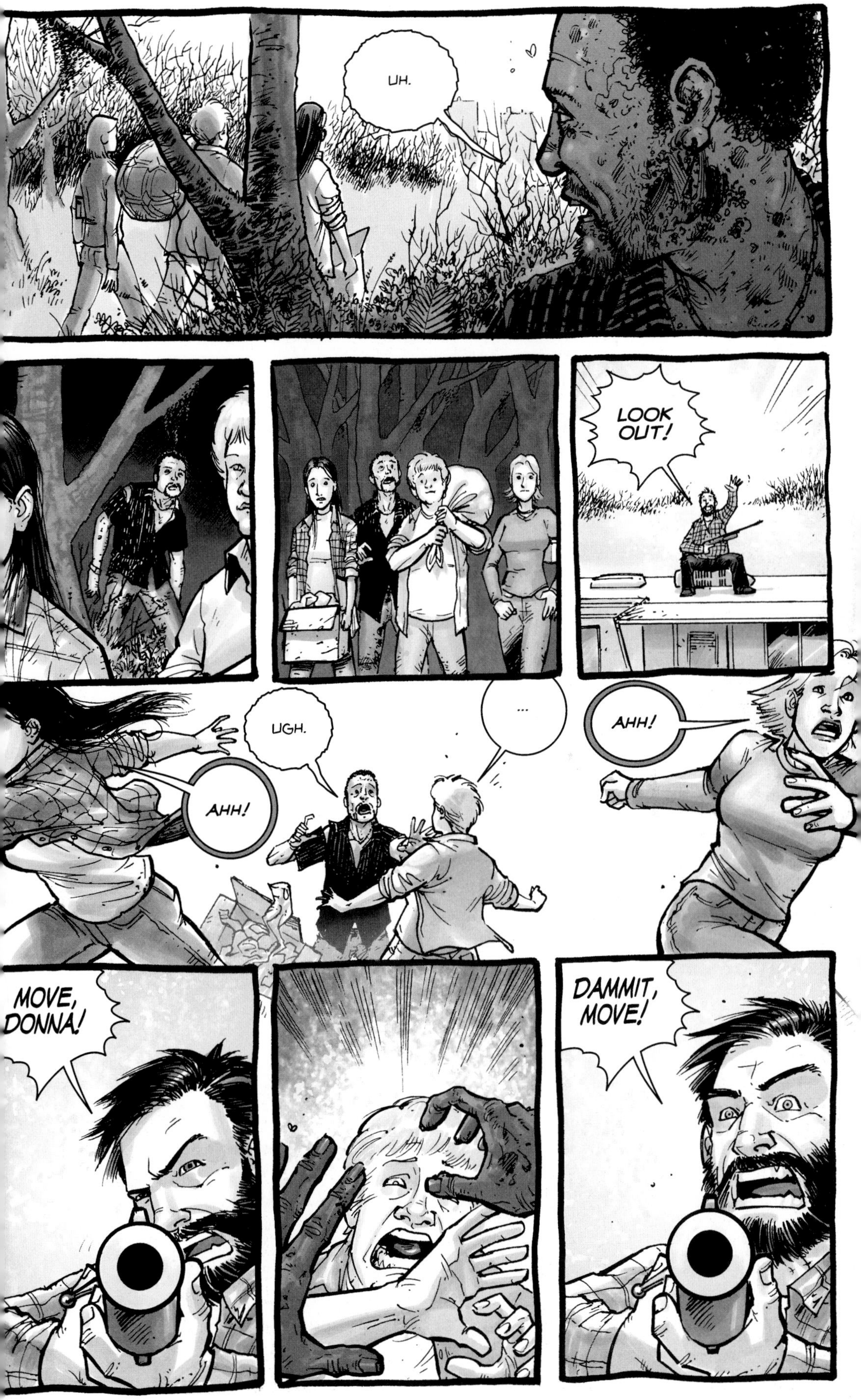
UH.
LOOK OUT!
AHH!
UGH.
...
AHH!
MOVE, DONNA!
DAMMIT, MOVE!

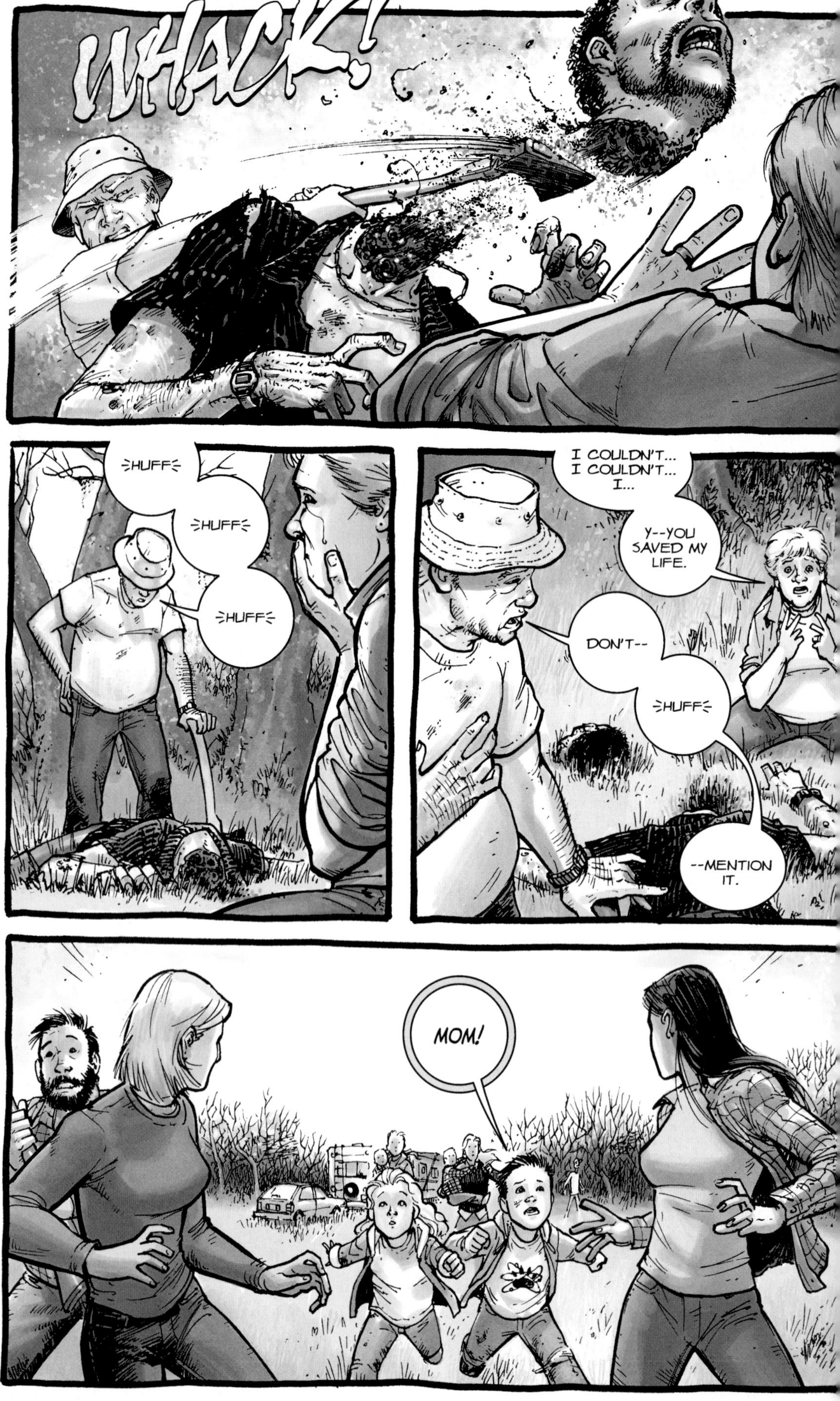
WHACK!
HUFF
HUFF
HUFF
I COULDN'T... I COULDN'T... I...
Y--YOU SAVED MY LIFE.
DON'T--
HUFF
--MENTION IT.
MOM!

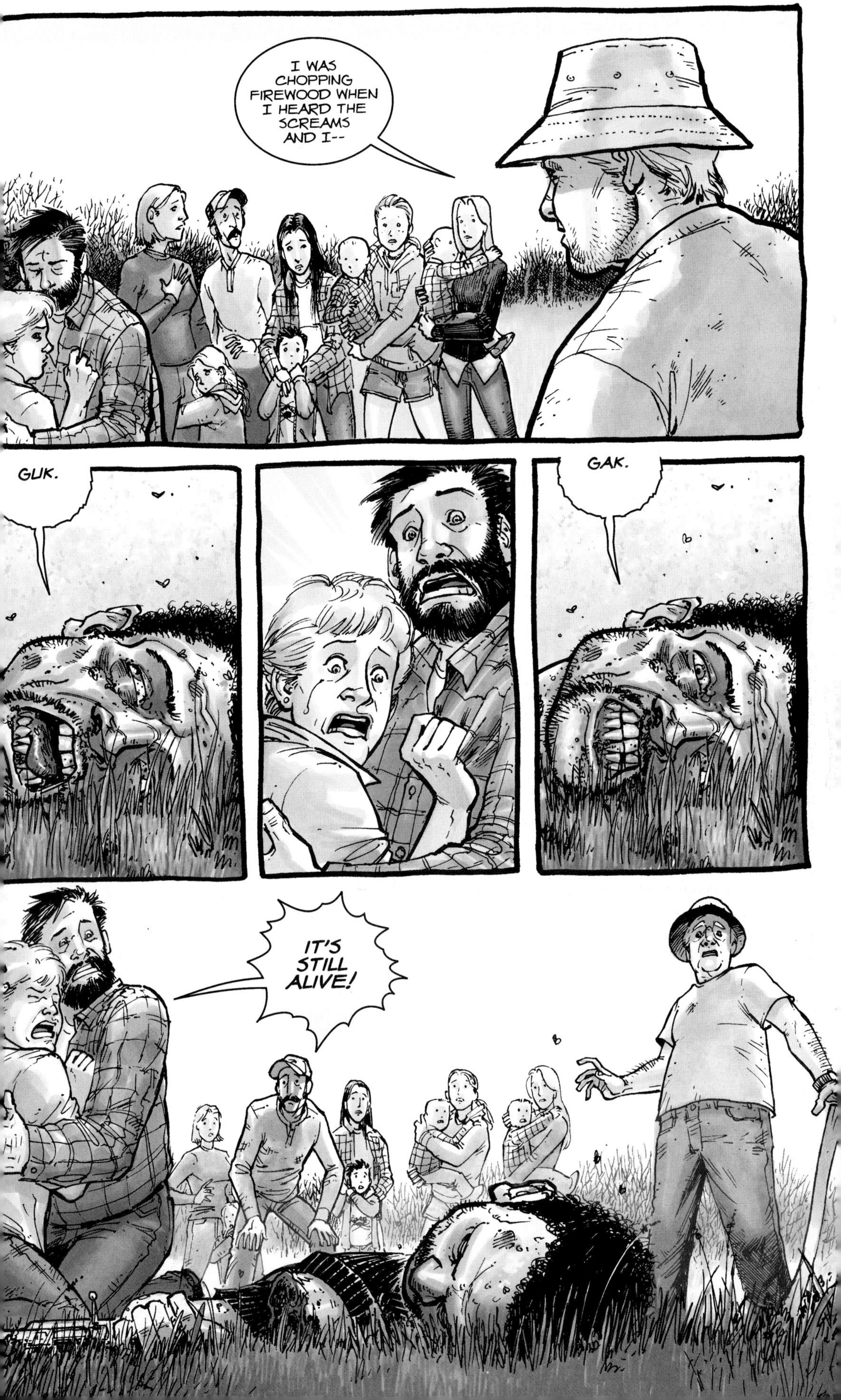
I WAS CHOPPING FIREWOOD WHEN I HEARD THE SCREAMS AND I--
GUK.
GAK.
IT'S STILL ALIVE!

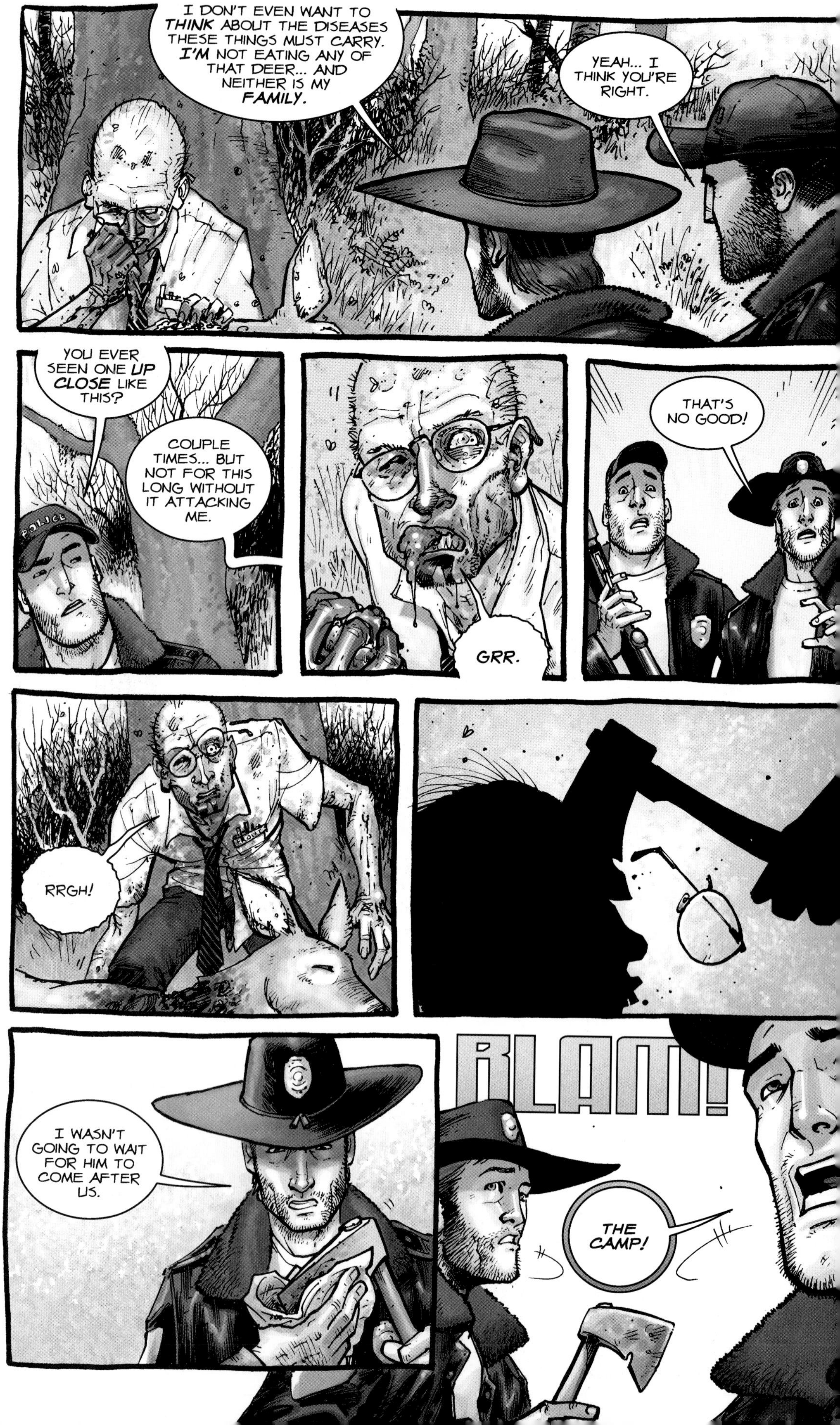
I DON'T EVEN WANT TO THINK ABOUT THE DISEASES THESE THINGS MUST CARRY. I'M NOT EATING ANY OF THAT DEER... AND NEITHER IS MY FAMILY.
YEAH... I THINK YOU'RE RIGHT.
YOU EVER SEEN ONE UP CLOSE LIKE THIS?
POLICE
COUPLE TIMES... BUT NOT FOR THIS LONG WITHOUT IT ATTACKING ME.
GRR.
THAT'S NO GOOD!
RRGH!
I WASN'T GOING TO WAIT FOR HIM TO COME AFTER US.
BLAM!
THE CAMP!

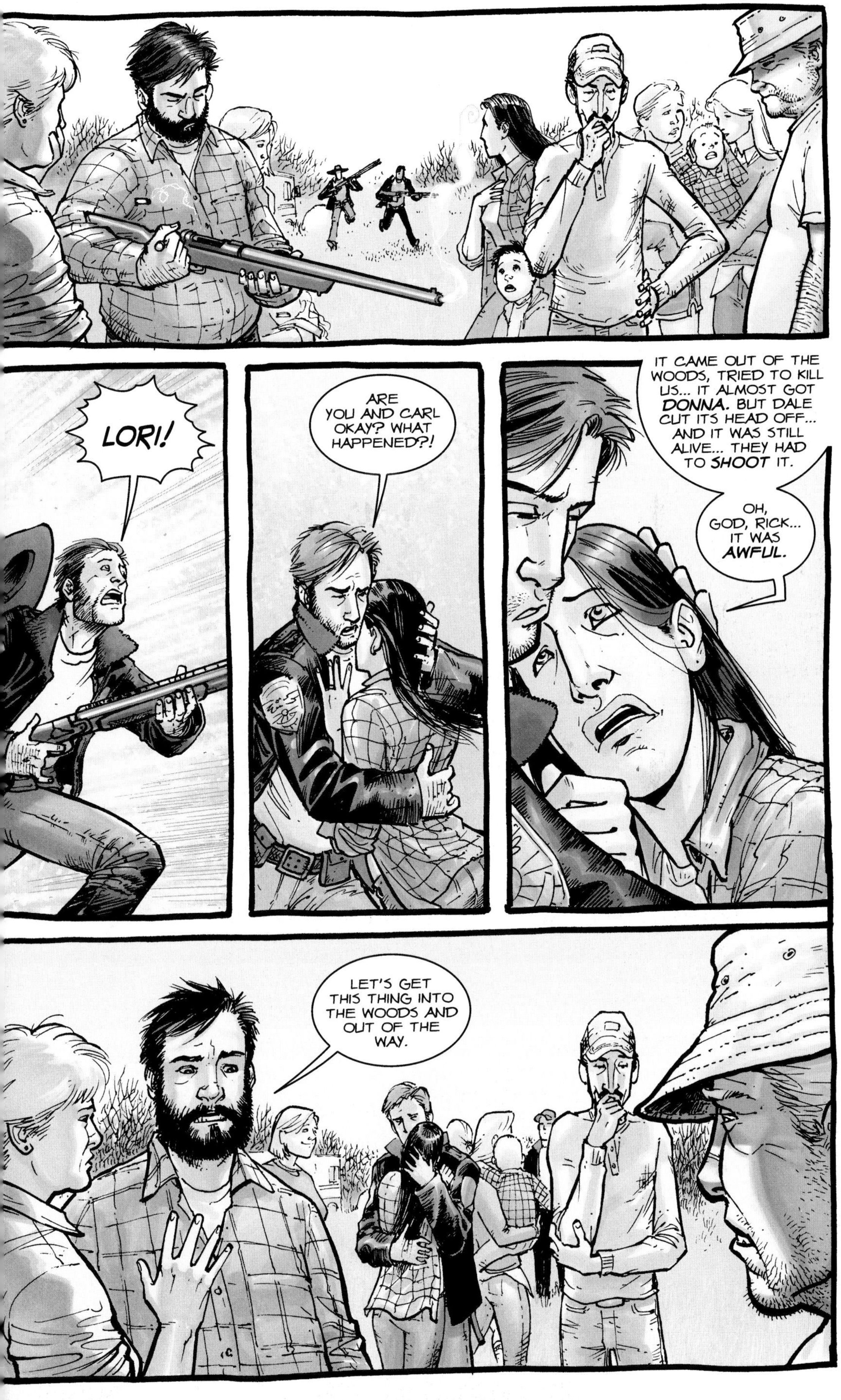
LORI!
ARE YOU AND CARL OKAY? WHAT HAPPENED?!
IT CAME OUT OF THE WOODS, TRIED TO KILL US... IT ALMOST GOT DONNA. BUT DALE CUT ITS HEAD OFF... AND IT WAS STILL ALIVE... THEY HAD TO SHOOT IT.
OH, GOD, RICK... IT WAS AWFUL.
LET'S GET THIS THING INTO THE WOODS AND OUT OF THE WAY.

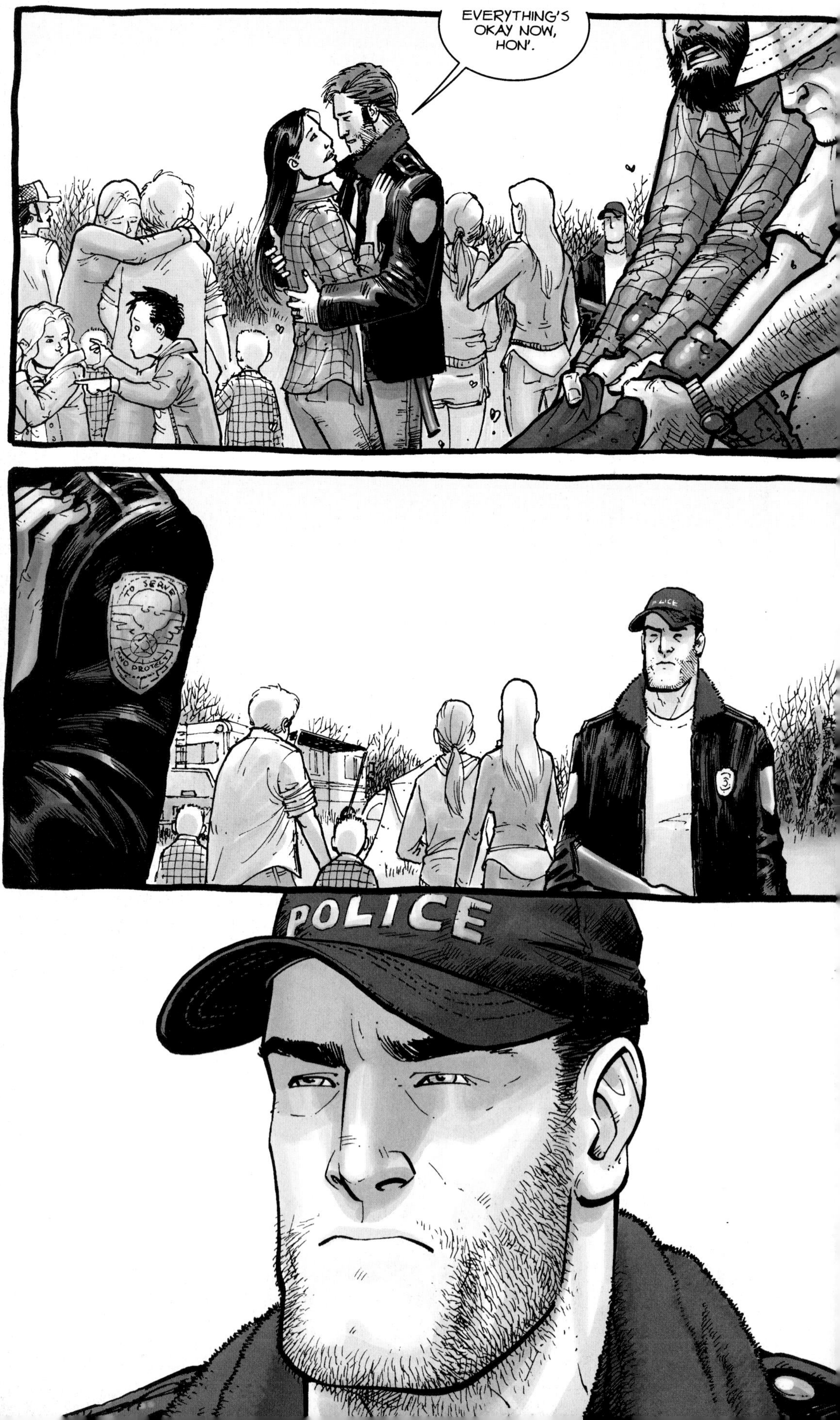
EVERYTHING'S OKAY NOW, HON'.
TO SERVE AND PROTECT
POLICE

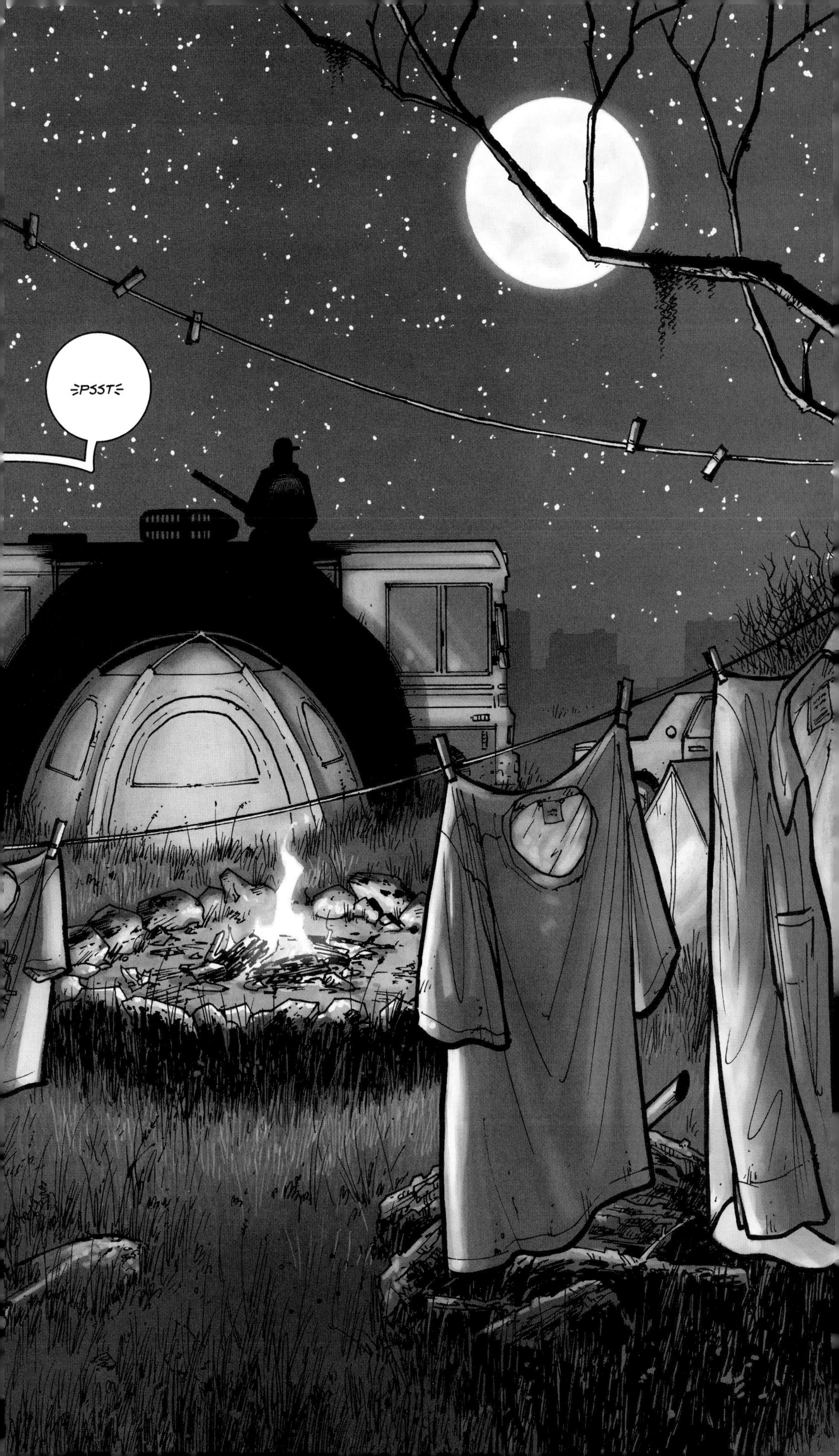
PSST

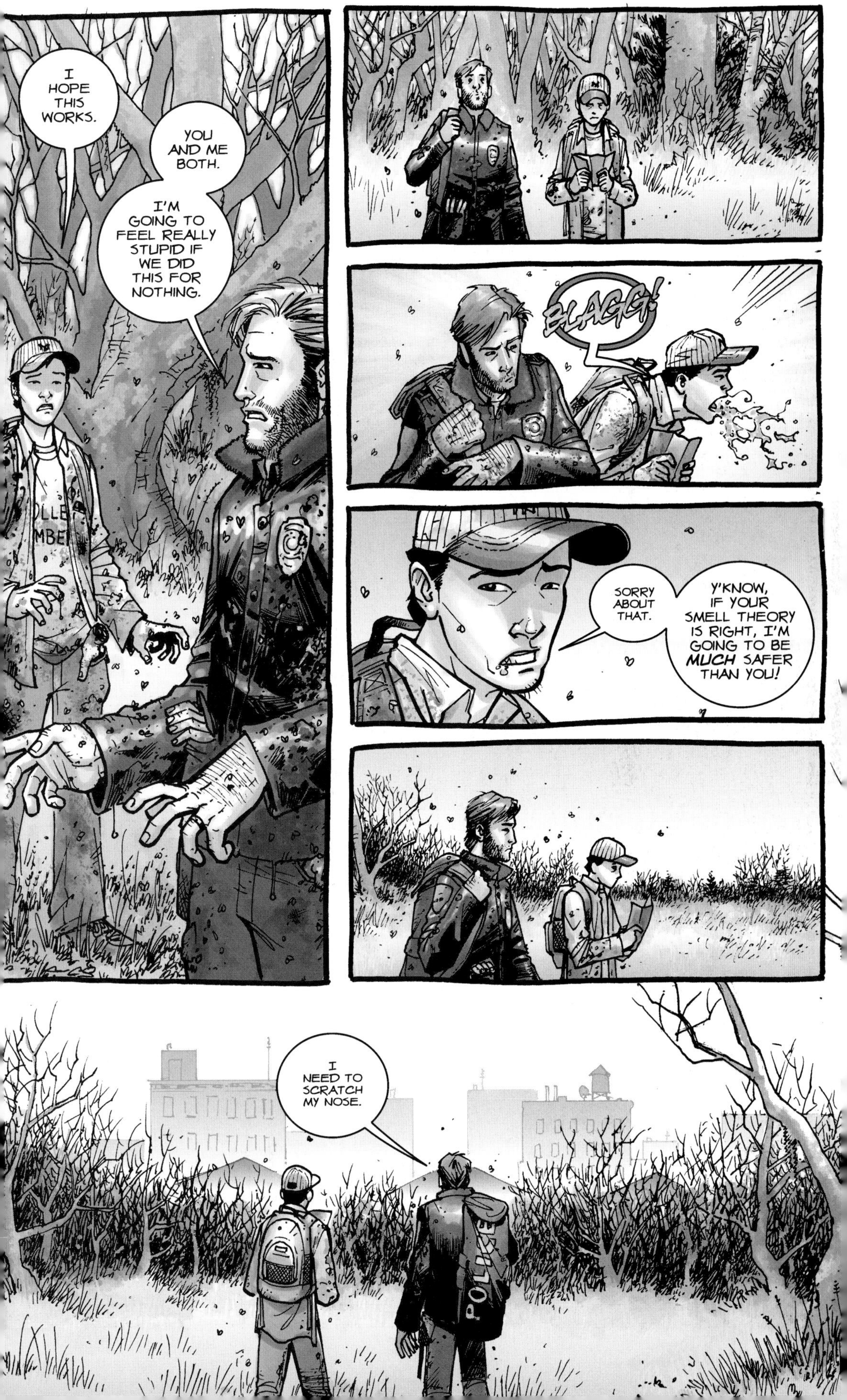
I HOPE THIS WORKS.
YOU AND ME BOTH.
I'M GOING TO FEEL REALLY STUPID IF WE DID THIS FOR NOTHING.
BLAGG!
SORRY ABOUT THAT.
Y'KNOW, IF YOUR SMELL THEORY IS RIGHT, I'M GOING TO BE MUCH SAFER THAN YOU!
I NEED TO SCRATCH MY NOSE.

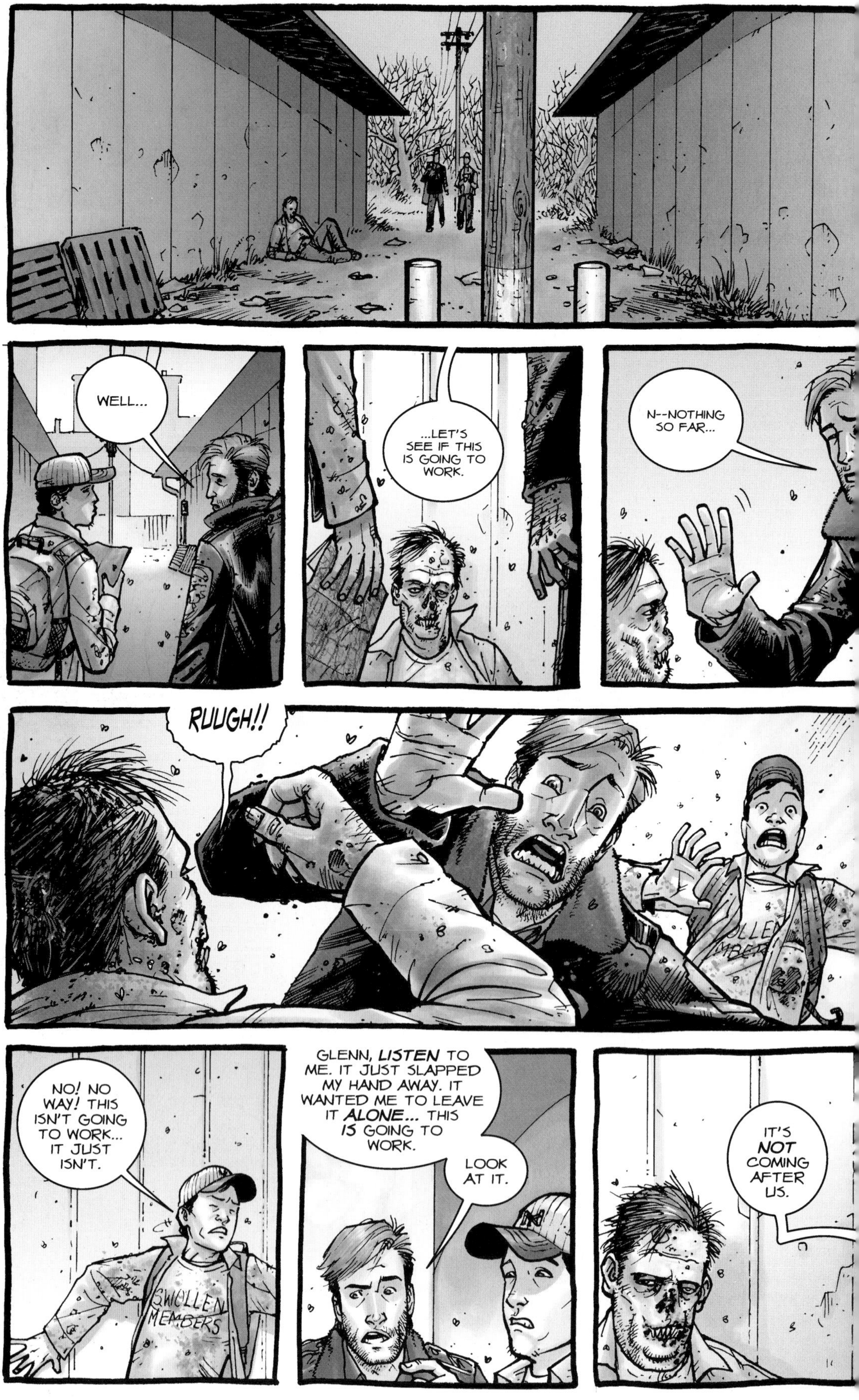
WELL...
...LET'S SEE IF THIS IS GOING TO WORK.
N--NOTHING SO FAR...
RUUGH!!
NO! NO WAY! THIS ISN'T GOING TO WORK... IT JUST ISN'T.
GLENN, LISTEN TO ME. IT JUST SLAPPED MY HAND AWAY. IT WANTED ME TO LEAVE IT ALONE... THIS IS GOING TO WORK.
LOOK AT IT.
IT'S NOT COMING AFTER US.

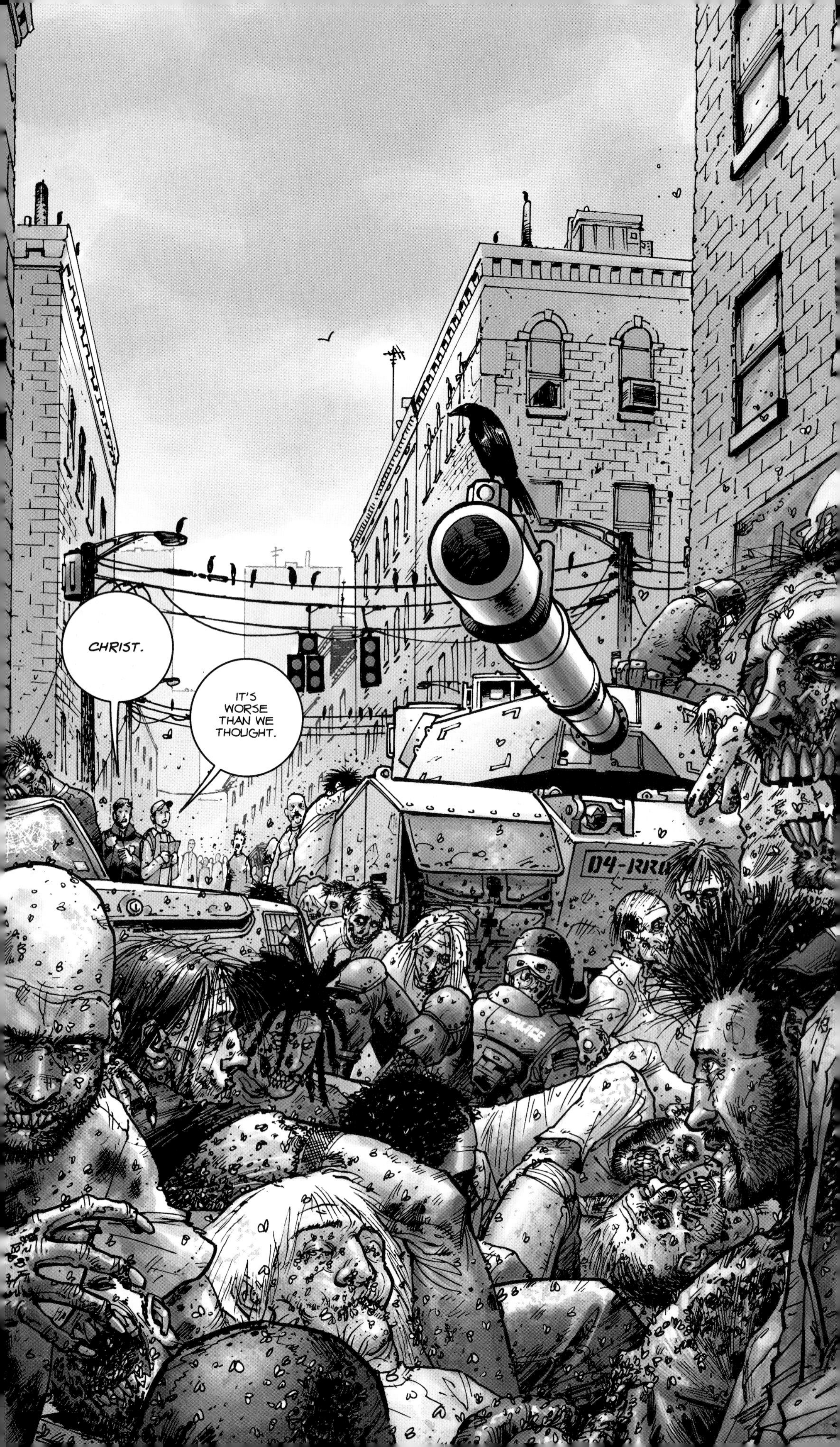
CHRIST.
IT'S WORSE THAN WE THOUGHT.
04-RRU
POLICE

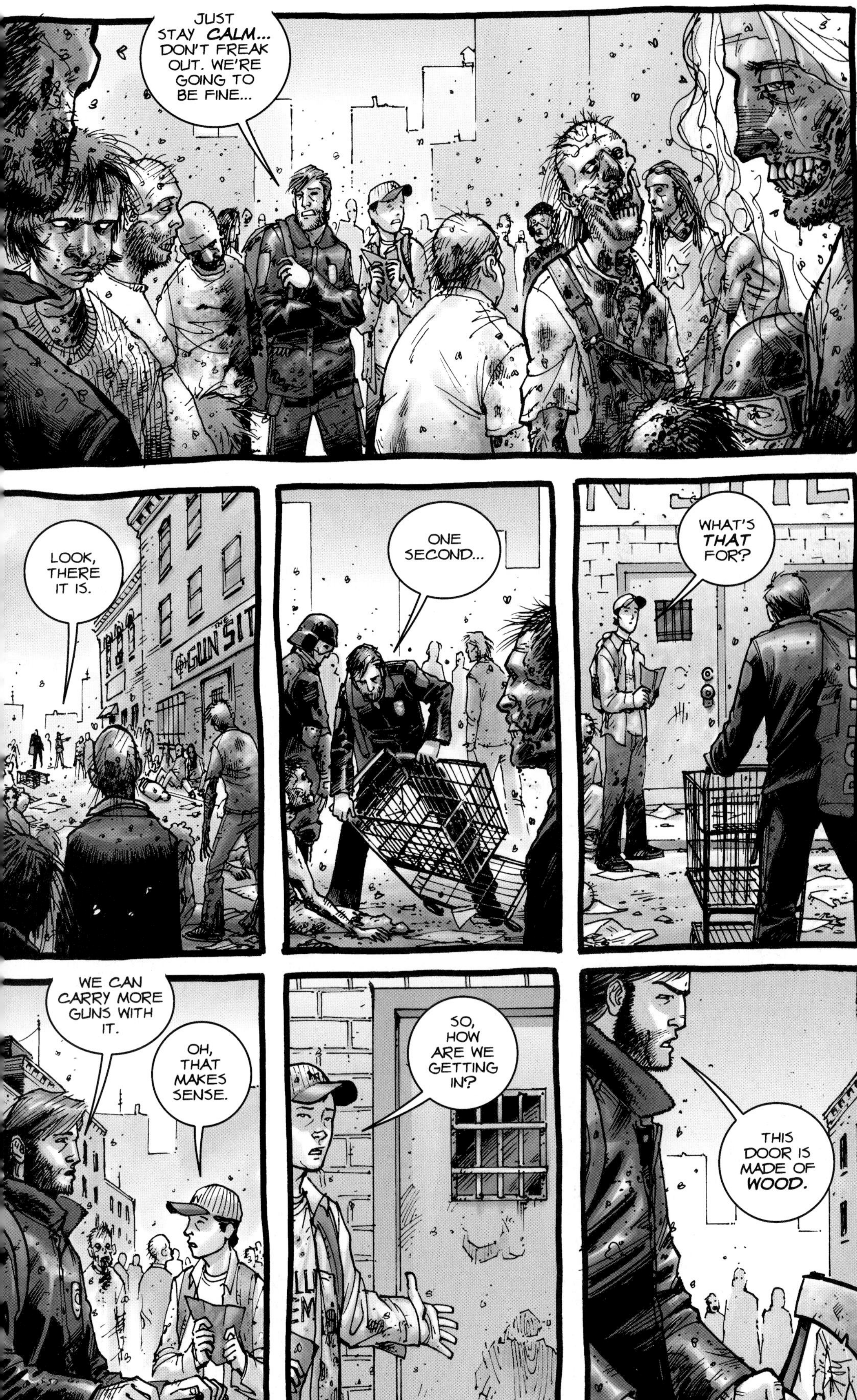
JUST STAY CALM... DON'T FREAK OUT. WE'RE GOING TO BE FINE...
LOOK, THERE IT IS.
GUN SIT
ONE SECOND...
WHAT'S THAT FOR?
WE CAN CARRY MORE GUNS WITH IT.
OH, THAT MAKES SENSE.
SO, HOW ARE WE GETTING IN?
THIS DOOR IS MADE OF WOOD.

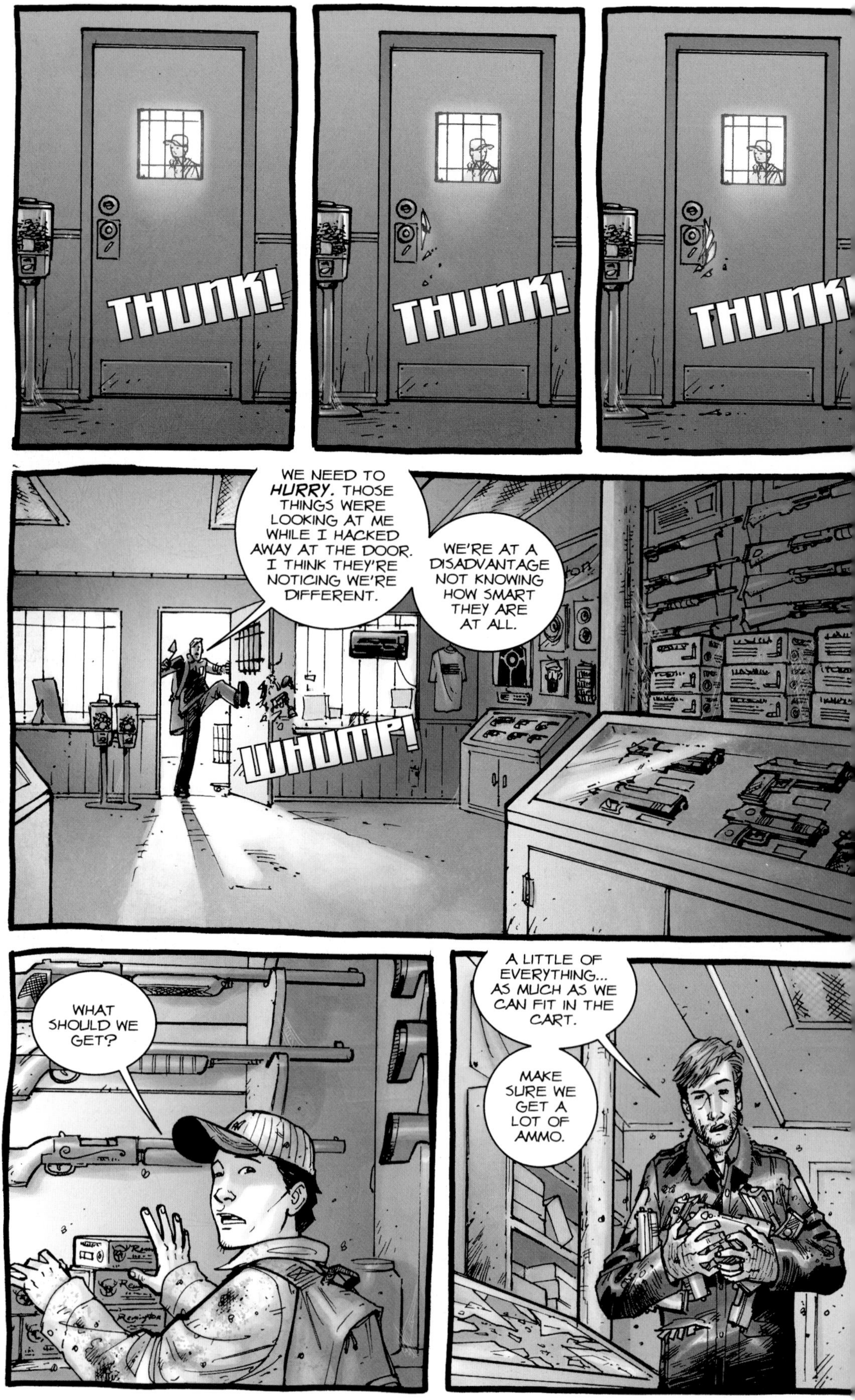
THUNK!
THUNK!
THUNK!
WE NEED TO HURRY. THOSE THINGS WERE LOOKING AT ME WHILE I HACKED AWAY AT THE DOOR. I THINK THEY'RE NOTICING WE'RE DIFFERENT.
WE'RE AT A DISADVANTAGE NOT KNOWING HOW SMART THEY ARE AT ALL.
WHUMP!
WHAT SHOULD WE GET?
A LITTLE OF EVERYTHING... AS MUCH AS WE CAN FIT IN THE CART.
MAKE SURE WE GET A LOT OF AMMO.

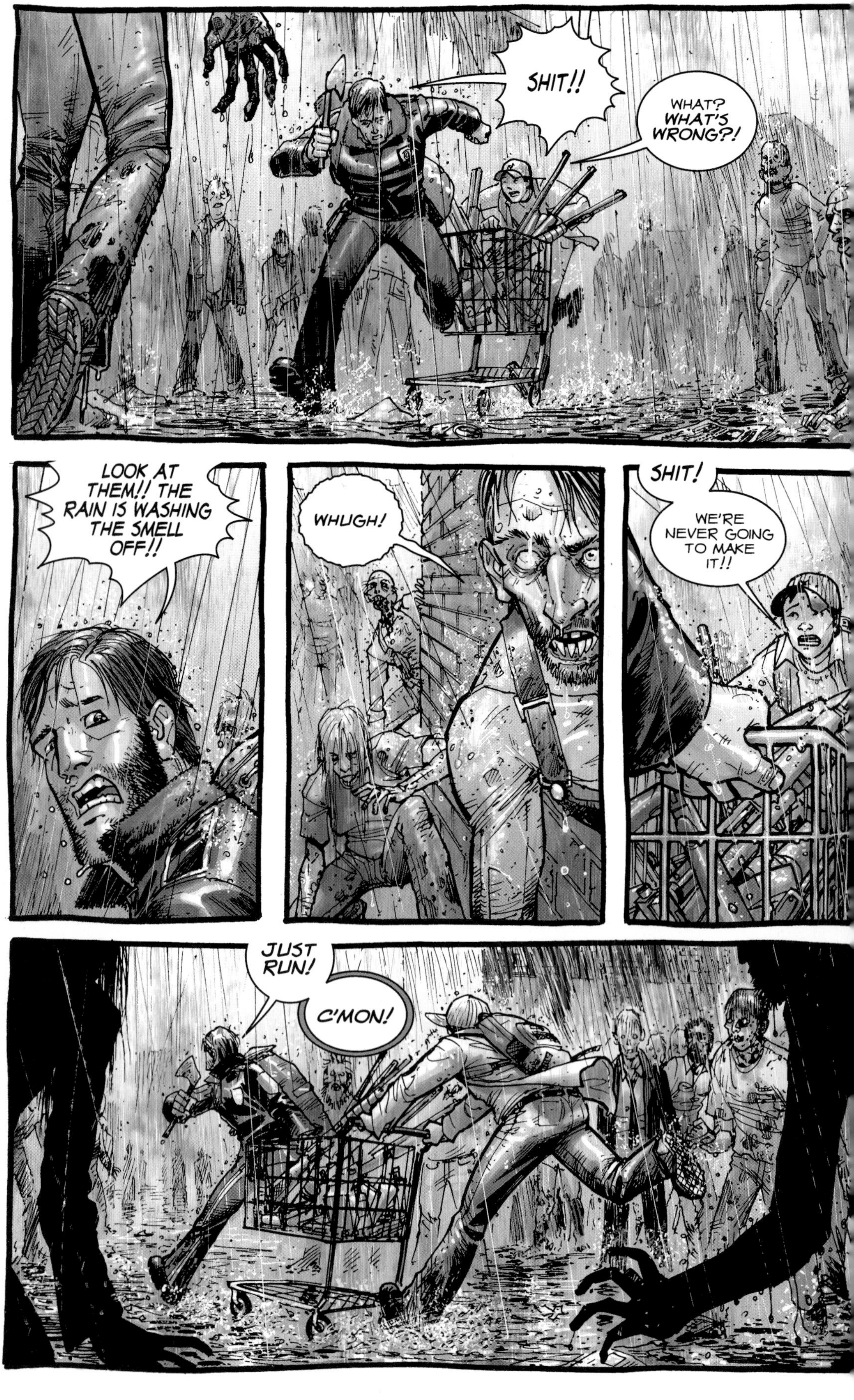
SHIT!!
WHAT? WHAT'S WRONG?!
LOOK AT THEM!! THE RAIN IS WASHING THE SMELL OFF!!
WHUGH!
SHIT!
WE'RE NEVER GOING TO MAKE IT!!
JUST RUN!
C'MON!

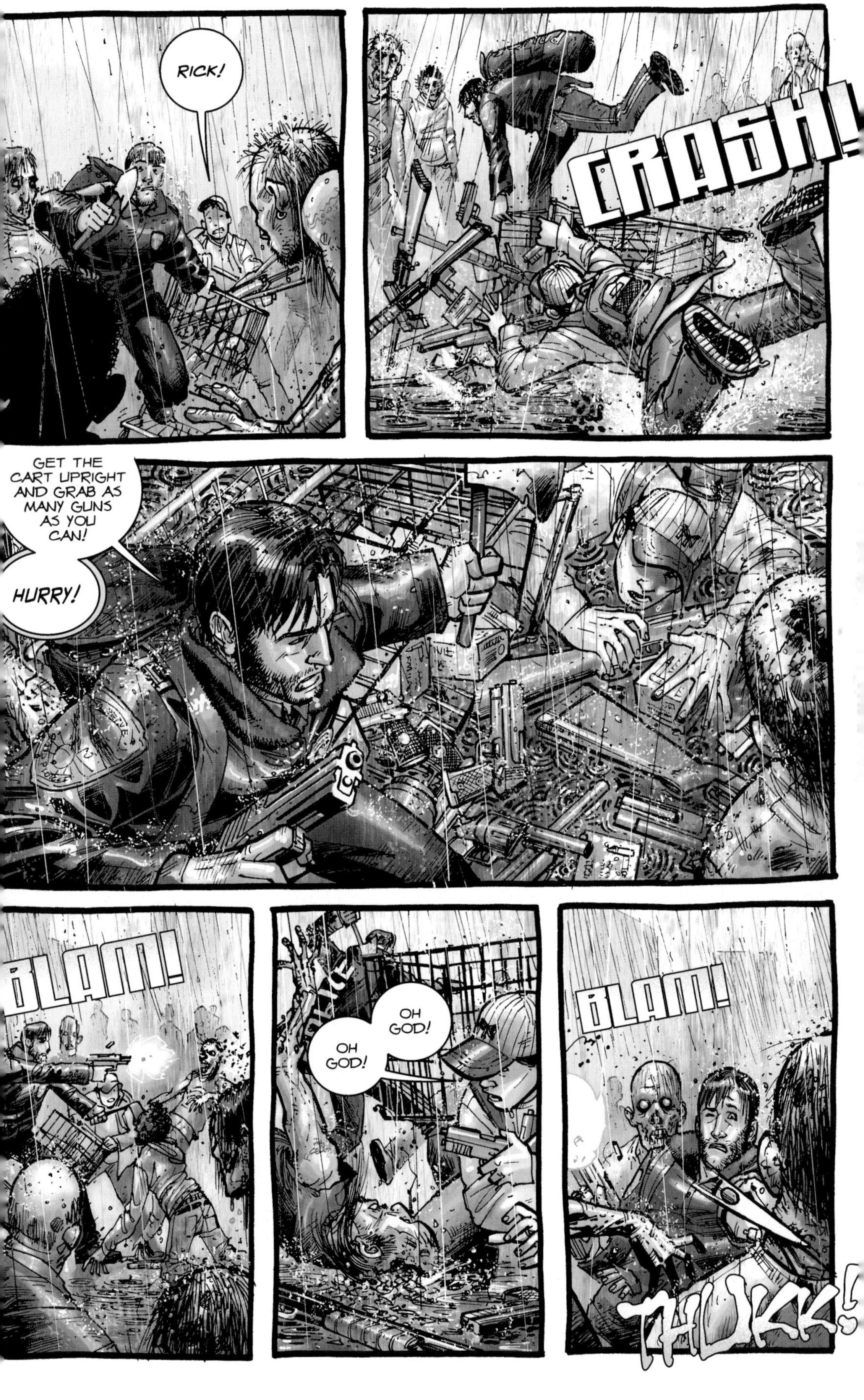
RICK!
CRASH!
GET THE CART UPRIGHT AND GRAB AS MANY GUNS AS YOU CAN!
HURRY!
BLAM!
OH GOD!
OH GOD!
BLAM!
THUKK!

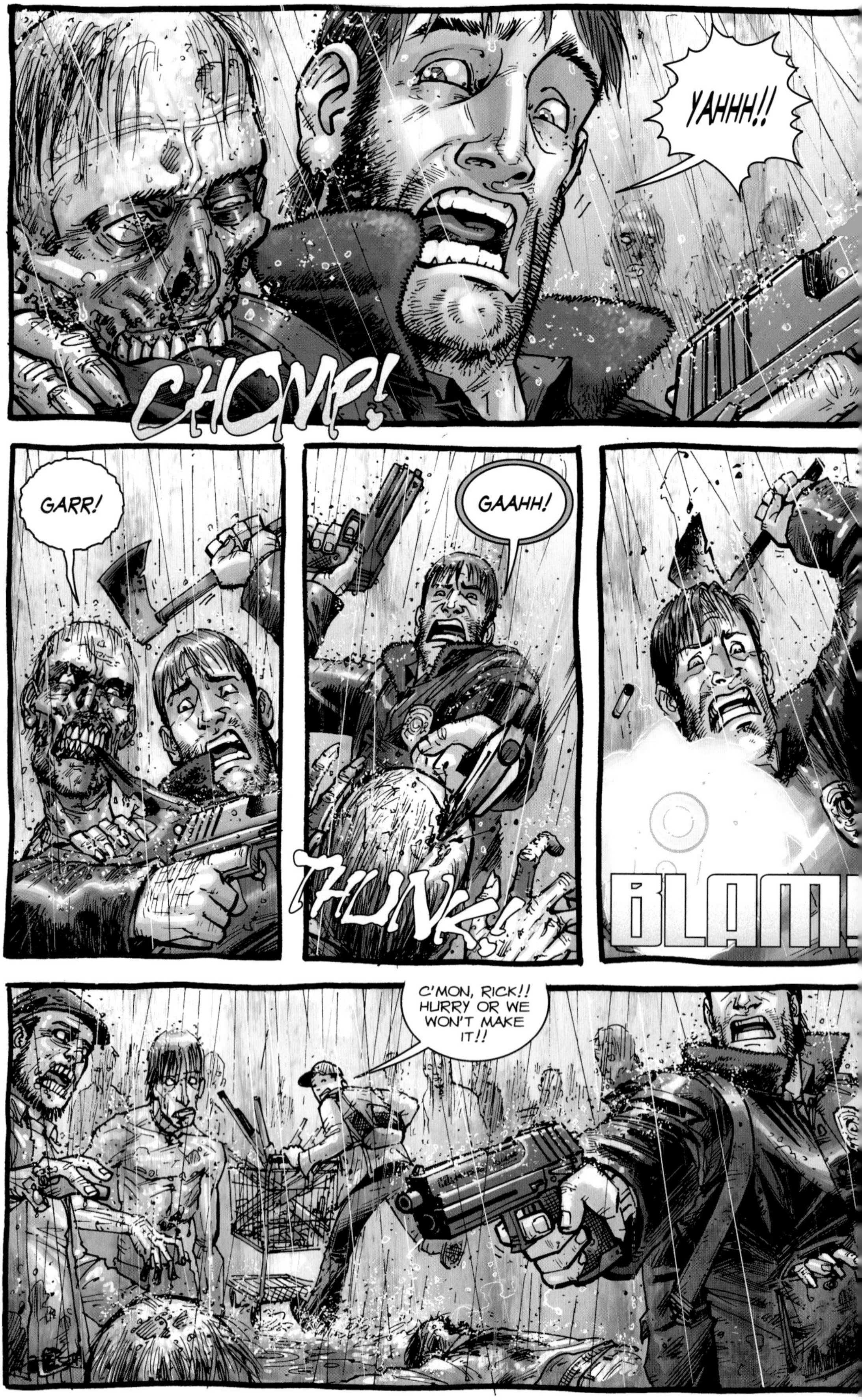
YAHHH!!
CHOMP!
GARR!
GAAHH!
THUNK!
BLAM!
C'MON, RICK!! HURRY OR WE WON'T MAKE IT!!

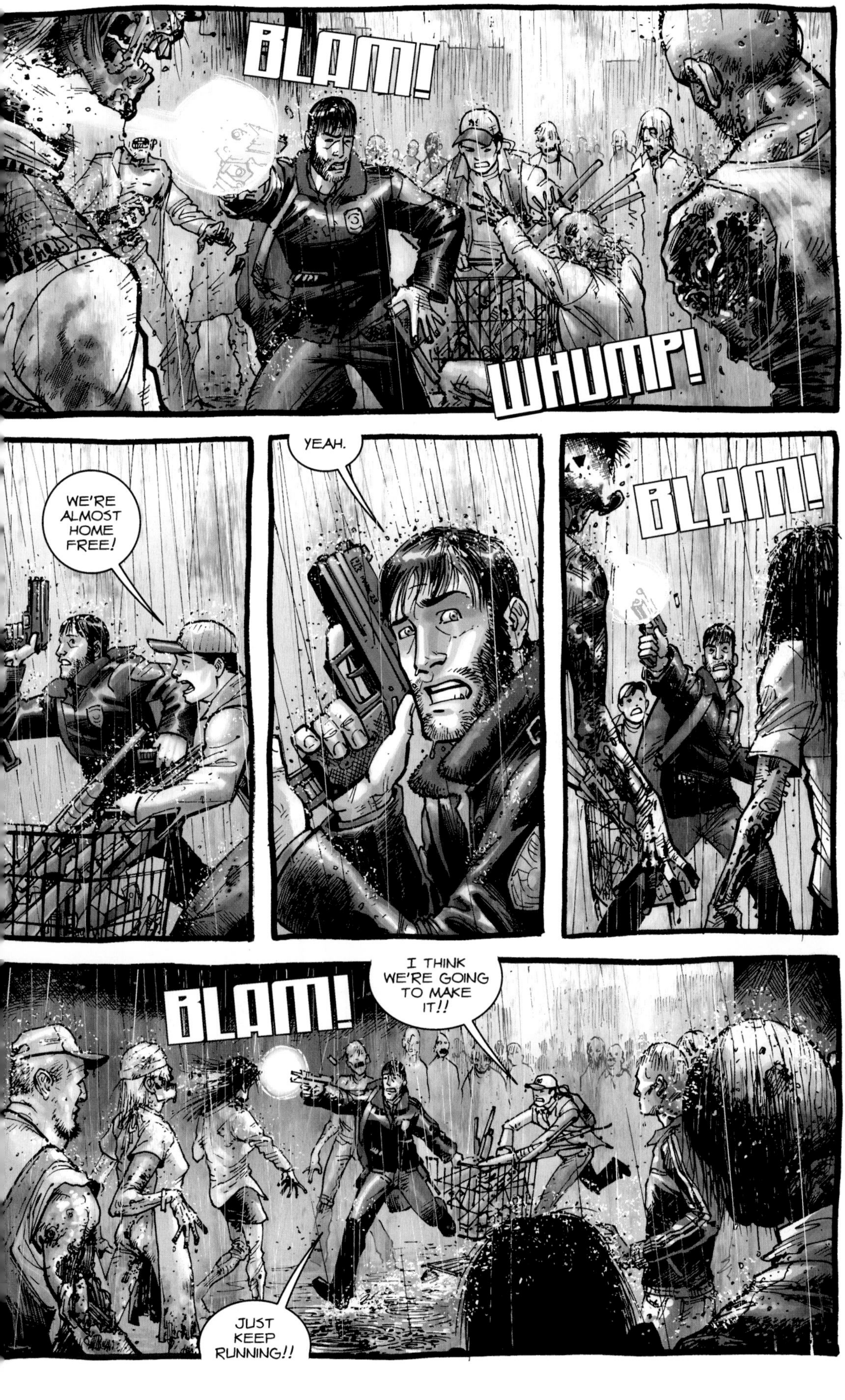
BLAM!
WHUMP!
WE'RE ALMOST HOME FREE!
YEAH.
BLAM!
BLAM!
I THINK WE'RE GOING TO MAKE IT!!
JUST KEEP RUNNING!!

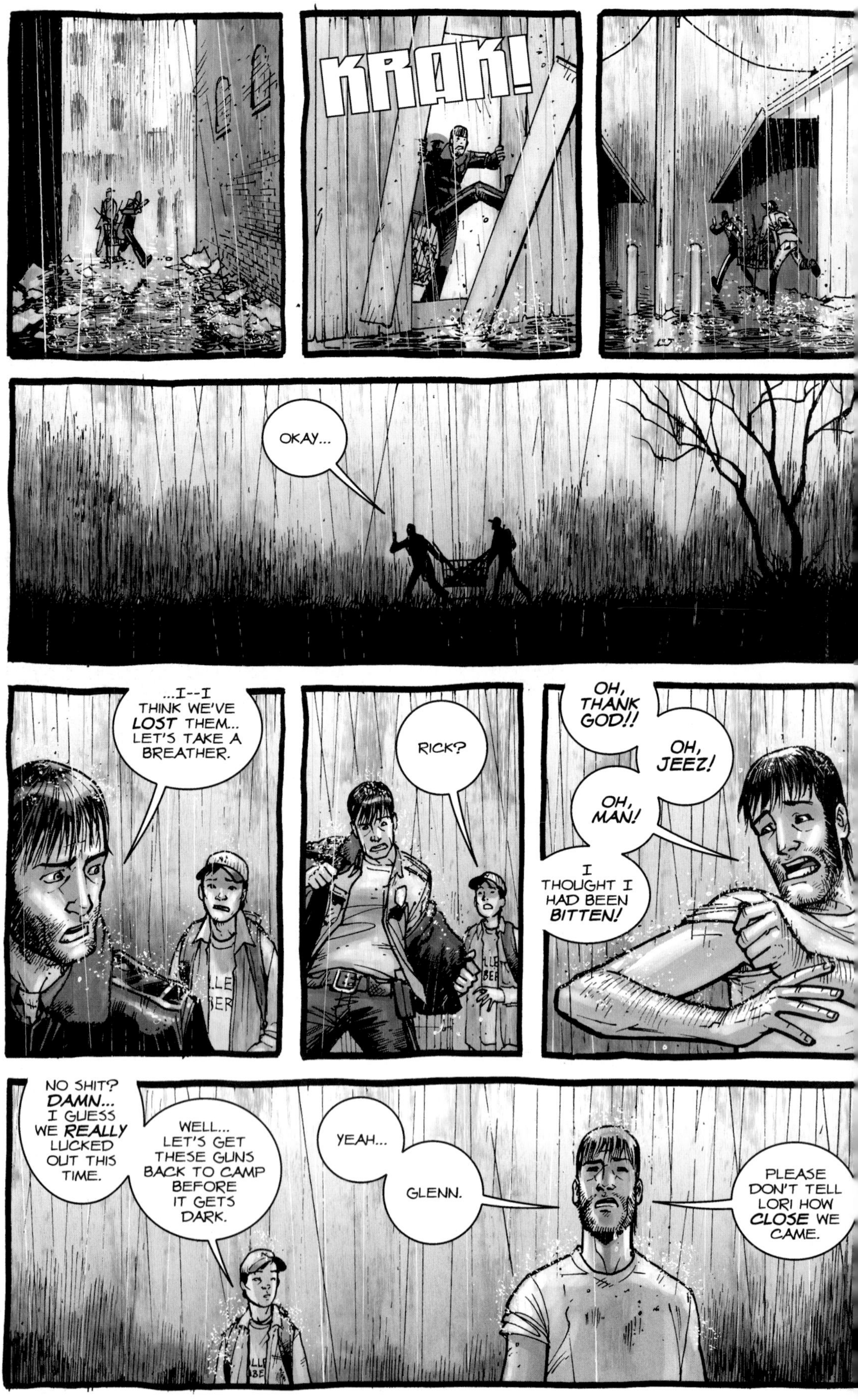
KRAK!
OKAY...
...I--I THINK WE'VE LOST THEM... LET'S TAKE A BREATHER.
RICK?
OH, THANK GOD!!
OH, JEEZ!
OH, MAN!
I THOUGHT I HAD BEEN BITTEN!
NO SHIT? DAMN... I GUESS WE REALLY LUCKED OUT THIS TIME.
WELL... LET'S GET THESE GUNS BACK TO CAMP BEFORE IT GETS DARK.
YEAH...
GLENN.
PLEASE DON'T TELL LORI HOW CLOSE WE CAME.

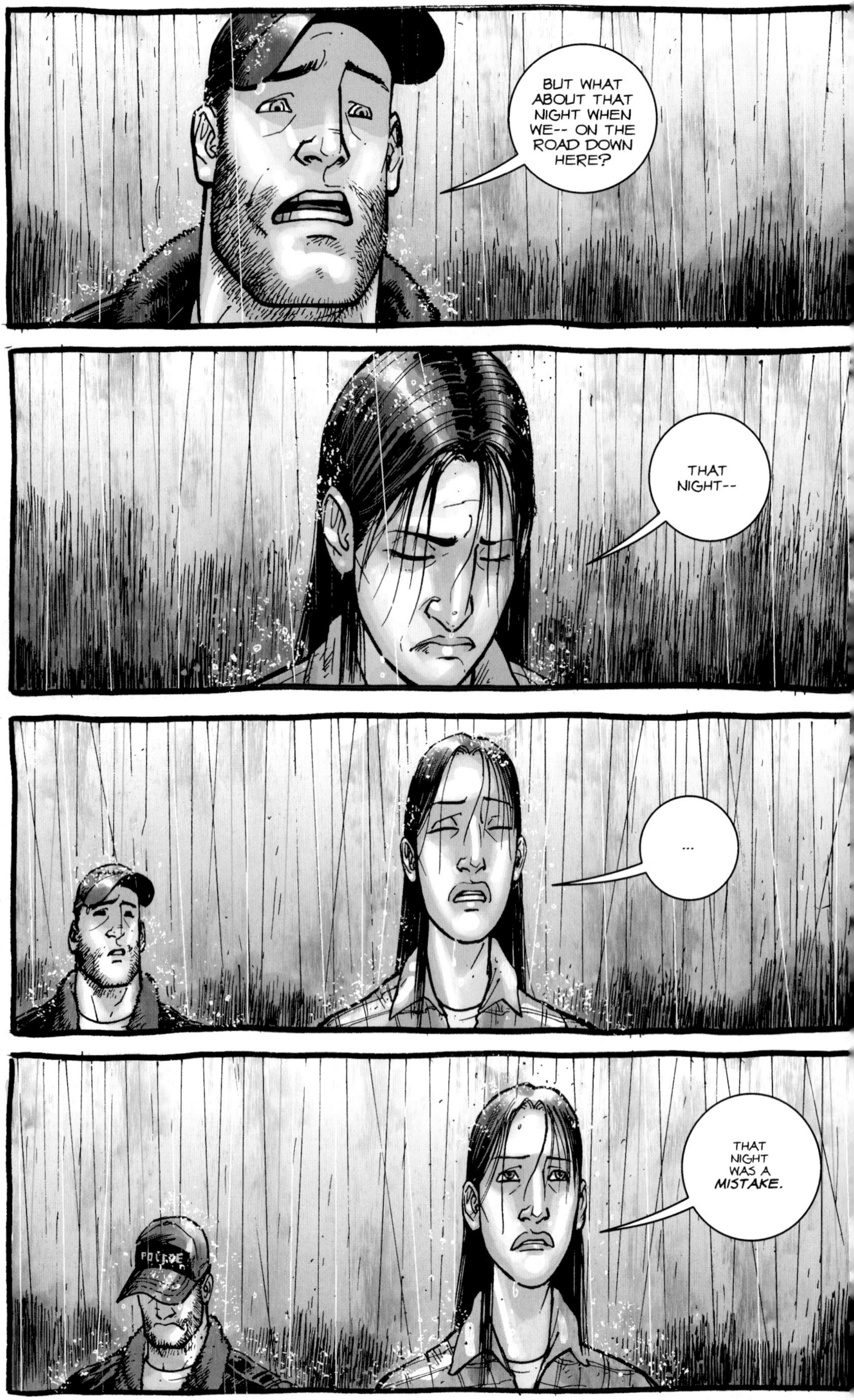
BUT WHAT ABOUT THAT NIGHT WHEN WE-- ON THE ROAD DOWN HERE?
THAT NIGHT--
...
THAT NIGHT WAS A *MISTAKE.*

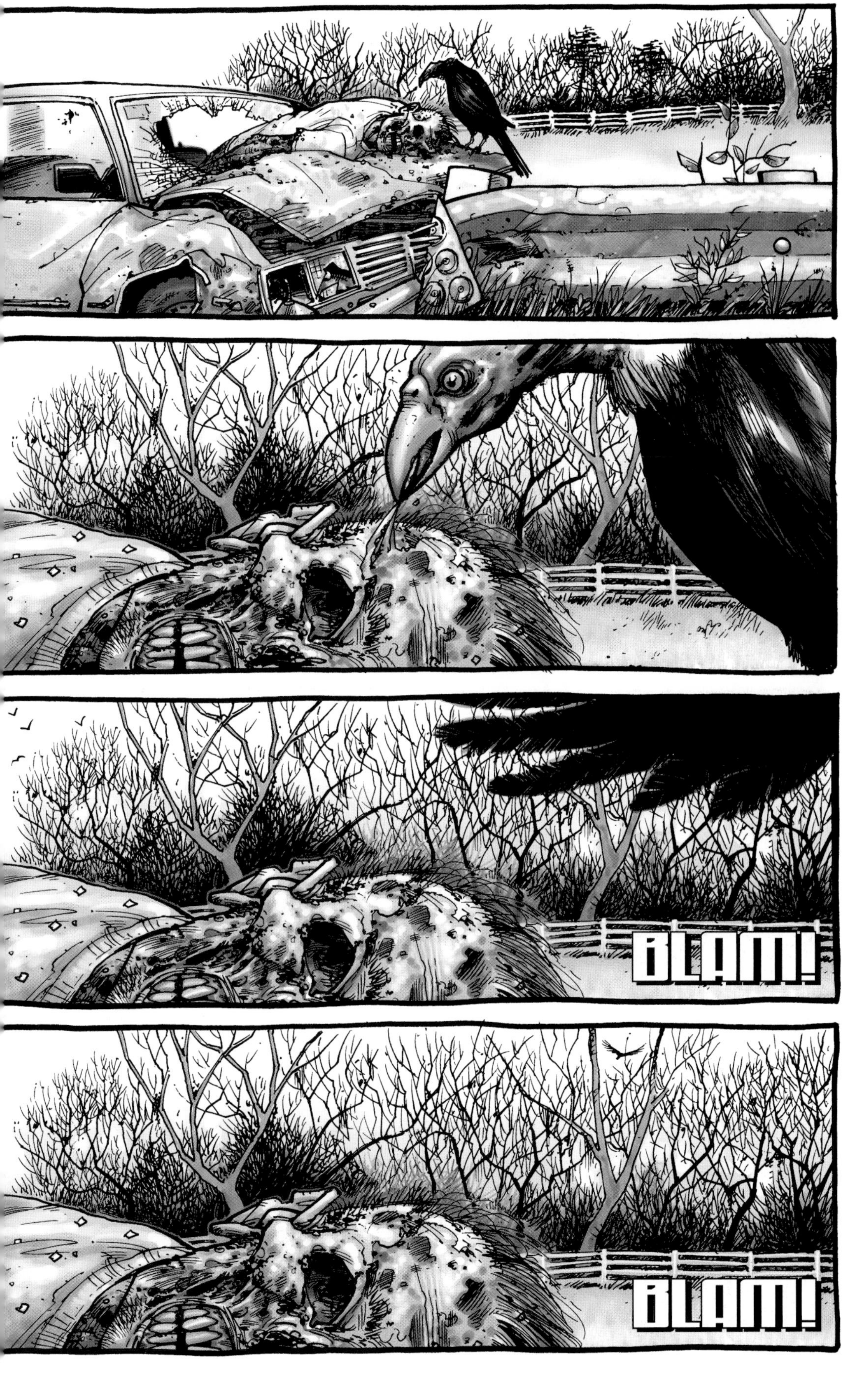
BLAM!
BLAM!

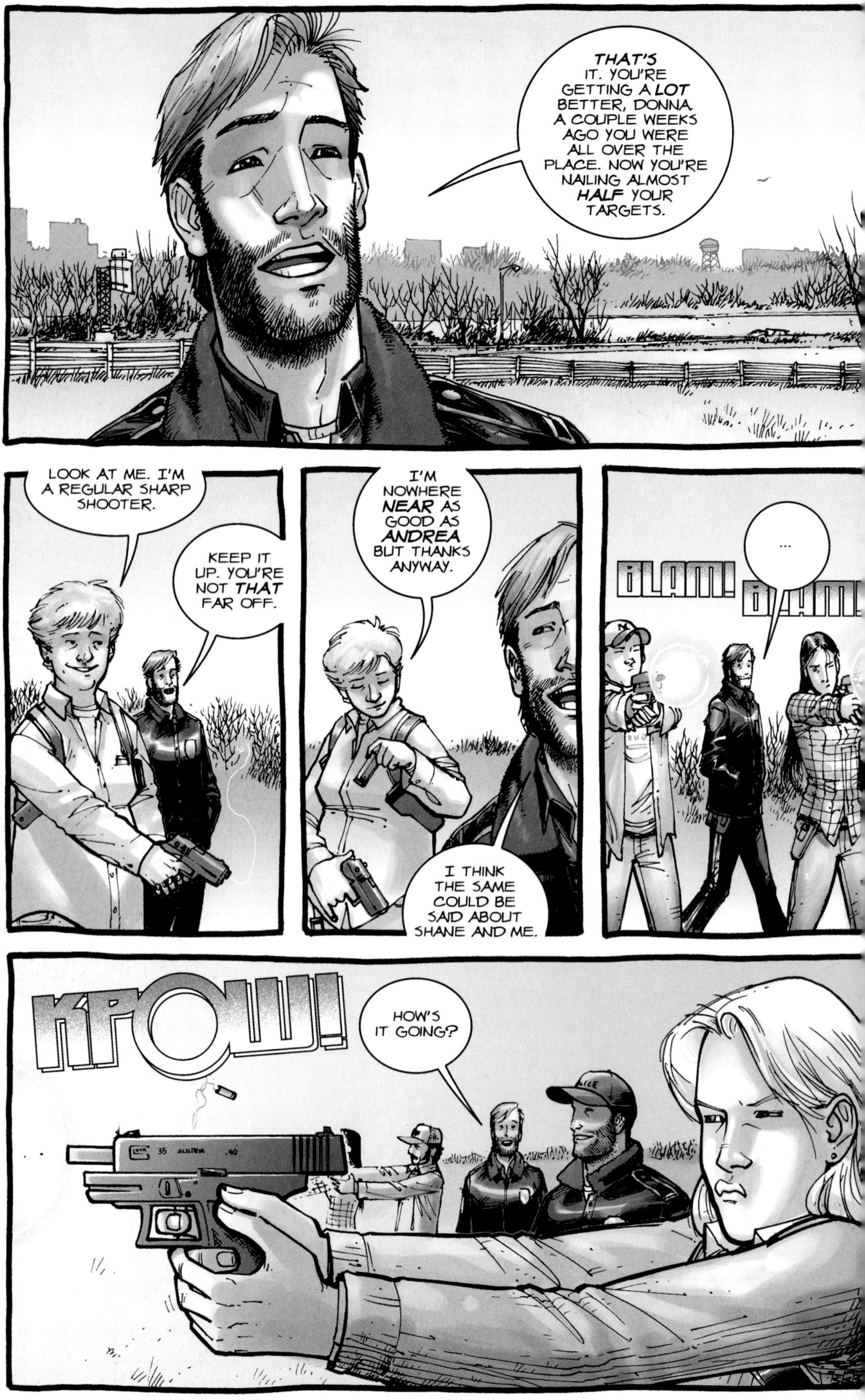
THAT'S IT. YOU'RE GETTING A LOT BETTER, DONNA. A COUPLE WEEKS AGO YOU WERE ALL OVER THE PLACE. NOW YOU'RE NAILING ALMOST HALF YOUR TARGETS.
LOOK AT ME. I'M A REGULAR SHARP SHOOTER.
KEEP IT UP. YOU'RE NOT THAT FAR OFF.
I'M NOWHERE NEAR AS GOOD AS ANDREA BUT THANKS ANYWAY.
I THINK THE SAME COULD BE SAID ABOUT SHANE AND ME.
BLAM!
...
KPOW!
HOW'S IT GOING?

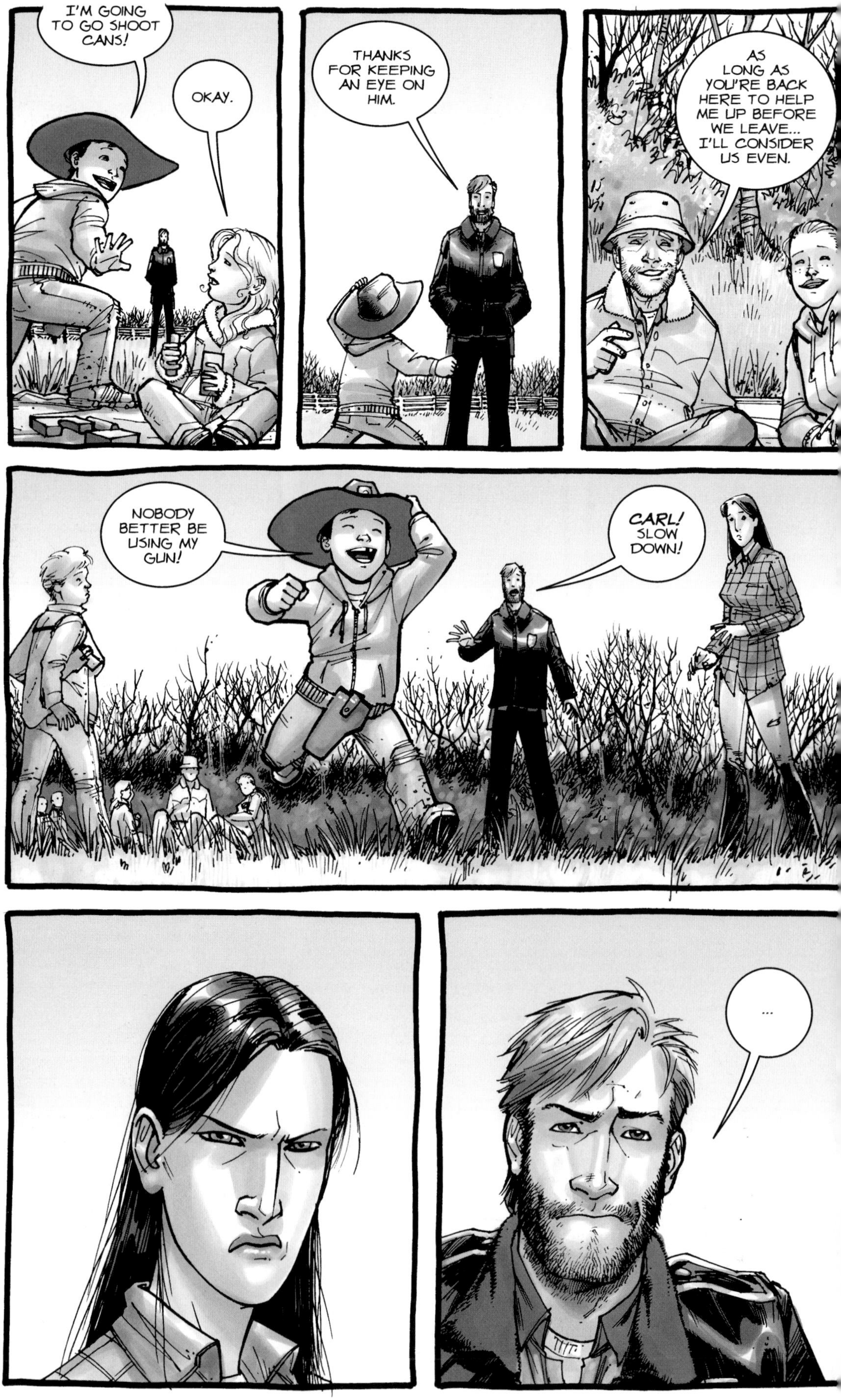
I'M GOING TO GO SHOOT CANS!
OKAY.
THANKS FOR KEEPING AN EYE ON HIM.
AS LONG AS YOU'RE BACK HERE TO HELP ME UP BEFORE WE LEAVE... I'LL CONSIDER US EVEN.
NOBODY BETTER BE USING MY GUN!
CARL! SLOW DOWN!
...

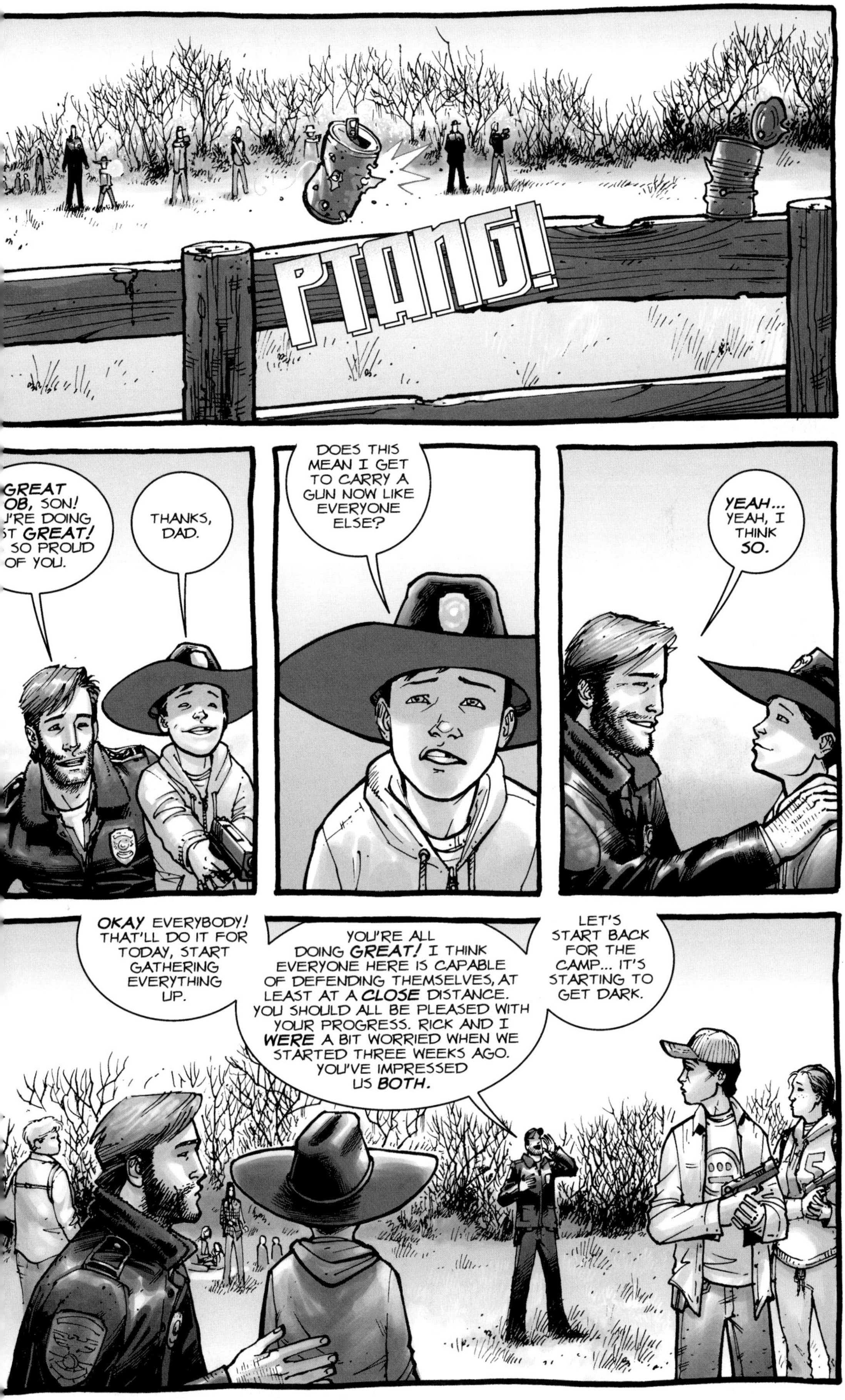
PTANG!
GREAT OB, SON! U'RE DOING ST GREAT! SO PROUD OF YOU.
THANKS, DAD.
DOES THIS MEAN I GET TO CARRY A GUN NOW LIKE EVERYONE ELSE?
YEAH... YEAH, I THINK SO.
OKAY EVERYBODY! THAT'LL DO IT FOR TODAY, START GATHERING EVERYTHING UP.
YOU'RE ALL DOING GREAT! I THINK EVERYONE HERE IS CAPABLE OF DEFENDING THEMSELVES, AT LEAST AT A CLOSE DISTANCE. YOU SHOULD ALL BE PLEASED WITH YOUR PROGRESS. RICK AND I WERE A BIT WORRIED WHEN WE STARTED THREE WEEKS AGO. YOU'VE IMPRESSED US BOTH.
LET'S START BACK FOR THE CAMP... IT'S STARTING TO GET DARK.

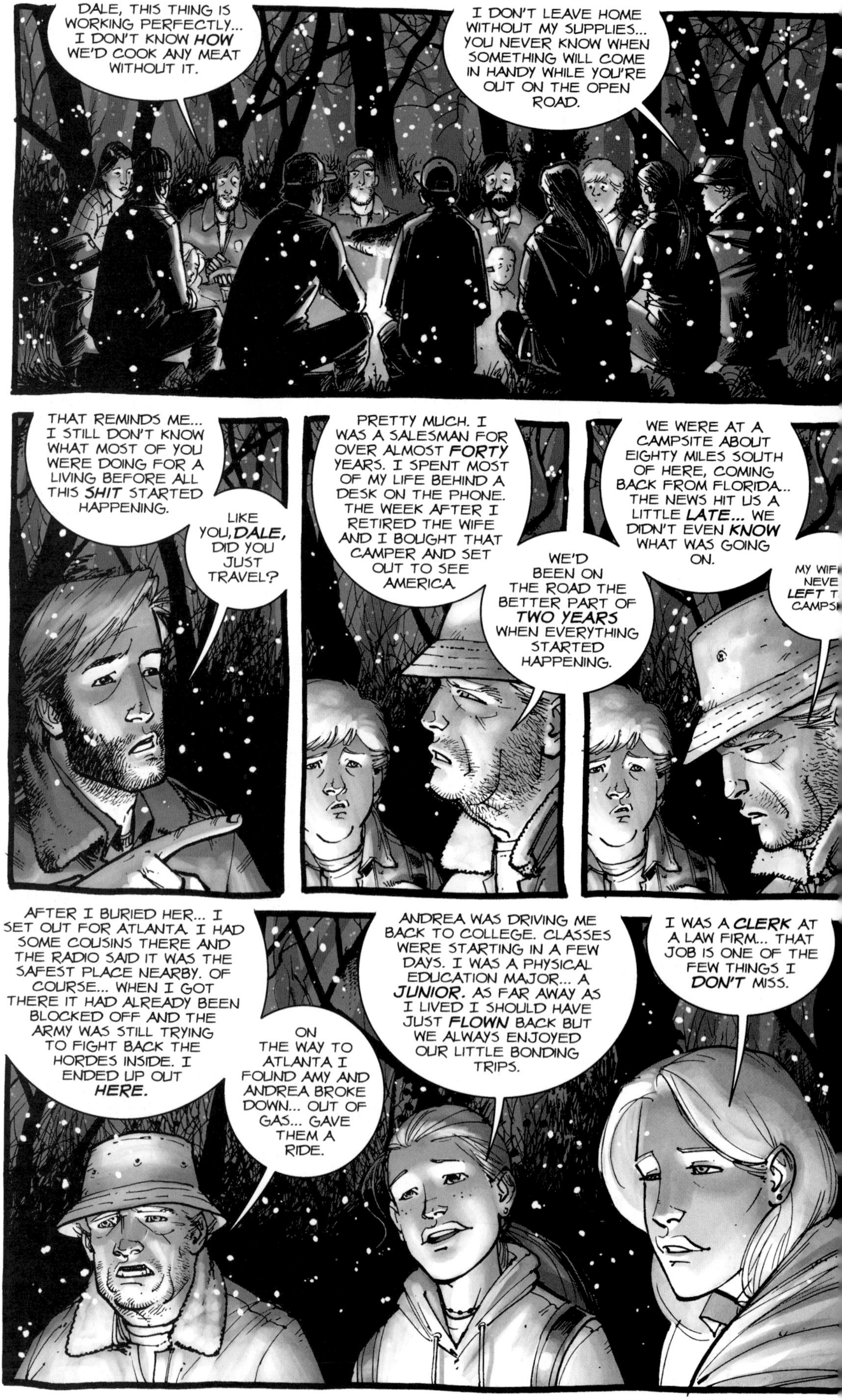

DALE, THIS THING IS WORKING PERFECTLY... I DON'T KNOW HOW WE'D COOK ANY MEAT WITHOUT IT.
I DON'T LEAVE HOME WITHOUT MY SUPPLIES... YOU NEVER KNOW WHEN SOMETHING WILL COME IN HANDY WHILE YOU'RE OUT ON THE OPEN ROAD.
THAT REMINDS ME... I STILL DON'T KNOW WHAT MOST OF YOU WERE DOING FOR A LIVING BEFORE ALL THIS SHIT STARTED HAPPENING.
LIKE YOU, DALE, DID YOU JUST TRAVEL?
PRETTY MUCH. I WAS A SALESMAN FOR OVER ALMOST FORTY YEARS. I SPENT MOST OF MY LIFE BEHIND A DESK ON THE PHONE. THE WEEK AFTER I RETIRED THE WIFE AND I BOUGHT THAT CAMPER AND SET OUT TO SEE AMERICA.
WE'D BEEN ON THE ROAD THE BETTER PART OF TWO YEARS WHEN EVERYTHING STARTED HAPPENING.
WE WERE AT A CAMPSITE ABOUT EIGHTY MILES SOUTH OF HERE, COMING BACK FROM FLORIDA... THE NEWS HIT US A LITTLE LATE... WE DIDN'T EVEN KNOW WHAT WAS GOING ON.
AFTER I BURIED HER... I SET OUT FOR ATLANTA. I HAD SOME COUSINS THERE AND THE RADIO SAID IT WAS THE SAFEST PLACE NEARBY. OF COURSE... WHEN I GOT THERE IT HAD ALREADY BEEN BLOCKED OFF AND THE ARMY WAS STILL TRYING TO FIGHT BACK THE HORDES INSIDE. I ENDED UP OUT HERE.
ON THE WAY TO ATLANTA I FOUND AMY AND ANDREA BROKE DOWN... OUT OF GAS... GAVE THEM A RIDE.
ANDREA WAS DRIVING ME BACK TO COLLEGE. CLASSES WERE STARTING IN A FEW DAYS. I WAS A PHYSICAL EDUCATION MAJOR... A JUNIOR. AS FAR AWAY AS I LIVED I SHOULD HAVE JUST FLOWN BACK BUT WE ALWAYS ENJOYED OUR LITTLE BONDING TRIPS.
I WAS A CLERK AT A LAW FIRM... THAT JOB IS ONE OF THE FEW THINGS I DON'T MISS.

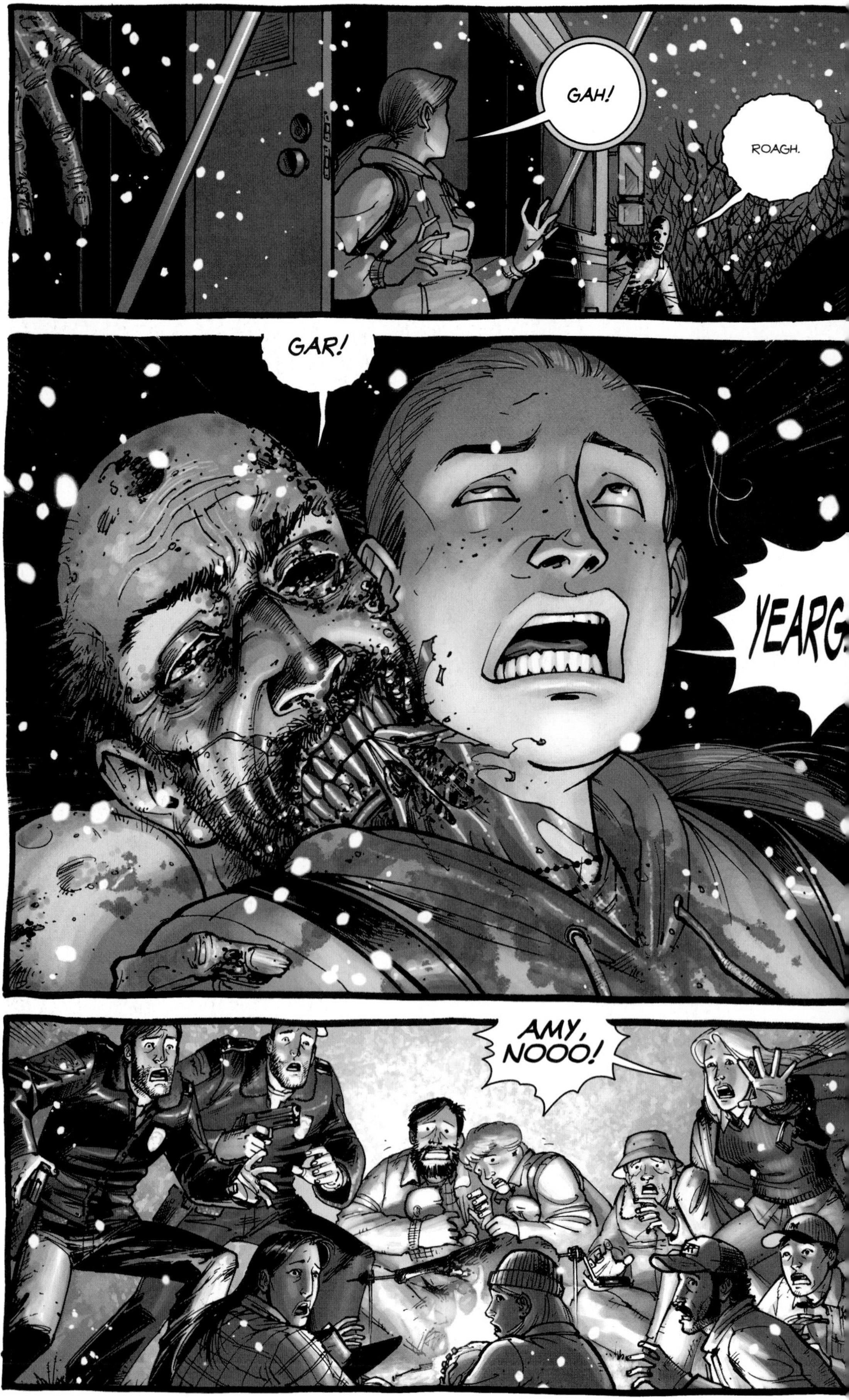
GAH!
ROAGH.
GAR!
YEARG
AMY, NOOO!

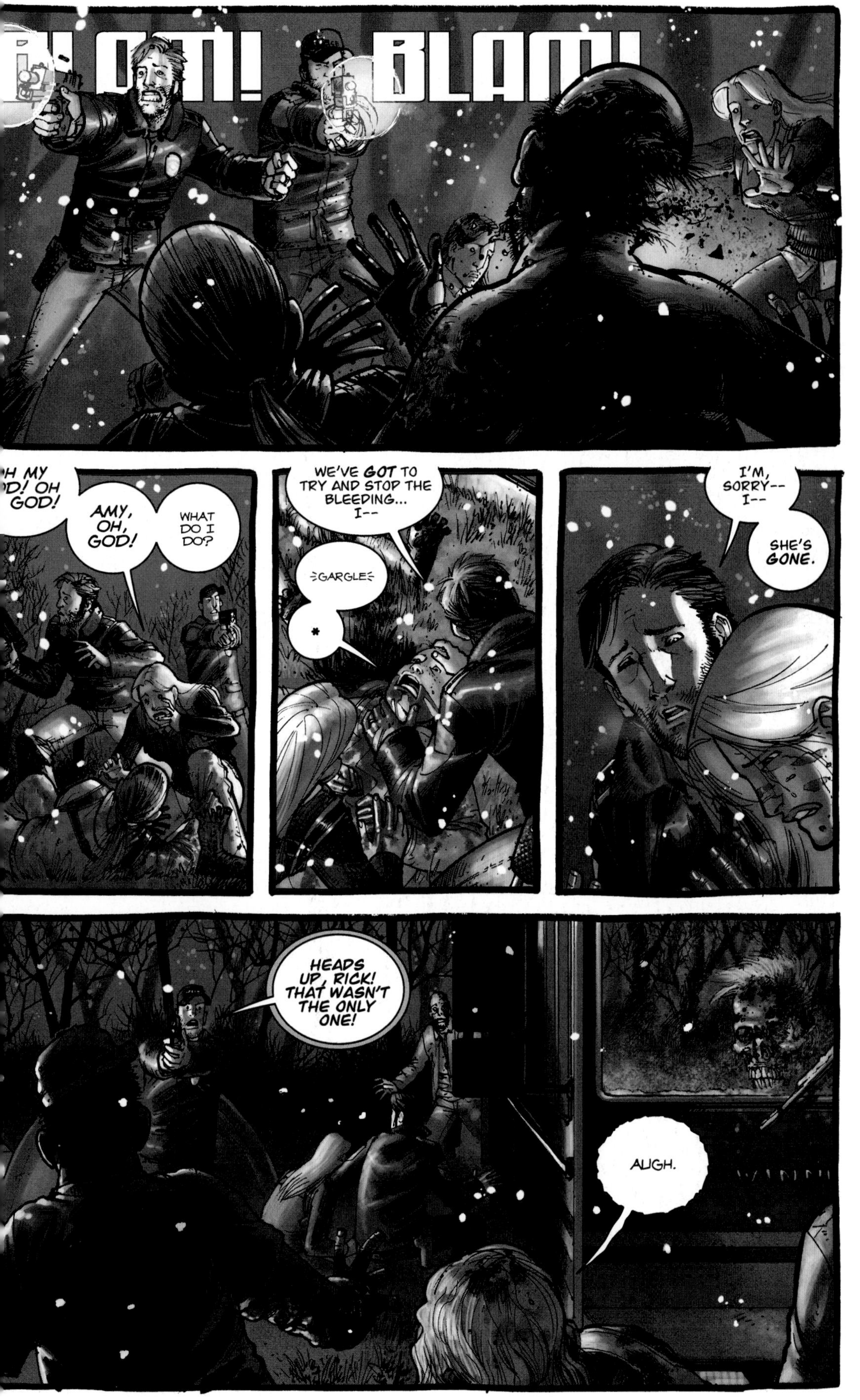
BLAM! BLAM!
OH MY GOD! OH GOD!
AMY, OH, GOD!
WHAT DO I DO?
WE'VE GOT TO TRY AND STOP THE BLEEDING... I--
GARGLE
*
I'M, SORRY-- I--
SHE'S GONE.
HEADS UP, RICK! THAT WASN'T THE ONLY ONE!
AUGH.

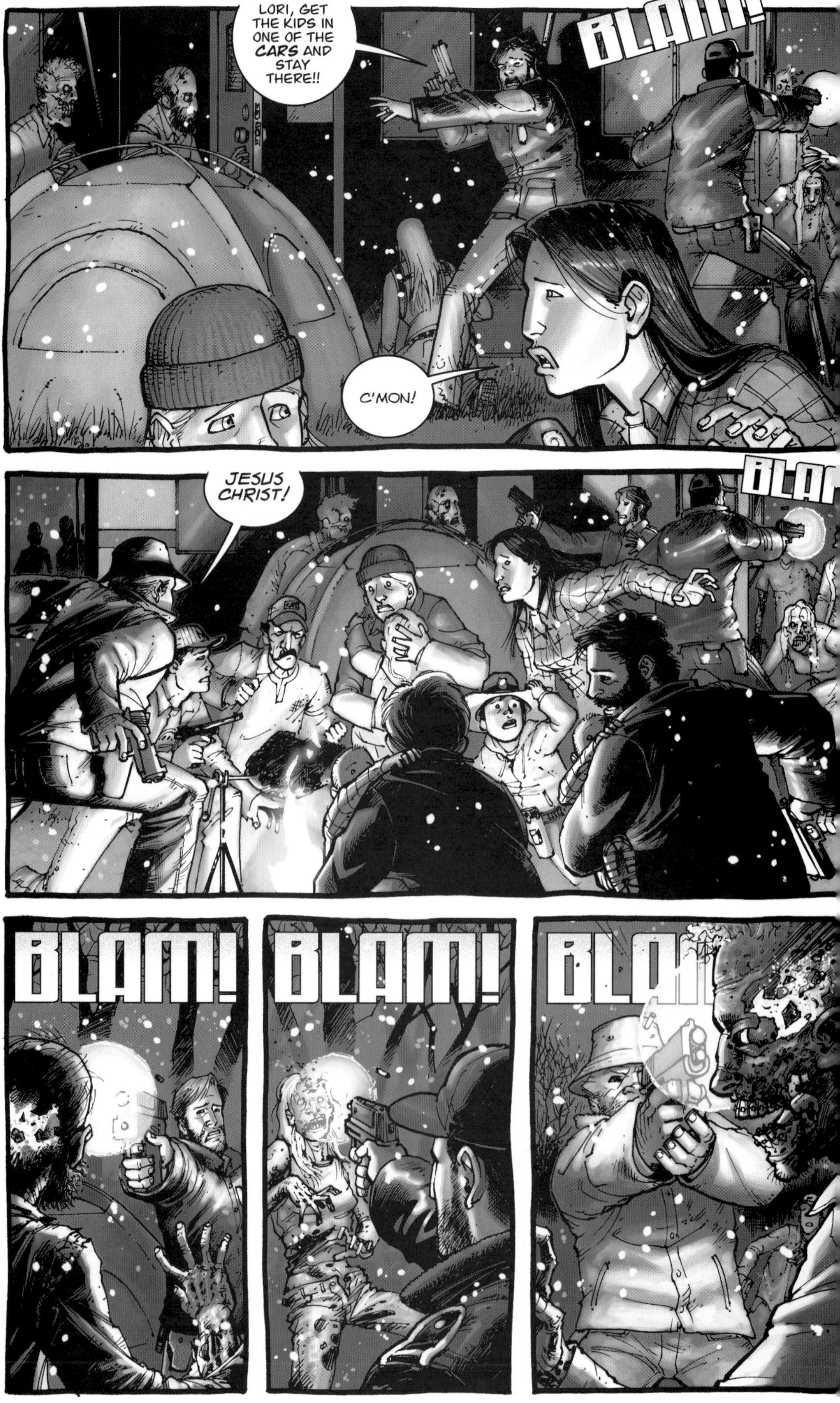
LORI, GET THE KIDS IN ONE OF THE CARS AND STAY THERE!!
BLAM!
C'MON!
JESUS CHRIST!
BLAM!
BLAM!
BLAM!

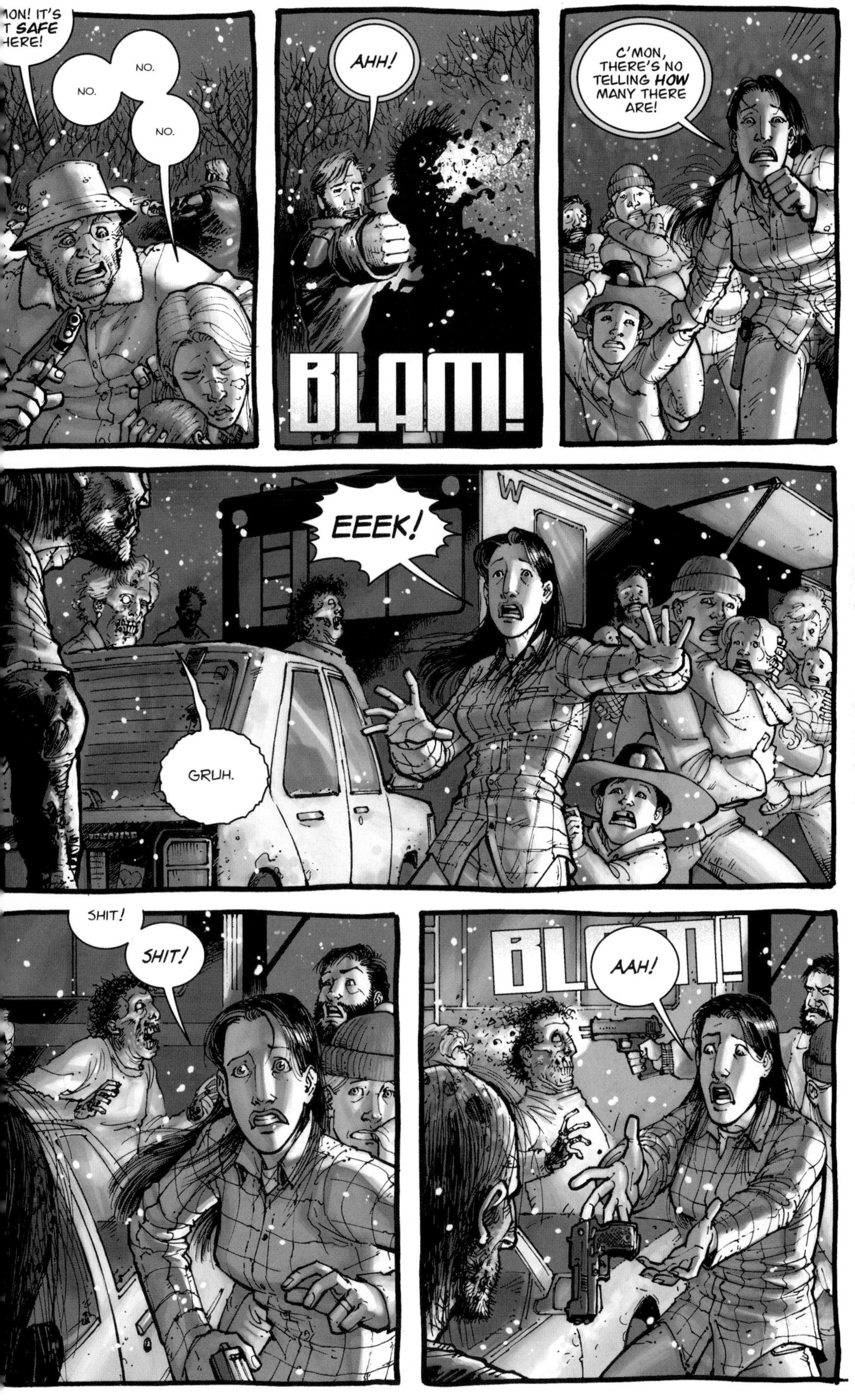

MON! IT'S
T SAFE
HERE!
NO.
NO.
NO.
AHH!
BLAM!
C'MON, THERE'S NO TELLING HOW MANY THERE ARE!
EEEK!
GRUH.
SHIT!
SHIT!
BLAM!
AAH!

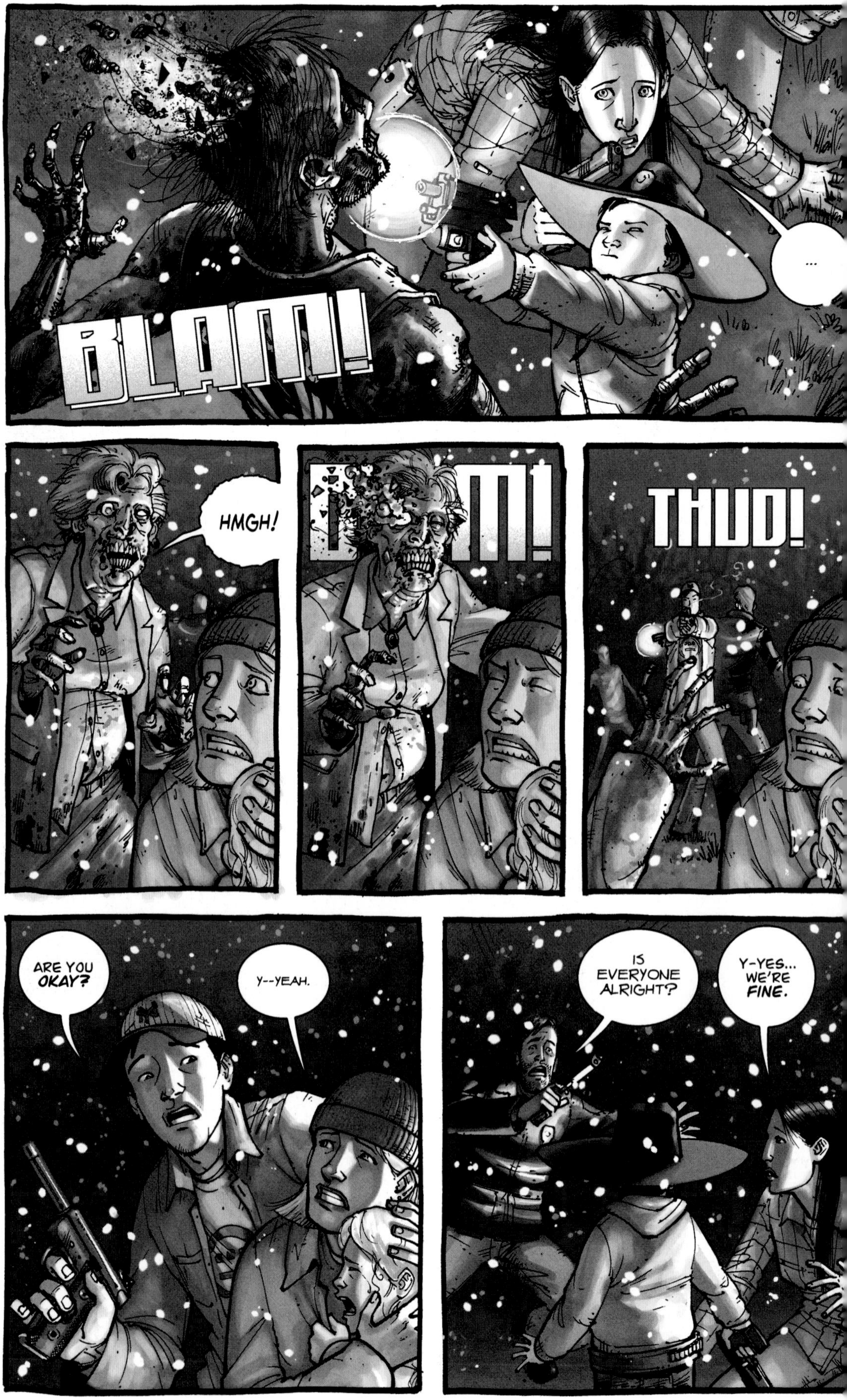
BLAM!
...
HMGH!
M!
THUD!
ARE YOU OKAY?
Y--YEAH.
IS EVERYONE ALRIGHT?
Y-YES... WE'RE FINE.

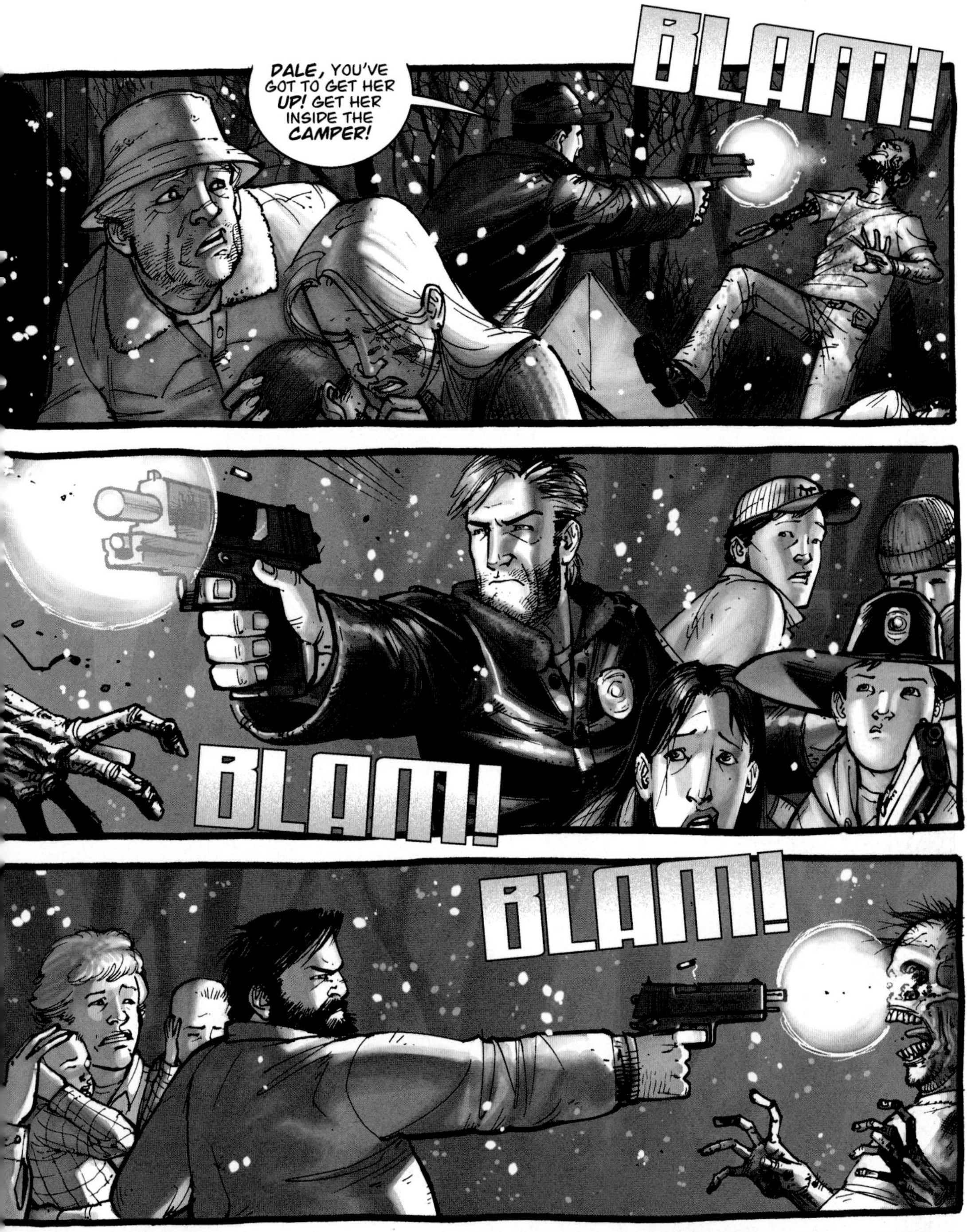
BLAM!
DALE, YOU'VE GOT TO GET HER UP! GET HER INSIDE THE CAMPER!
BLAM!
BLAM!
RUHH!
BLAM!

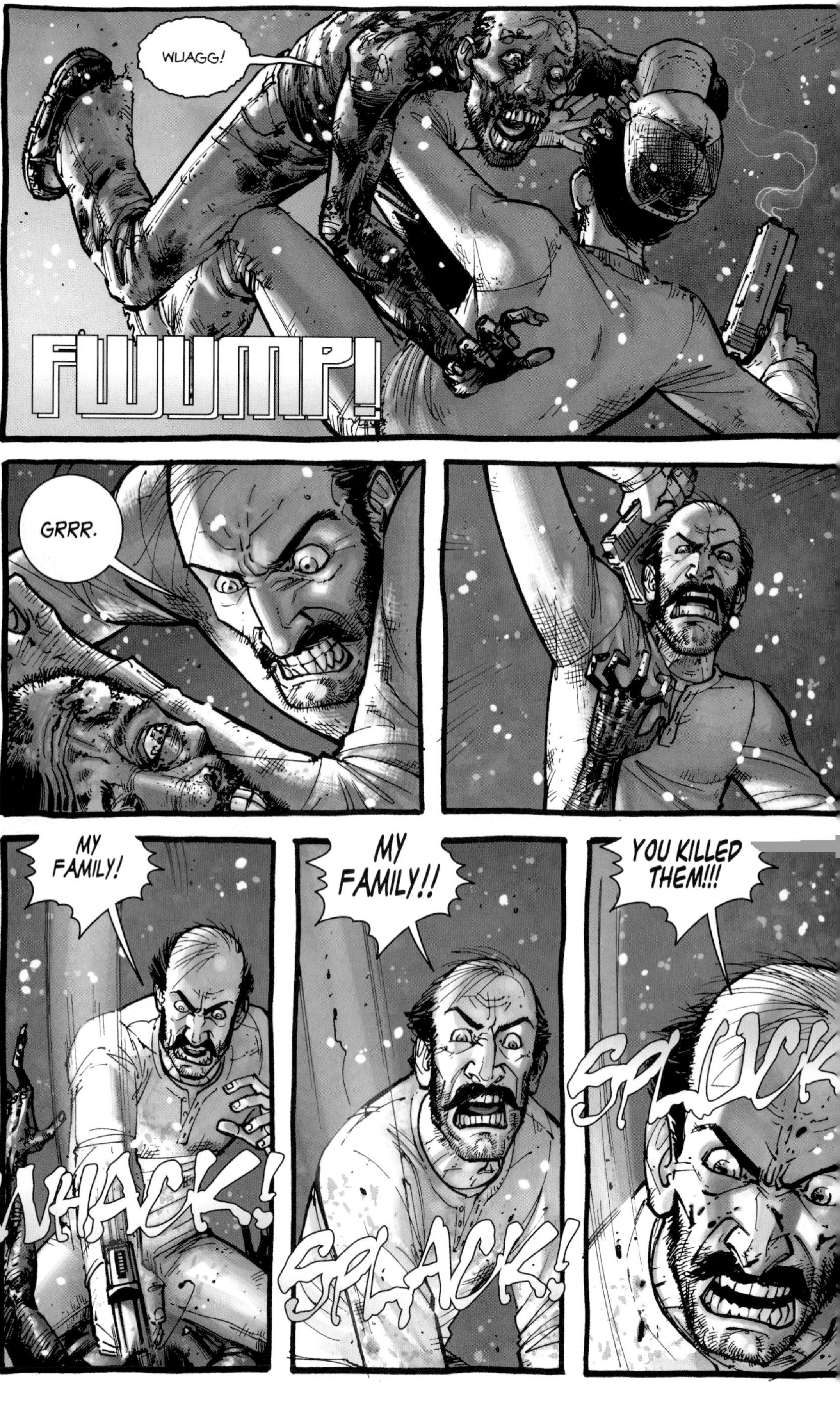

WUAGG!
FWUMP!
GRRR.
MY FAMILY!
WHACK!
MY FAMILY!!
SPLACK!
YOU KILLED THEM!!!

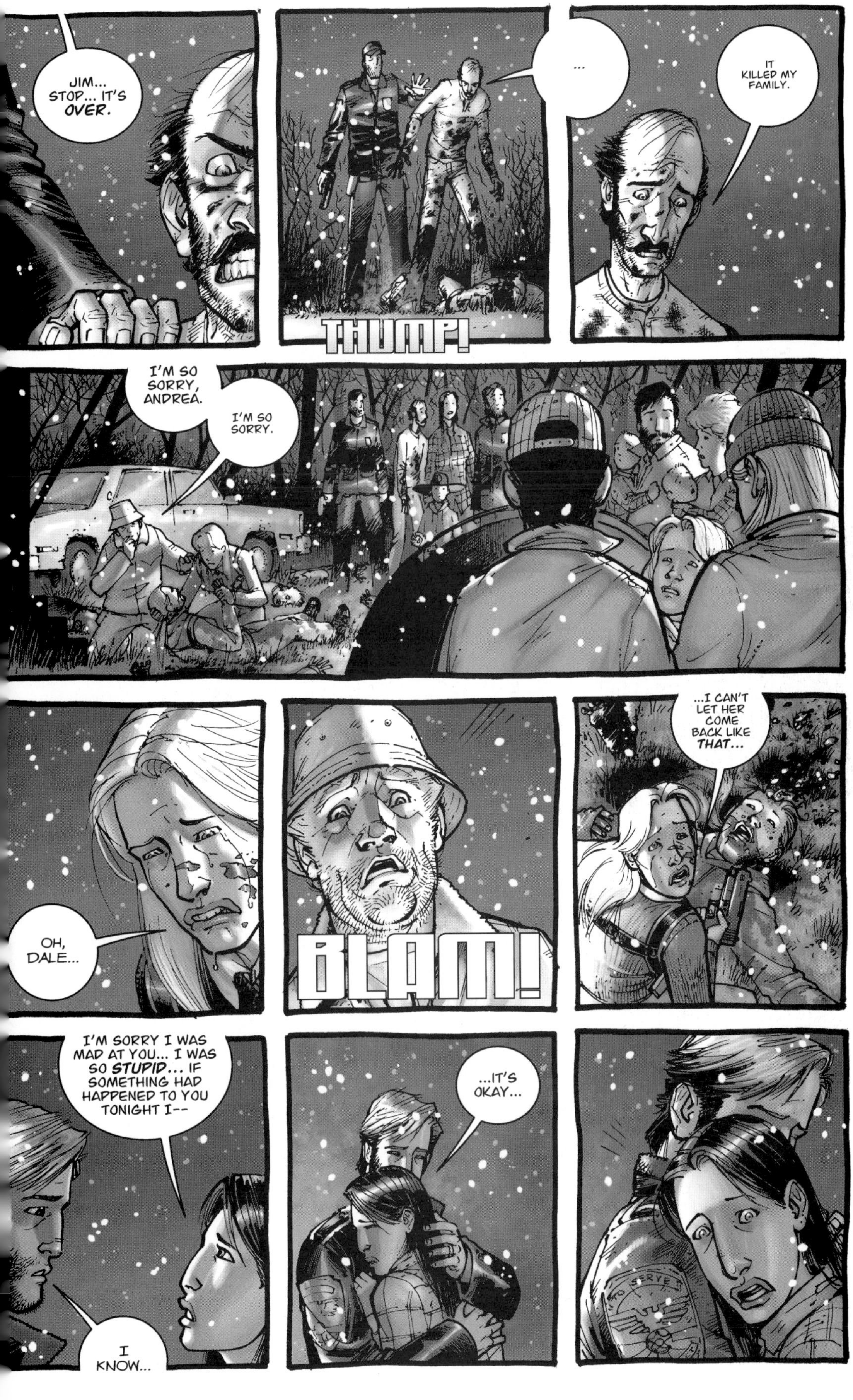
JIM... STOP... IT'S OVER.
...
IT KILLED MY FAMILY.
THUMP!
I'M SO SORRY, ANDREA.
I'M SO SORRY.
OH, DALE...
BLAM!
...I CAN'T LET HER COME BACK LIKE THAT...
I'M SORRY I WAS MAD AT YOU... I WAS SO STUPID... IF SOMETHING HAD HAPPENED TO YOU TONIGHT I--
I KNOW...
...IT'S OKAY...

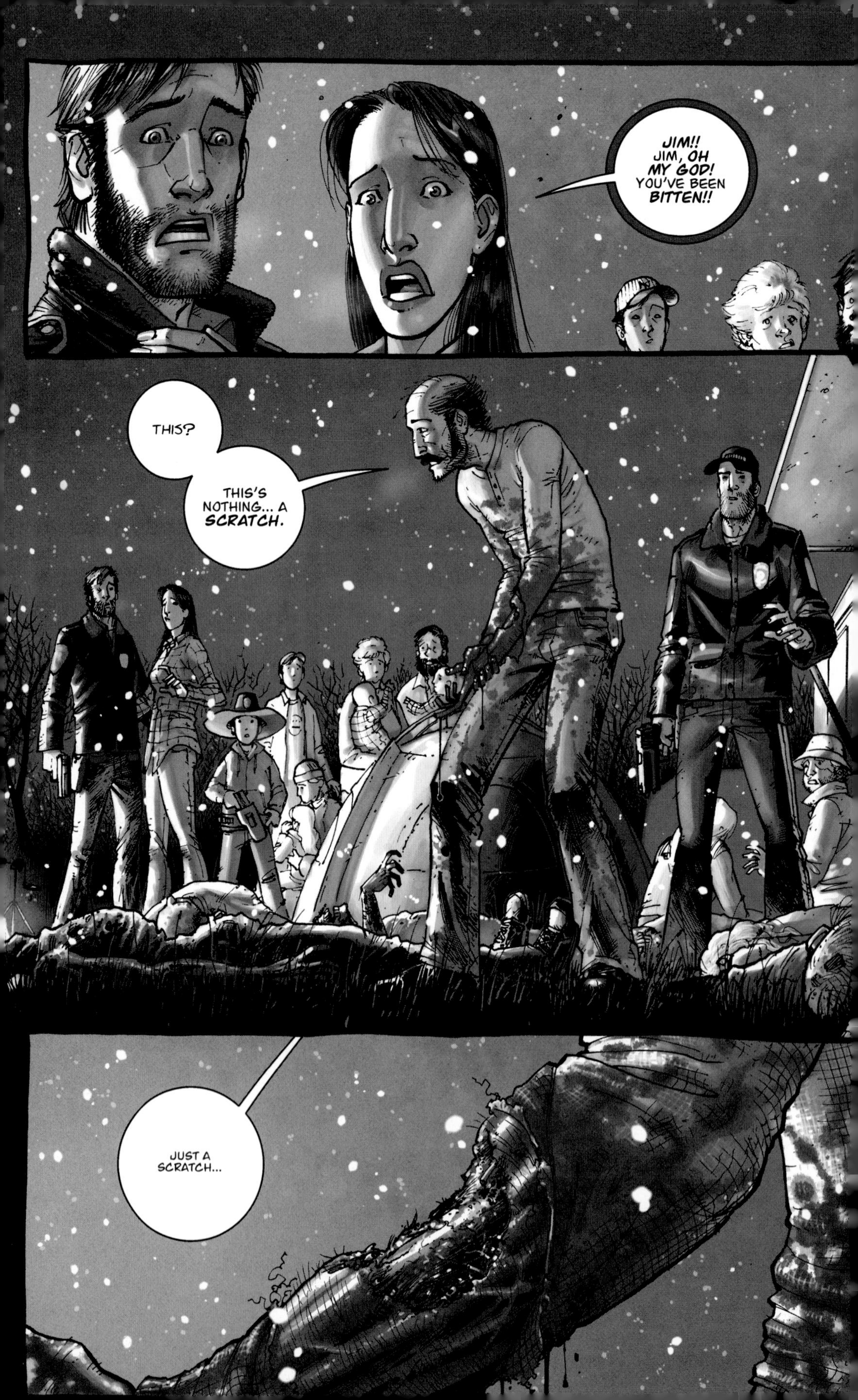
JIM!! JIM, OH MY GOD! YOU'VE BEEN BITTEN!!
THIS?
THIS'S NOTHING... A SCRATCH.
JUST A SCRATCH...

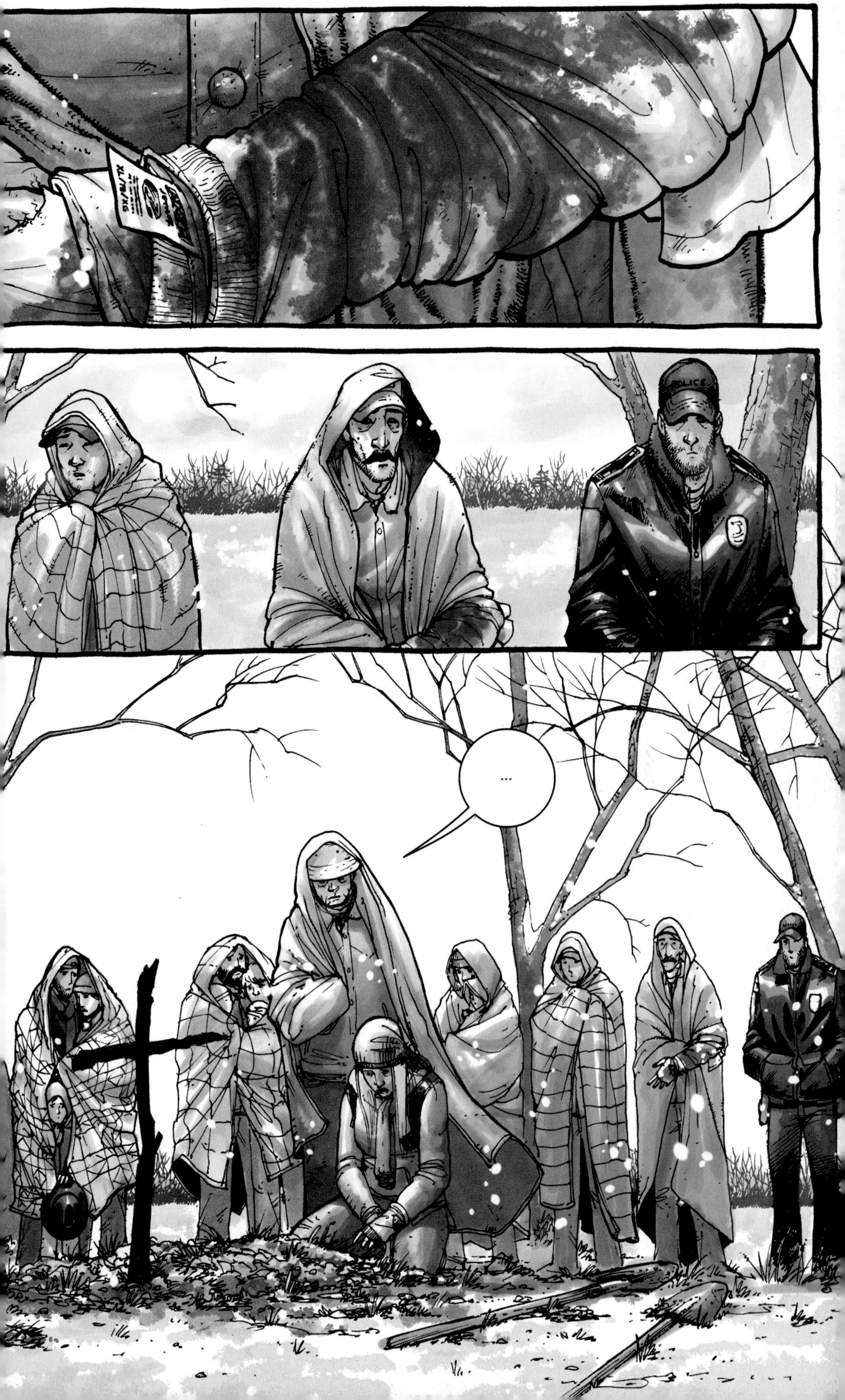
...

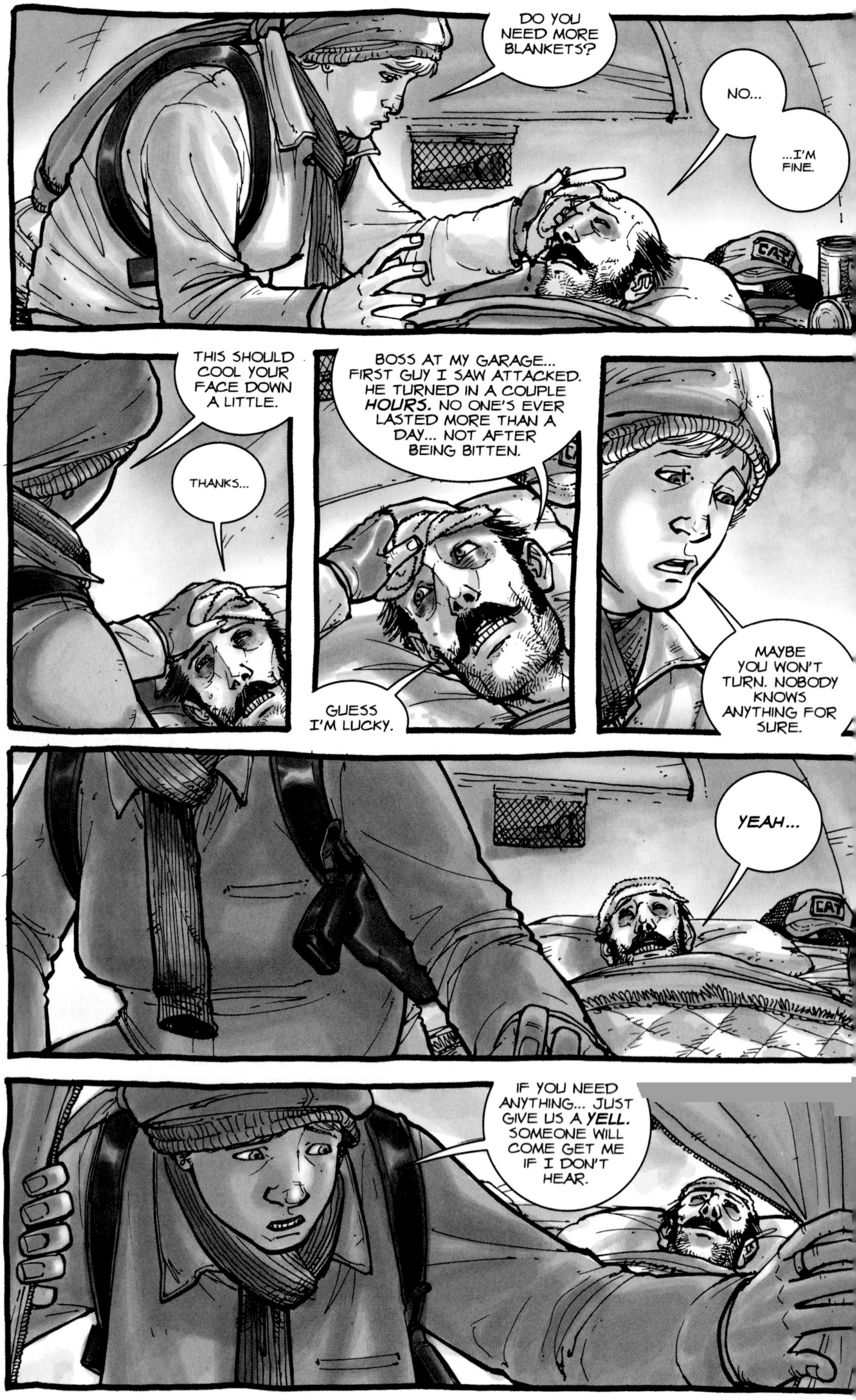
DO YOU NEED MORE BLANKETS?
NO...
...I'M FINE.
THIS SHOULD COOL YOUR FACE DOWN A LITTLE.
THANKS...
BOSS AT MY GARAGE... FIRST GUY I SAW ATTACKED. HE TURNED IN A COUPLE HOURS. NO ONE'S EVER LASTED MORE THAN A DAY... NOT AFTER BEING BITTEN.
GUESS I'M LUCKY.
MAYBE YOU WON'T TURN. NOBODY KNOWS ANYTHING FOR SURE.
YEAH...
IF YOU NEED ANYTHING... JUST GIVE US A YELL. SOMEONE WILL COME GET ME IF I DON'T HEAR.

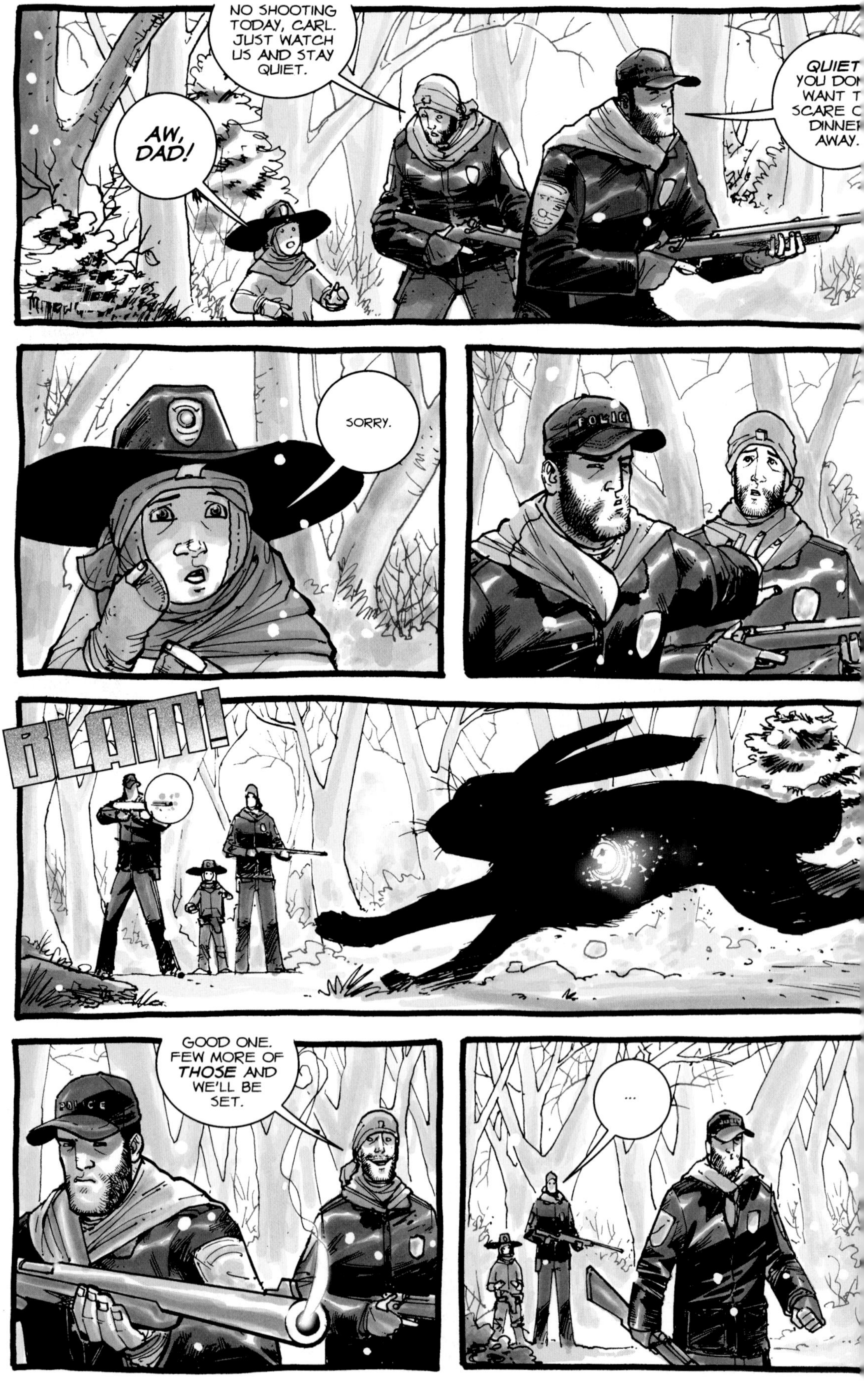

NO SHOOTING TODAY, CARL. JUST WATCH US AND STAY QUIET.
AW, DAD!
QUIET YOU DON WANT T SCARE O DINNER AWAY.
SORRY.
POLICE
BLAM!
GOOD ONE. FEW MORE OF THOSE AND WE'LL BE SET.
POLICE
...

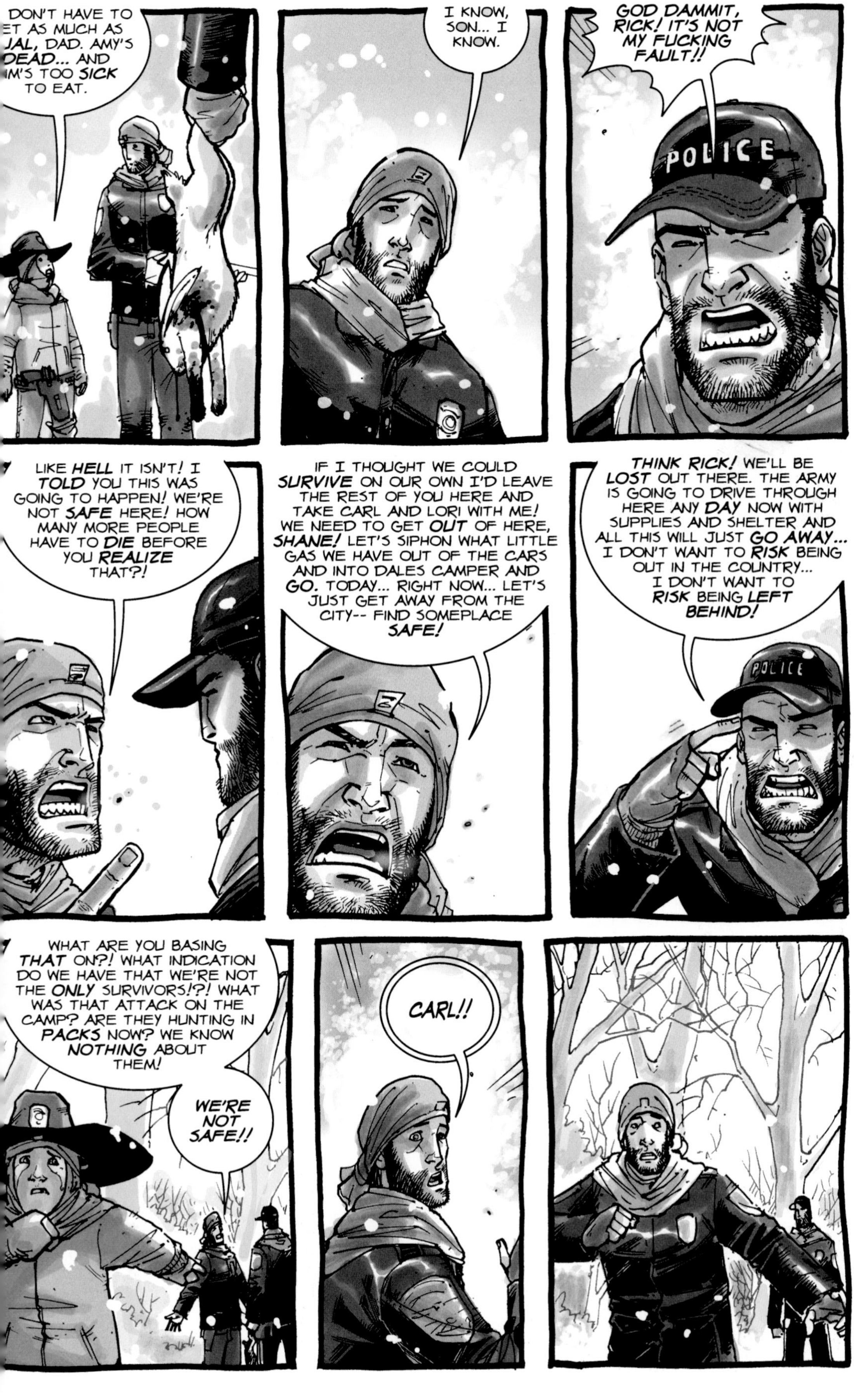

DON'T HAVE TO ET AS MUCH AS JAL, DAD. AMY'S DEAD... AND IM'S TOO SICK TO EAT.
I KNOW, SON... I KNOW.
GOD DAMMIT, RICK! IT'S NOT MY FUCKING FAULT!!
POLICE
LIKE HELL IT ISN'T! I TOLD YOU THIS WAS GOING TO HAPPEN! WE'RE NOT SAFE HERE! HOW MANY MORE PEOPLE HAVE TO DIE BEFORE YOU REALIZE THAT?!
IF I THOUGHT WE COULD SURVIVE ON OUR OWN I'D LEAVE THE REST OF YOU HERE AND TAKE CARL AND LORI WITH ME! WE NEED TO GET OUT OF HERE, SHANE! LET'S SIPHON WHAT LITTLE GAS WE HAVE OUT OF THE CARS AND INTO DALES CAMPER AND GO. TODAY... RIGHT NOW... LET'S JUST GET AWAY FROM THE CITY-- FIND SOMEPLACE SAFE!
THINK RICK! WE'LL BE LOST OUT THERE. THE ARMY IS GOING TO DRIVE THROUGH HERE ANY DAY NOW WITH SUPPLIES AND SHELTER AND ALL THIS WILL JUST GO AWAY... I DON'T WANT TO RISK BEING OUT IN THE COUNTRY... I DON'T WANT TO RISK BEING LEFT BEHIND!
POLICE
WHAT ARE YOU BASING THAT ON?! WHAT INDICATION DO WE HAVE THAT WE'RE NOT THE ONLY SURVIVORS!?! WHAT WAS THAT ATTACK ON THE CAMP? ARE THEY HUNTING IN PACKS NOW? WE KNOW NOTHING ABOUT THEM!
WE'RE NOT SAFE!!
CARL!!

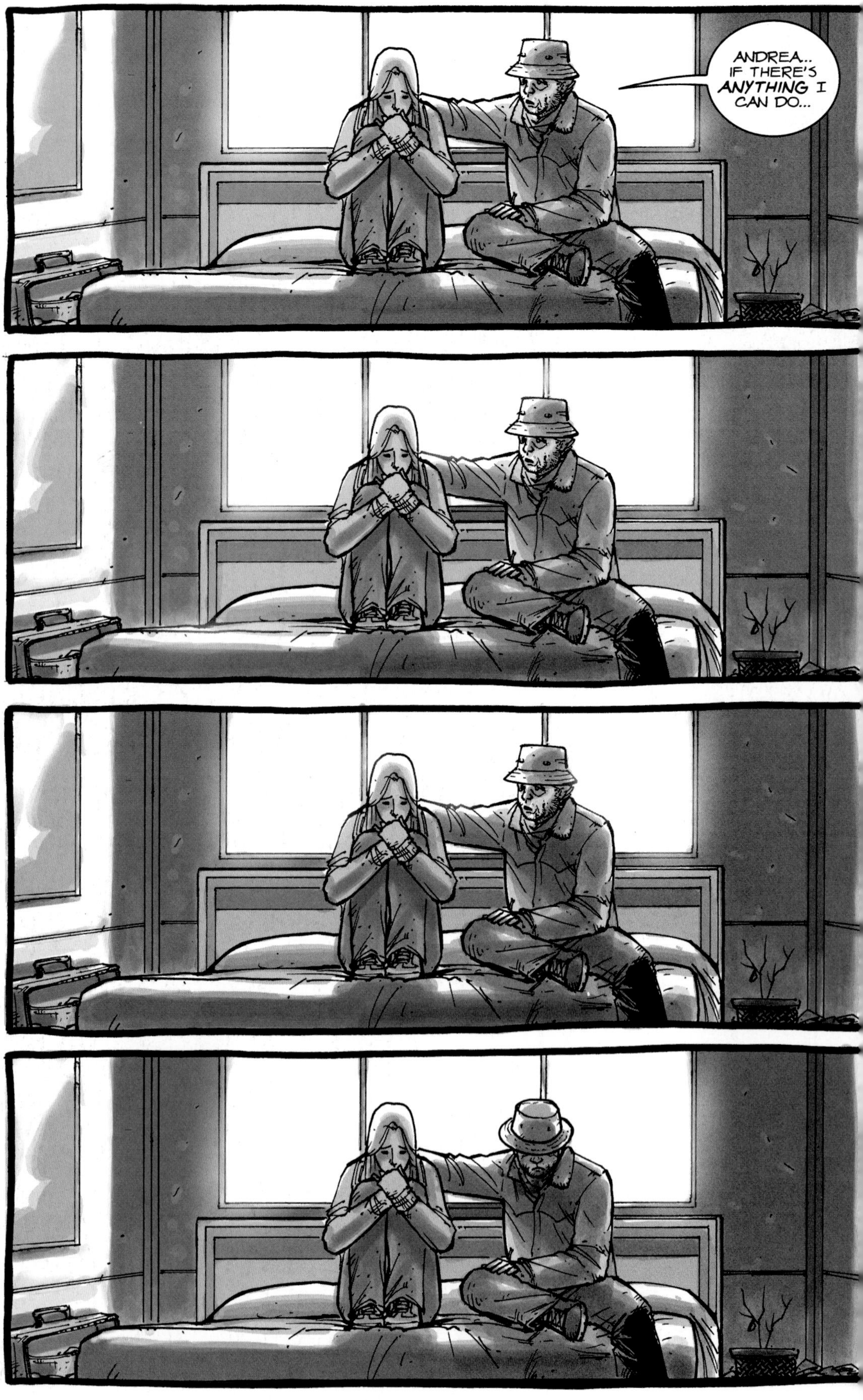
ANDREA.. IF THERE'S ANYTHING I CAN DO...

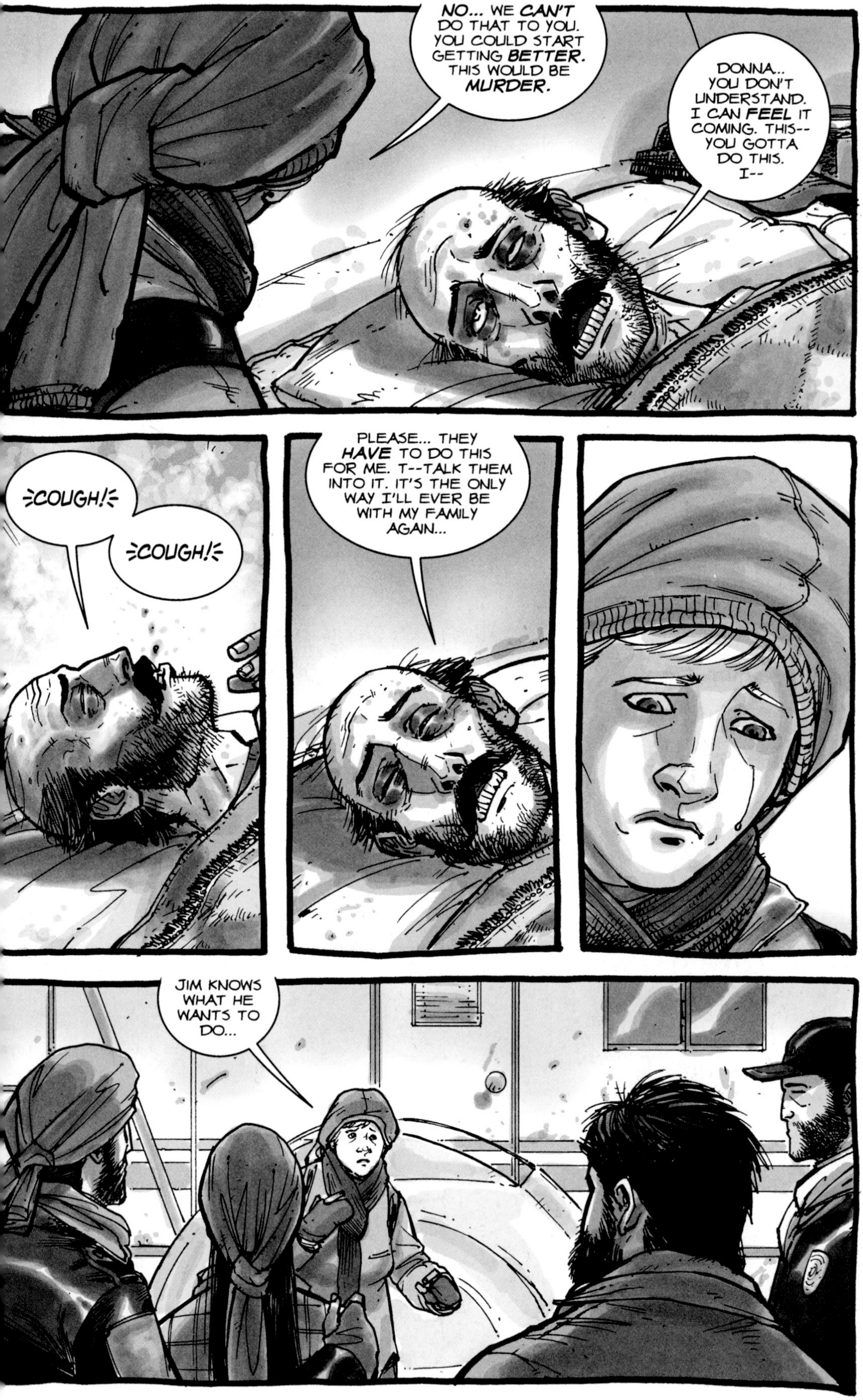
NO... WE CAN'T DO THAT TO YOU. YOU COULD START GETTING BETTER. THIS WOULD BE MURDER.
DONNA.. YOU DON'T UNDERSTAND. I CAN FEEL IT COMING. THIS-- YOU GOTTA DO THIS. I--
COUGH!
COUGH!
PLEASE... THEY HAVE TO DO THIS FOR ME. T--TALK THEM INTO IT. IT'S THE ONLY WAY I'LL EVER BE WITH MY FAMILY AGAIN...
JIM KNOWS WHAT HE WANTS TO DO...

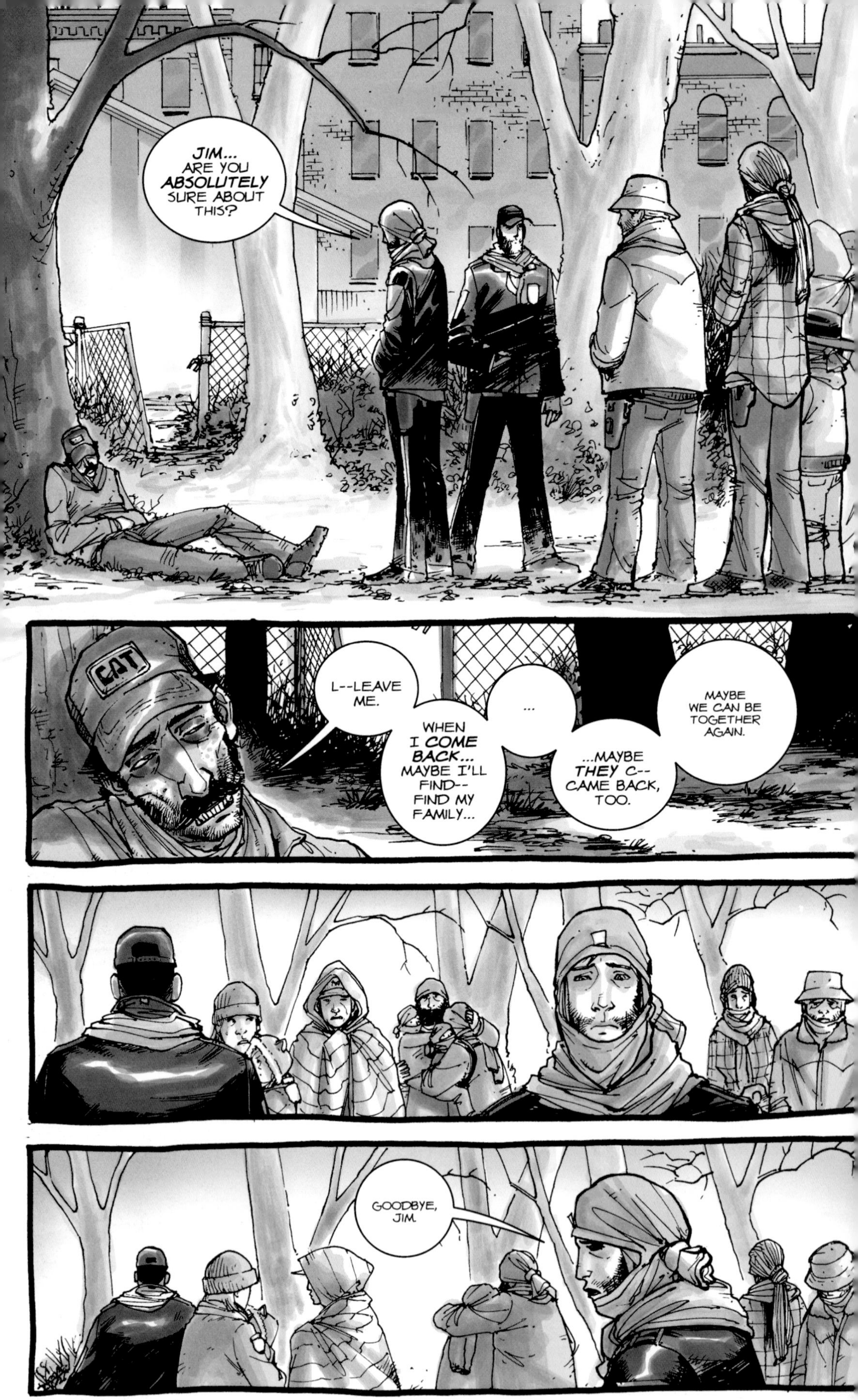
JIM... ARE YOU ABSOLUTELY SURE ABOUT THIS?
L--LEAVE ME.
WHEN I COME BACK... MAYBE I'LL FIND-- FIND MY FAMILY...
...
...MAYBE THEY C-- CAME BACK, TOO.
MAYBE WE CAN BE TOGETHER AGAIN.
GOODBYE, JIM.

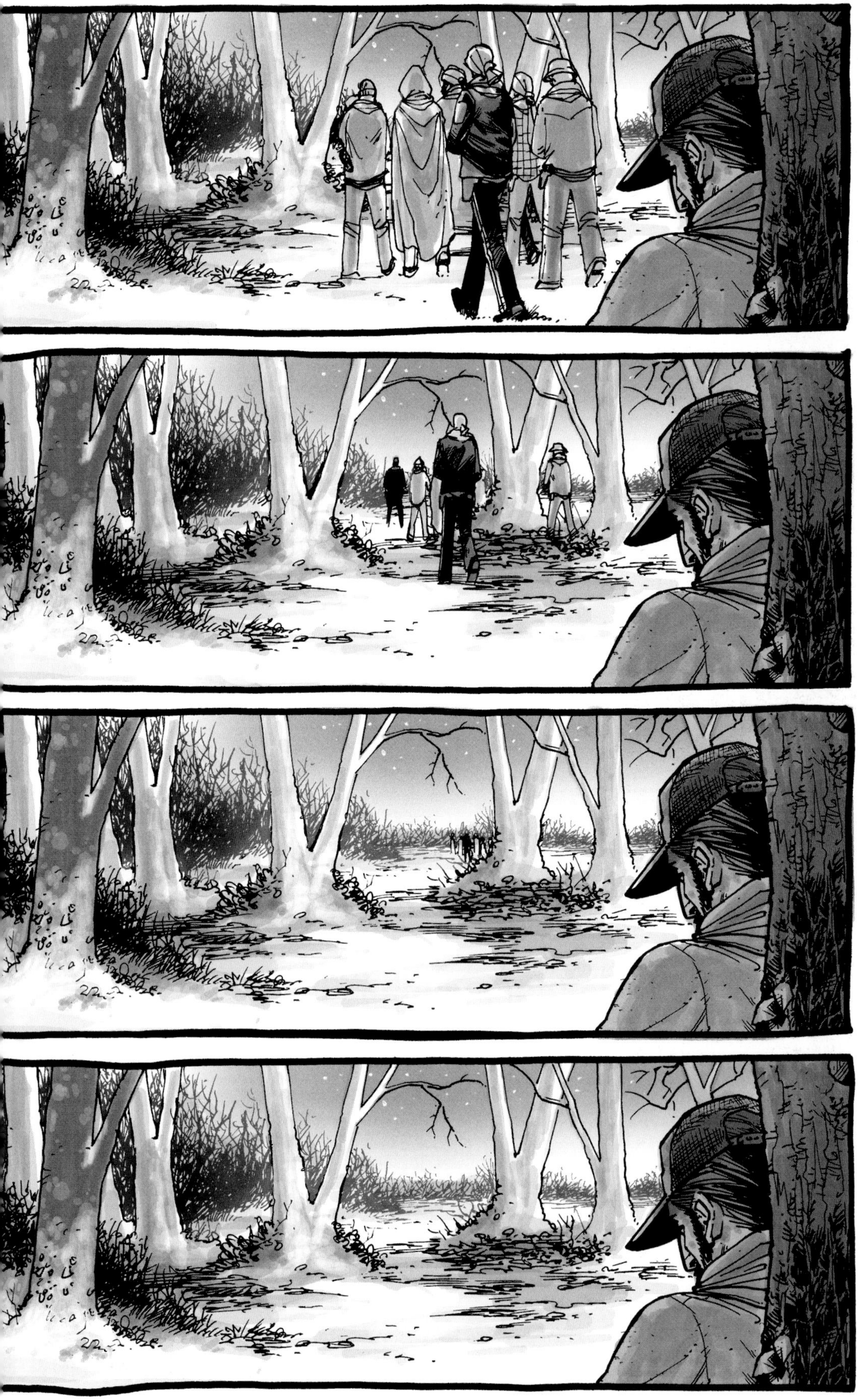

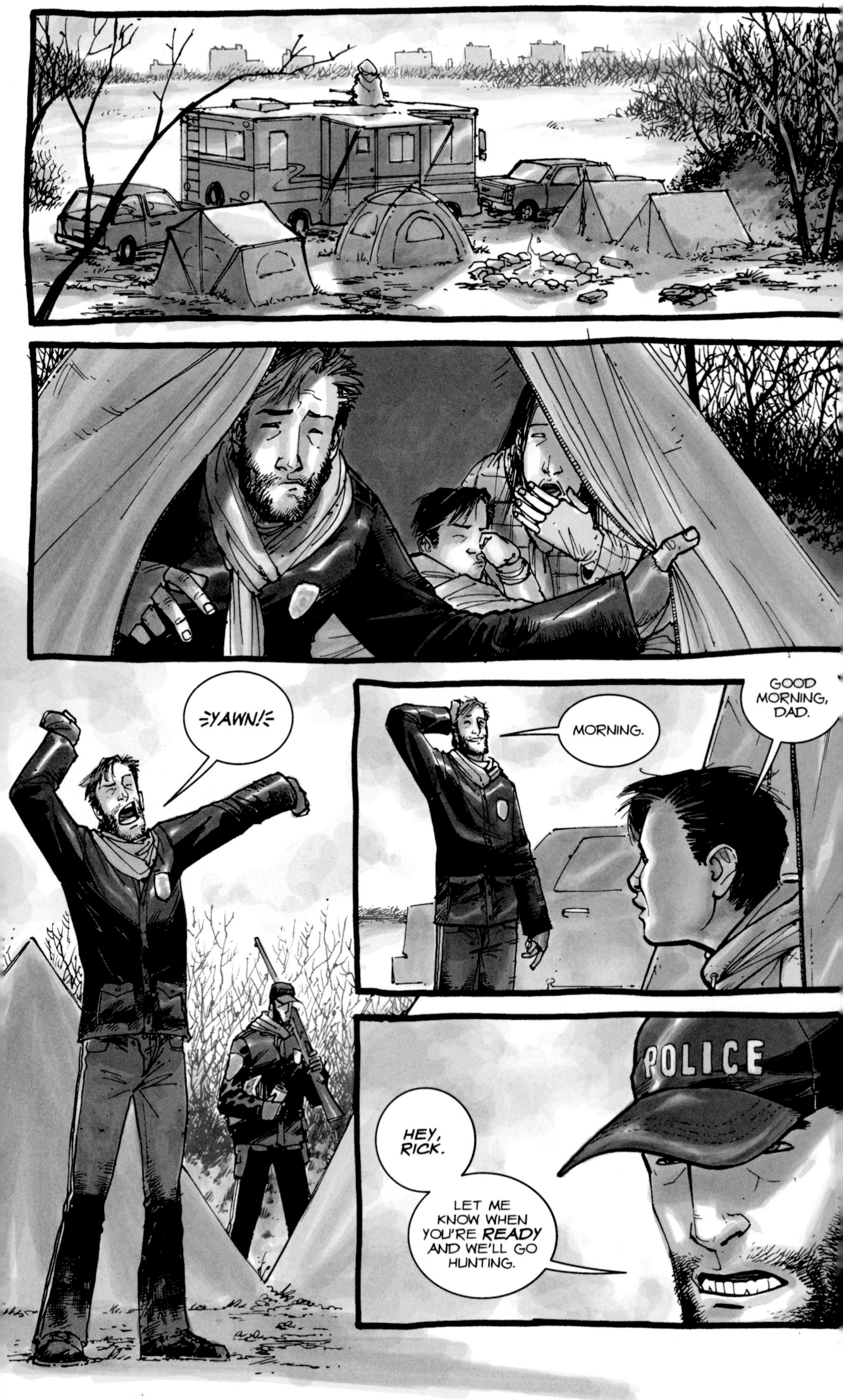

YAWN!
MORNING.
GOOD MORNING, DAD.
HEY, RICK.
LET ME KNOW WHEN YOU'RE READY AND WE'LL GO HUNTING.

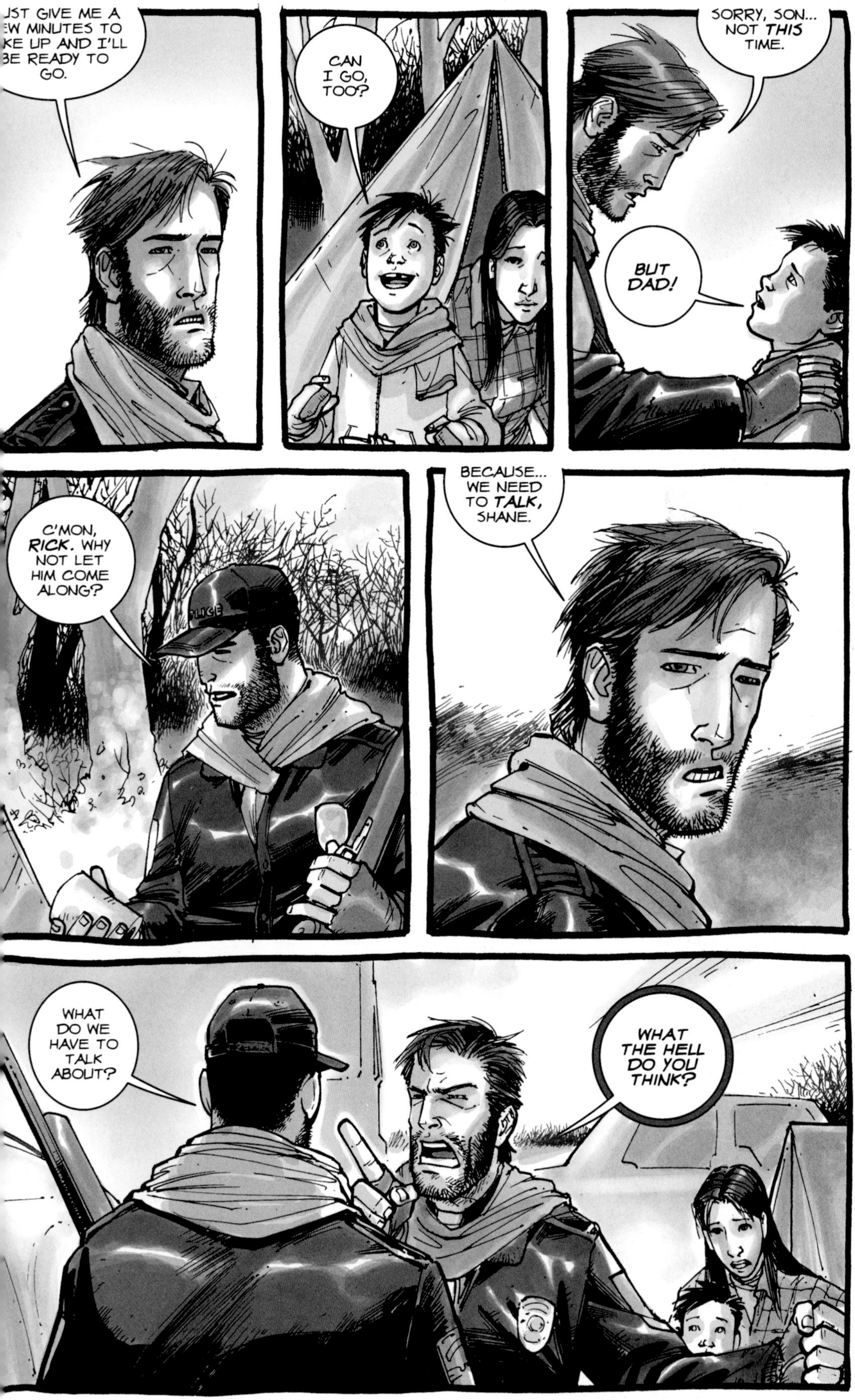

JUST GIVE ME A FEW MINUTES TO WAKE UP AND I'LL BE READY TO GO.
CAN I GO, TOO?
SORRY, SON... NOT THIS TIME.
BUT DAD!
C'MON, RICK. WHY NOT LET HIM COME ALONG?
BECAUSE... WE NEED TO TALK, SHANE.
WHAT DO WE HAVE TO TALK ABOUT?
WHAT THE HELL DO YOU THINK?

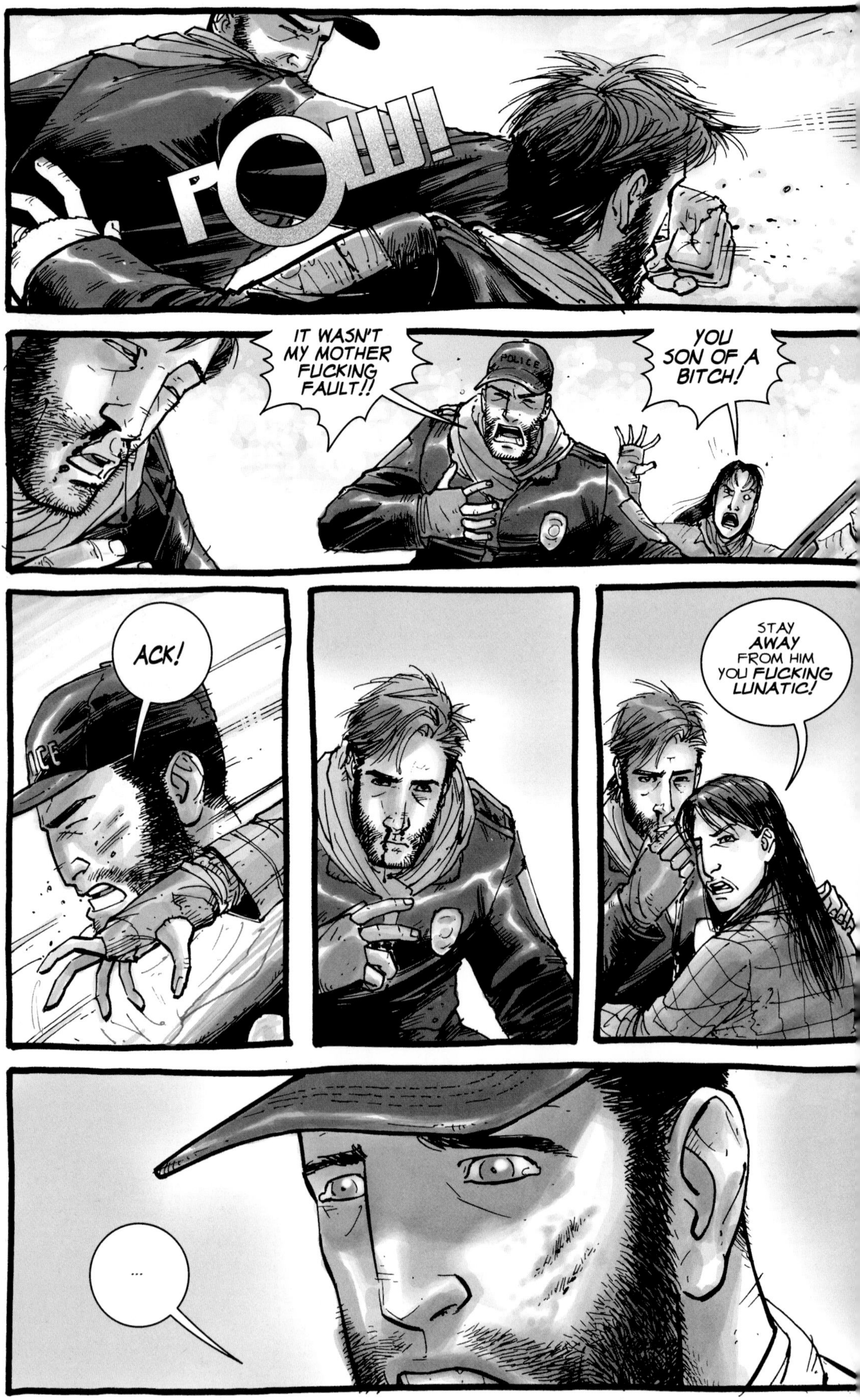
POW!
IT WASN'T MY MOTHER FUCKING FAULT!!
YOU SON OF A BITCH!
ACK!
STAY AWAY FROM HIM YOU FUCKING LUNATIC!
...

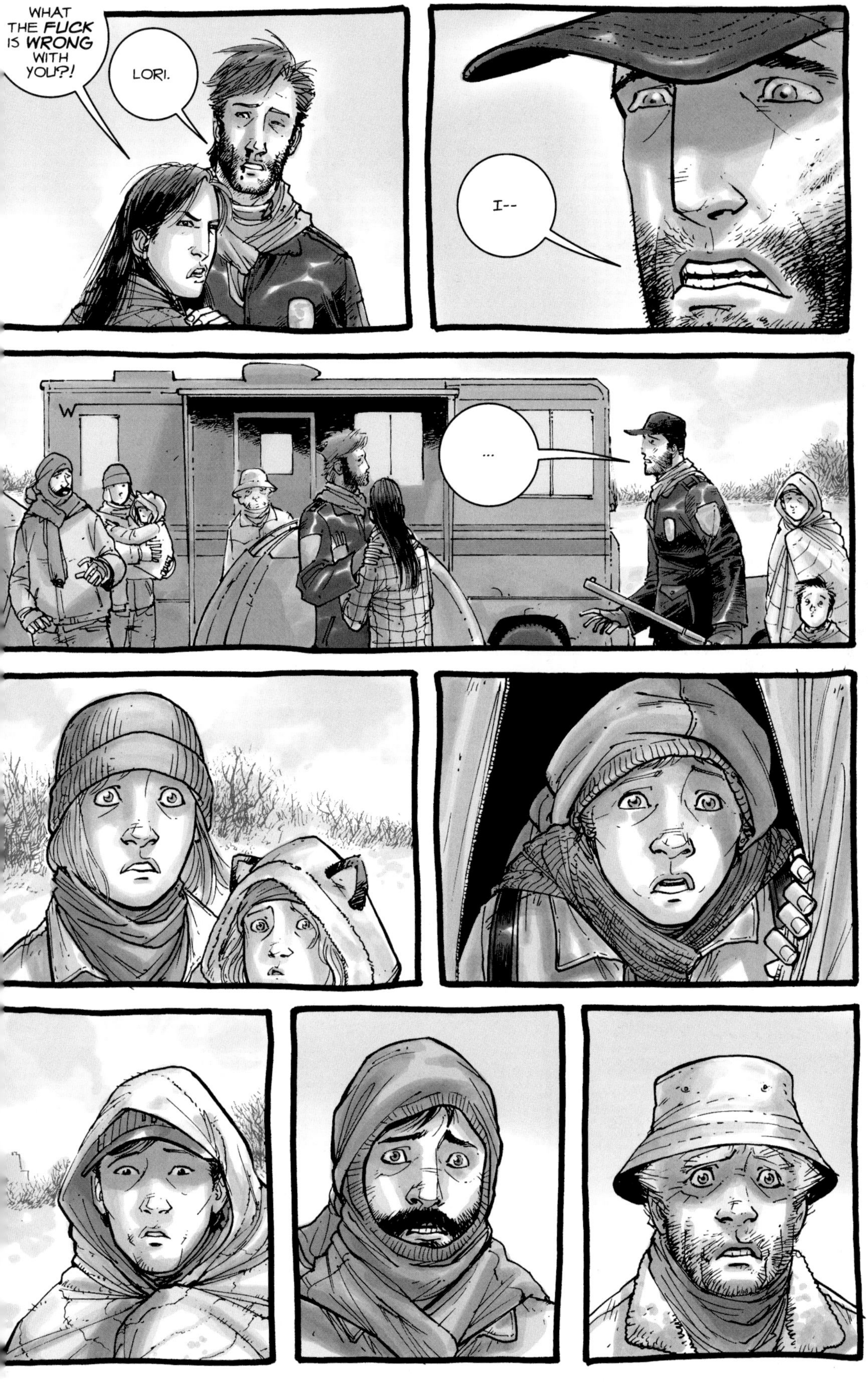
WHAT THE FUCK IS WRONG WITH YOU?!
LORI.
I--
...

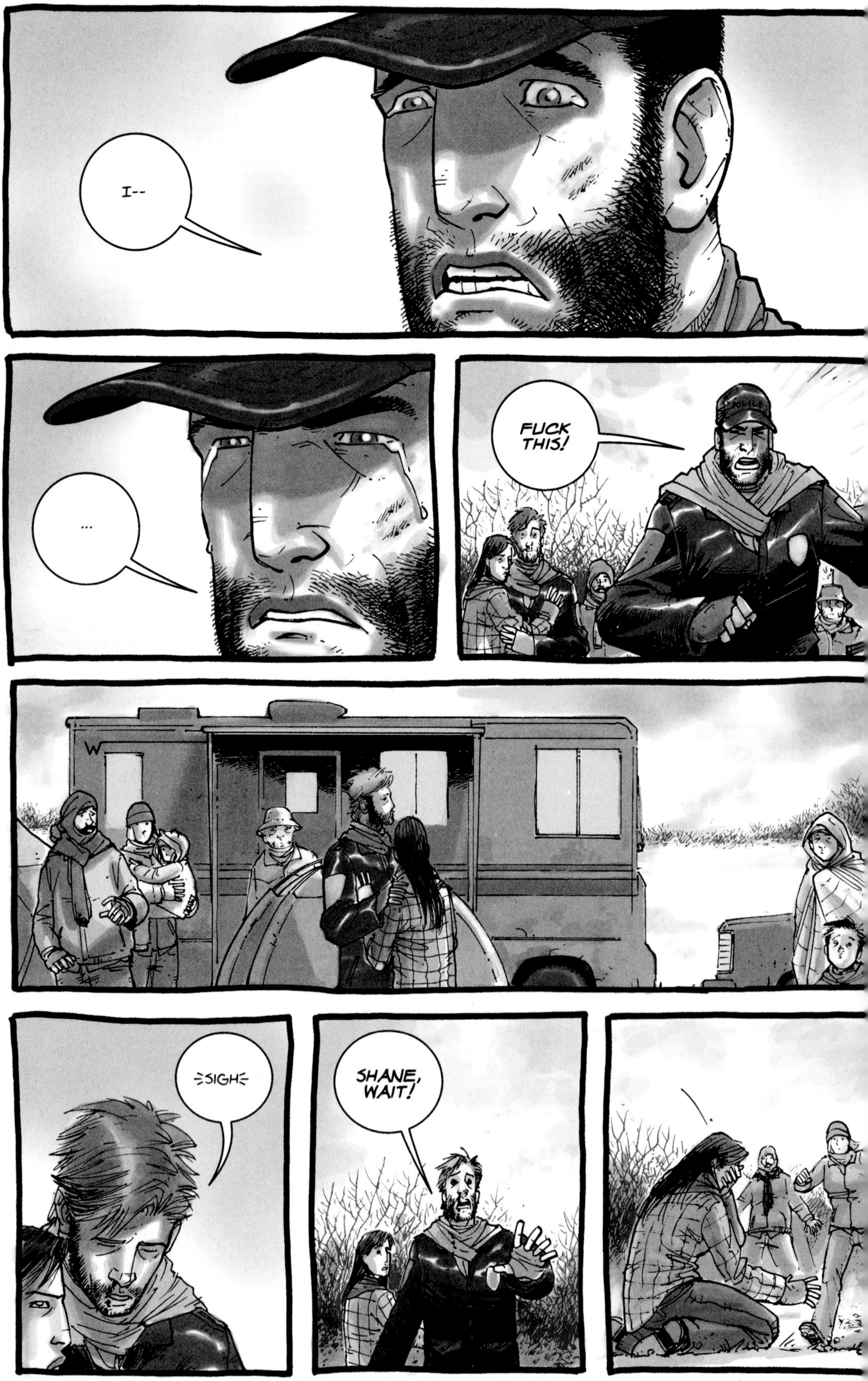
I--
...
FUCK THIS!
SIGH
SHANE, WAIT!

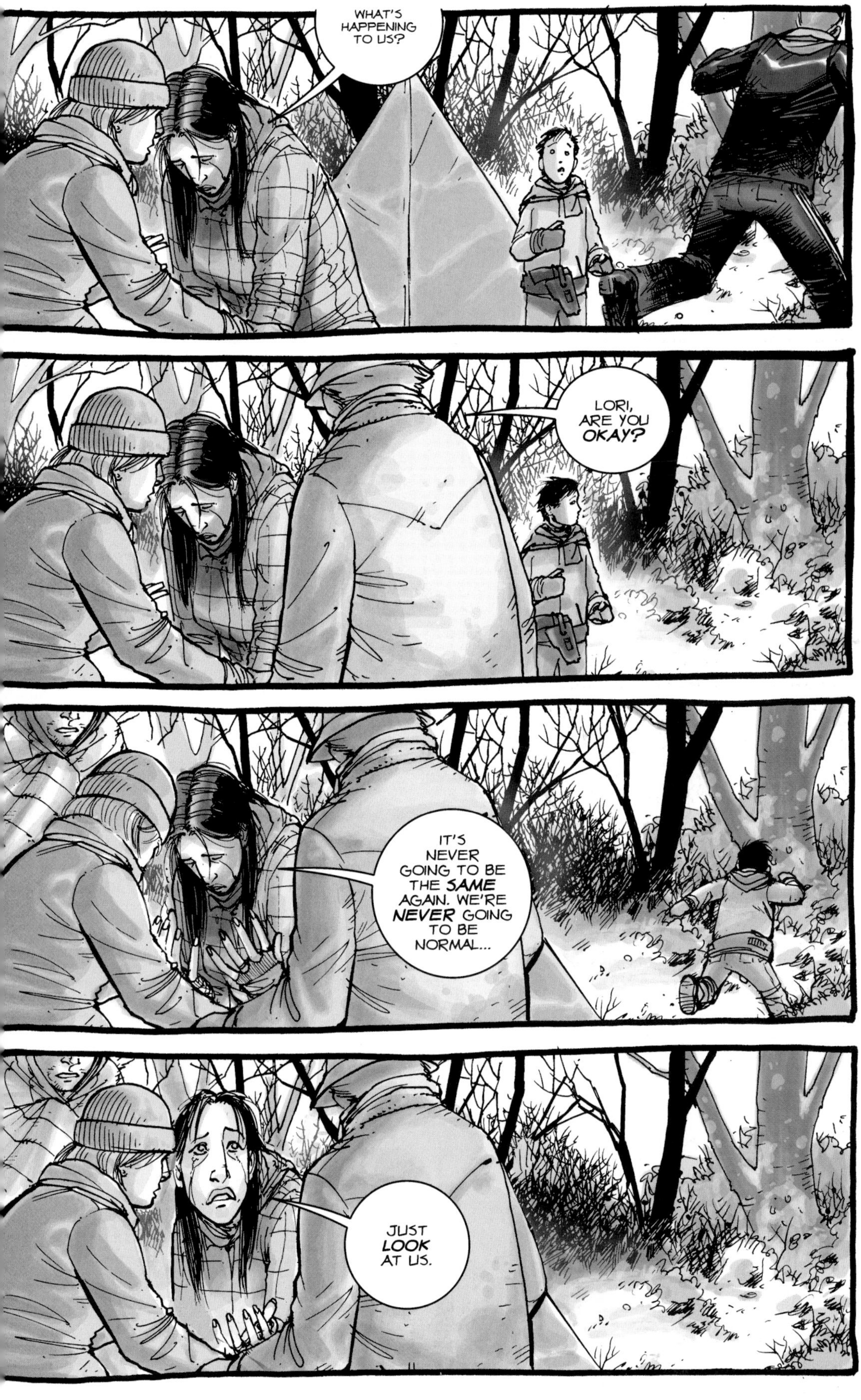
WHAT'S HAPPENING TO US?
LORI, ARE YOU OKAY?
IT'S NEVER GOING TO BE THE SAME AGAIN. WE'RE NEVER GOING TO BE NORMAL...
JUST LOOK AT US.

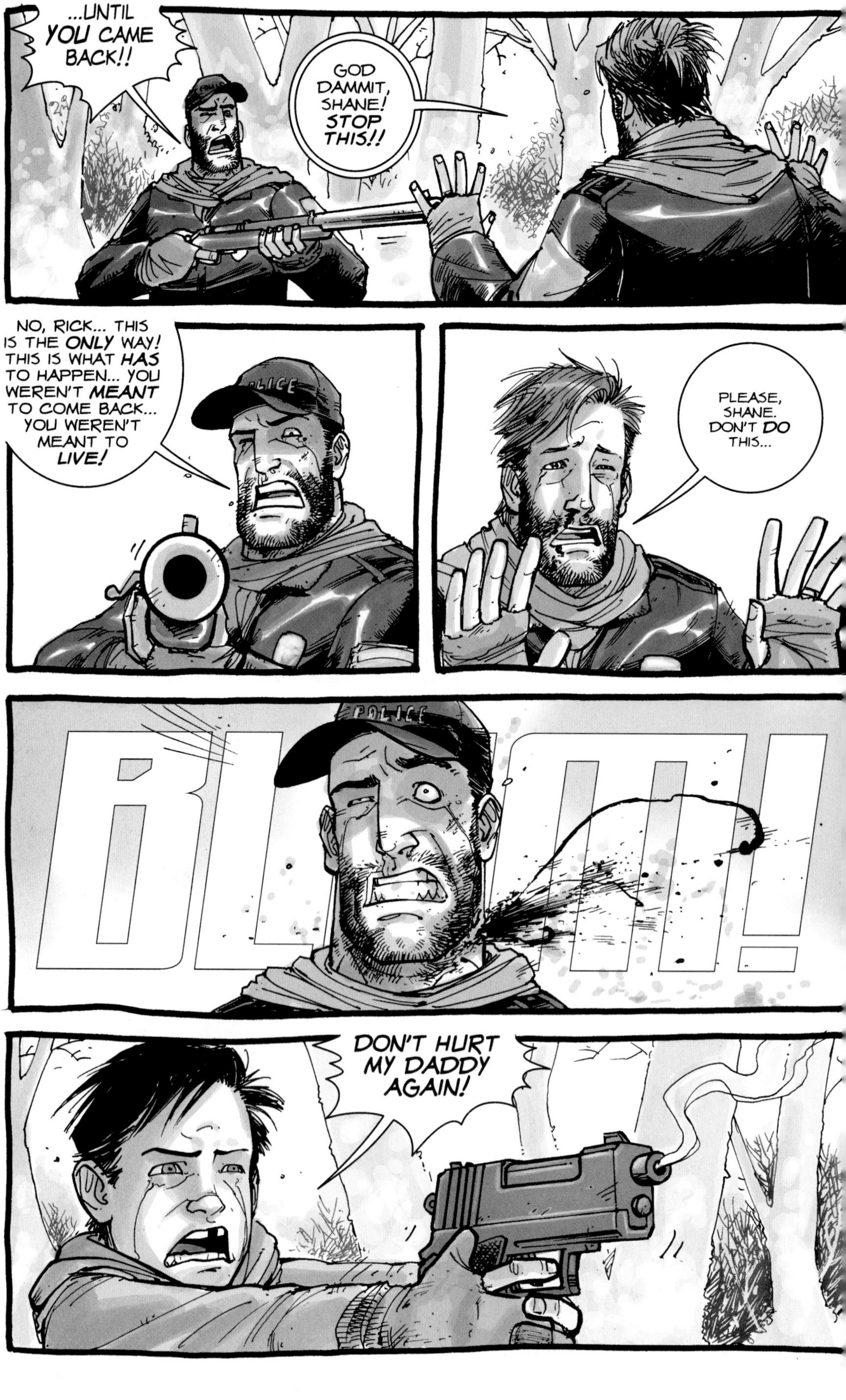
...UNTIL YOU CAME BACK!!
GOD DAMMIT, SHANE! STOP THIS!!
NO, RICK... THIS IS THE ONLY WAY! THIS IS WHAT HAS TO HAPPEN... YOU WEREN'T MEANT TO COME BACK... YOU WEREN'T MEANT TO LIVE!
PLEASE, SHANE. DON'T DO THIS...
DON'T HURT MY DADDY AGAIN!